What Readers Are Saying About *The Wilderness Companion:*

"And from the days of John the Baptist until now the kingdom of heaven suffereth violence, and the violent take it by force." (Matthew 11:12) Have you ever wondered what this "violent force" looks like? <u>*The Wilderness Companion*</u> is the living example of such violence lived out. This book is about the violent seizure of the Kingdom of God, and the events that surround refusing to let go at any cost.

I believe this book is essential in preparing you for your own wilderness journeys. It is a straightforward and honest look at real experiences in the wilderness in all of its humanity and spirituality. It is commonly said, *"Experience is the best teacher"*, but I tell you, *"Other people's experiences are the best instruction, but you still have to do the lesson!"* Wise counsel and encouragement in your journey await you in this book of the events of the wilderness experiences of Glynda Lomax.

The founders of the Biosphere projects in the Arizona desert set out to create the perfect ecosystem for natural life to thrive and be studied. A curious thing happened in the decades that followed, as healthy trees growing in ideal conditions began to fall over by themselves. Though the trees had no disease and grew remarkably faster than their wild counterparts, because they had no wind in their protected environment, they became top-heavy and never developed roots.

The winds of change are blowing across America and the world. Right now the Spirit of God is readying the people of God, because a storm is coming. This book is a tool in God's hand to speak into your wilderness experience, and to "flesh out" an example of what a wilderness experience looks and feels like in our modern world. The focus of this book is not upon Glynda or her struggles, not even on what good spiritual fruit it produces, but on our Wilderness Companion: the Lord Jesus Christ Himself.

- Brian D. McClafferty, (DoorOfPrayer.blogspot.com)

I have watched Glynda's YouTube videos, read her blog posts, and listened to her Blog Talk Radio shows. I thought I knew what to expect before reading her book. I was pleasantly surprised. In "*The Wilderness Companion*", she takes the time to delve deeply into the nuances of her faith walks.

It is easy to pawn off faith as to only being for biblical characters like Elijah, John the Baptist, or the apostles. They seem so distant, so holy, so out of touch with today's reality. This lends to the excuse that faith is not for today. Glynda absolutely demolishes that excuse in this book. Glynda is a real flesh and blood, living, breathing person that lives now, and she lives by real biblical faith - NOW!

She records in detail her thoughts and struggles that happened during her roller coaster faith walks in the wilderness. It reads so warm and relaxed as if she is across the kitchen table talking to a close friend. It is also suspenseful. I kept turning the page wondering what she going to do, say, or pray next.

Her book relates to many of the struggles I have had with faith. I am sure it will relate to you as well. Her brutal honesty opens up a new dimension of understanding about faith in today's world. In conclusion, she addresses the seven temptations that rear their head when on a wilderness walk. The importance of being aware of these temptations and how to deal with them cannot be over emphasized.

Don't wait until you are in the wilderness to read *The Wilderness Companion*.

— *Conrad Carriker, (www.bethefew.com)*

Having not known I was going through a "wilderness experience" of my own while proofing this book, I broke out in tears one night when I realized the magnitude of how great the Lord is to have moved Glynda Lomax to write this book!

The Wilderness Companion is a book about Glynda's own raw pain, her personal challenges, failures and great victories intermingled with Words from the Lord she received as she goes through "The Wilderness". The Wilderness is those extremely hard times in life when we struggle to hear God's voice let alone not die.

In this book you will see the heart of God for His people in the way He cares for one of His daughters. In *The Wilderness Companion,* Glynda recalls how she started hearing and obeying the voice of God in her most desperate trials. From there she gives us guidelines of what to do and what not to do while in these harsh lessons so that, if followed, our times in the deserts will be shortened and we can avoid some of the pitfalls she had to endure.

This book is packed with real-life, down-to-earth experiences accompanied with REAL bona fide wisdom from God *(anyone with a half a spirit would bear witness to the things in this book being truly from God!!)* This book is highly anointed and, if applied, will help greatly to prepare us for the time to come! God bless you, Glynda Lomax, as you bare all to teach us. Thank you for writing this book. It has changed my life. My whole perspective of everything to do with God has been greatly strengthened. Well done, Glynda Lomax! Well done!

- Cindy (Smith) Biddle, former Journalist, Plano Star Courier

The
Wilderness
Companion

A Road Map To
Guide You Through
the Desert Times of
Your Life

Glynda Lomax

Mass Market Edition, 2012

International Standard Book Number
ISBN 13: 978-1470144623
ISBN 10: 147014462X

Edited by Brian D. McClafferty and Cindy *(Smith)* Biddle

Cover Design by Jason Alexander, Lead Designer, www.ExpertSubjects.com

Printed in the United States of America

DEDICATION

Though there are several people I could dedicate this book to, there is only one who truly made it happen. I dedicate it to Jesus Christ, the Lord of Lords, King of Kings, and Lord of my life forever. May all praise, honor and glory be to You forevermore. I am nothing in myself, and anything that is good in me, I owe to You.

Acknowledgements

Fifteen years ago, the Lord spoke to me to begin writing down everything He spoke to or showed me, saying I would "need it to tell the story." I never asked what the story was, and until He spoke to me to write this book, I never knew. Although I had the story in all those pages, it took many more people to bring it all together and make this book happen.

I would like to extend my deep gratitude to my beautiful Mother and sister Shirley, who have never stopped encouraging me to write over the years. Though there were others who encouraged me from time to time, you both believed in me when no one else did.

I would also like to thank my friends who have continually encouraged me through the many long nights it took to complete this book. You know who you are. I am so grateful for you all and truly blessed to have you as my friends.

I wish to thank especially those of you who saw the vision of God, and gave gifts to me that I might take the time needed to write it in its entirety. You know who you are. Without you, this book could not have happened.

My thanks to my dear friends Brian McClafferty, Cindy Biddle, David F. Branz, and Conrad Carriker, as well as my niece Stephanie Denton for all your help with proofreading and editing the story. This book would be much less pleasant to read without the excellent help and advice each of you contributed. Thank you for your service to the brethren, and to me as your fellow servant in helping to make *The Wilderness Companion* a reality.

I owe my gratitude also to the powerful mentors who have helped me in my walk, and to those who have walked various parts of this journey with me – thank you. I am who I am because each of you touched my life in some way, and I thank God for all of you.

May God richly reward each one of you with a mighty harvest for all you have sown into my life, and into *The Wilderness Companion.*

CONTENTS

PREFACE

As a Christian and an avid reader of Christian books, I have often wished I had a powerful testimony to share with others to glorify the Lord and help others find a closer walk with Him as well, but to be willing to have a testimony like that, you must be willing to stare down giants while holding only a sling and a tiny rock with which to slay them. You must be willing to face pain and decline in your natural body each day as you fight to keep your eyes on Jesus and believe for healing, or be willing to live with no steady source of income while you watch God miraculously provide for you again and again.

You must believe beyond any shadow of doubt that He is God, and you must trust Him over everything you have been taught in the world. You must be willing to risk everything you hold most dear, and all that makes you feel secure. You must be willing, like Peter, to step out of the boat and walk through places not made for walking. You must be willing like the Israelites, to walk for days and days into a desolate wasteland, carrying nothing but your faith and not knowing how you will feed yourself or your family. You must be willing to stake everything on your faith, to draw the line in the sand and stand firmly on the right side of it. Though you see nothing in the natural to hold you up, when Jesus softly says, "Come," you must be willing to obey Him, and take that terrifying step into the dark unknown.

I never expected my life would produce anything grand enough to write a book about. I was surprised when the Lord sent me a word through more than one person in one week in 2010, that He wanted me to start writing. For months I prayed and struggled to understand what the book was to be about. *What is it You want me to write about, Lord? What can I possibly know enough about to put into a book for You?*

Finally, late in 2011, the answer came.

I want you to tell others about The Wilderness. I want you to tell them about how I took care of you there.

This book is the story of my journeys through The Wilderness, through those desert places where everything is barren and dry. The desert places are not places of comfort. The heat is on, and nothing in your life is the same as it was before the desert, but it is there that you will learn more than ever before about yourself, and about your God.

You must be willing to continue walking in the heat, out of the security of your comfort zone, and stay there when there is nothing solid in your circumstances to stand on as the storms batter you, and the enemy does his utmost to terrify you. You have to be willing to lose relationships when people distance themselves from associating with you, when they mock and doubt and think you've lost your mind, and then walk away. In the midst of the wilderness, you must take your eyes off the backs of those walking away and the things you may lose and train your eyes on Jesus and keep saying, "What's the next step, Lord?" You have to know in your heart that Jesus said, "Come!" and keep walking in spite of being ridiculed, in spite of being abandoned, in spite of the fear and terror that rise up when nothing around you looks solid enough to plant your feet on. You must wholeheartedly believe in what you are doing and for whom, and keep putting one foot in front of the other until you come out the other side, having passed the test.

When the disciples decided to follow Jesus, they risked everything for what they believed. The earliest disciples were businessmen and family men. Without doubt, their friends must have questioned their decision. You know their spouses certainly did, since they were going up against the Pharisees, who had the power to influence others in the community against them and even had the power to do them harm. But they risked it all for what they knew to be truth, to help spread the news that Jesus was truly the Messiah, the Word made flesh to save the world from its sin and make a way for us all to go to Heaven and be with Him for all eternity.

In spite of the terror I encountered in my desert experiences, it was there that I learned to trust Him - *really* trust Him. Trust Him with everything and everyone that is important to me. You learn to trust Him even more when you thought you already did. He will stretch your faith until it can be stretched no more, and then He'll stretch it a little further. Like a rubber band pulled to its limit, you think surely you will break and all will be lost as you cling to Him with every ounce of faith you have inside you, and then He stretches you yet again.

The prize that waits at the end of a wilderness walk is priceless but this walk is not free. Wilderness walking will always cost you something. Often it costs you material things as we must all lighten our loads to make it up the narrow path - it gets narrower the higher up we go. But it will cost you more than that - it will cost you relationships, it will cost you your dreams, it will cost you your pride, it will cost you your reputation. In the end, it will cost you yourself. Every time we want to go up higher, we must look around for another part of ourselves to lay down. The Children of Israel, when they came out of Egypt, left behind homes, possessions, friendships - everything they had that they could not carry into the desert was left behind. Whether it was a lot in worldly terms or not, it was all they had and their life there was all they had ever known.

In a wilderness walk, God is trying you, refining you, proving you. But He is also proving Himself to you. He is proving that He and His word are both true. He is taking more of your fleshly nature, the part of you that wants the things of this world - out of the equation and filling that empty space with His glorious spirit. The end result is a lot less of you and a whole lot more of Him as well as an increased understanding of Him, that ultimately results in a powerful testimony that has the power to reach others for His Name's Sake.

A wilderness experience is something that happens in the lives of those who are about to be promoted to a new level of anointing, but the greatest reward of walking through the wilderness is a closer intimacy with the Lord. When you walk through fiery trials with someone and survive them, you have a closer bond with that person, because you experience things in the fire that you don't experience at other times of your life, and only others who have also walked through that fiery place truly understand. Like the brave men and women of the armed forces who have fought on the battlefields will tell you, intense battles tend to bring out both the best and the worst in each of us, and when you battle side by side with someone, you share both fear and courage. You weep tears of sorrow as well as tears of joy, but you weep them all together.

I pray my story will inspire you to reach a little higher, risk a little more, believe a little bit deeper than ever before.

WHAT THE WILDERNESS IS

The wilderness the Lord takes you through is not a physical place, but a place where you will learn things about yourself and about Him, that will strengthen your faith, and your walk with Him.

No matter how many times you go through this type of faith walk, each time it will challenge your faith all over again. Sometimes it challenges you to believe more completely, or for more of your provision. You may start out in the wilderness believing for lunch one day at a time, and end up believing for the income to pay all your expenses. Sometimes a new wilderness walk will challenge you to believe in an area where your faith has not been built up yet, such as physical healing.

You may think that if someone survives one walk where God provided for them miraculously for a whole year that they would never doubt His provision again, but that's not true. They will have more faith than they did before, but not necessarily enough faith to enter their next trek into the wilderness with complete confidence, and maybe not any faith at all in the area where they are tested the next time. God desires His people to continually grow in faith, to continually be strengthened in the knowledge of who He is, and that He is a loving Father, faithful to provide for His children.

I took my first walk through the wilderness years ago, in 1998. I had been walking closely with the Lord for less than two years when it happened. The Word had just been opened to me and I was struggling to know God better, and to get free from the many sins I had become bound up in before coming to know Christ at the age of thirty-six.

In the years that followed, I would take many more wilderness walks, some by my choice and some not by my choice.

Many times during my various trips through the wilderness, I have wished for a companion that would guide me, tell me what was happening and help me know what to do next, someone who could tell me where the pitfalls in my journey were. Obviously, the Lord is our companion at all times, but there are times when He is silent and we are unsure of what to do next. I needed advice, encouragement, someone else's experiences to relate to, scriptures for reference....something..., anything to help me survive that terrible desert place.

My story is not unusual, there are thousands of Christians today who have far greater testimonies than mine . So many of our brothers and sisters are being persecuted and dying for professing the Name of Christ even as you read this, and my story is nothing compared to the fires they have endured, but each story has the power to touch, to testify, to inspire - that is the power of the testimony.

The purpose of this book is to share with you what I have learned through my wilderness experiences. In sharing them, it is my prayer that your walks there will be a little less dark and terrifying, that you will walk with a little more faith than I did, that you will have the assurance of knowing even the desert places don't last forever. This too shall pass. It is my hope that by telling you my experiences in the wilderness, you will be encouraged in your own.

I PETER 1:6-7

IN THIS YOU REJOICE, THOUGH NOW FOR A LITTLE WHILE, IF NECESSARY, YOU HAVE BEEN GRIEVED BY VARIOUS TRIALS, SO THAT THE TESTED GENUINENESS OF YOUR FAITH—MORE PRECIOUS THAN GOLD THAT PERISHES THOUGH IT IS TESTED BY FIRE—MAY BE FOUND TO RESULT IN PRAISE AND GLORY AND HONOR AT THE REVELATION OF JESUS CHRIST.

CHAPTER 1 – HOW I FOUND CHRIST

Unlike many Christians I know, I was not raised in church, and attendance there was a very infrequent part of our lives. Mom had a strong belief in God, but no one talked much about Him at our house, though the living room usually had a Bible in it, and we were never allowed to place anything on top of it. We spent most of our time trying to survive my Dad's drinking. My father never said grace over our meals, but we didn't miss it, because we had never known anything else. We grew up moving around Northeast Texas, following my father's construction work. Moving so often, we had no long term friendships from our childhood that followed us through our lives. We had few friends period, not being able to bring friends home, because we could never be sure what would be happening there. The spring of my fifteenth year, we moved to the Texas Gulf Coast.

I met my husband Rick at a restaurant in Texas City, while waiting tables one summer to make money for school clothes. Our first meeting left me thinking he was completely obnoxious, and it would be two weeks before I accepted his invitation to go on a date. By our second date, we were completely in love. I dropped out of school and married him in January of the following year, a month before I turned sixteen. We moved every few months that first year, my husband trying to find a place where he could make enough money for us to survive. Eventually, we moved back to his home near St. Louis. That was where the abuse began. I was seven months pregnant with our daughter the first time he knocked me to the ground. After that, it never stopped. At first, it was every month or so, but by the time I left the marriage eleven years later, it was every week. I gave birth to our first child, a daughter, late the first year we were together. It would be almost six months before either of us could find work in the St. Louis area, and we nearly starved there. After finally finding jobs and working for a few months, we lost them, and decided it was time to move. A year and a half later, we had moved to Princeton, Texas, near my parents, and our son was born.

I first began dabbling in the occult and new age practices like candle gazing and reading tarot cards when I was nineteen after reading about them in a library book. For a while, I read every book I could find on occult practices, delving deeper, and eventually began reading about witchcraft, learning how to cast spells. I never joined a coven, preferring to practice alone. Not living near a big city, I knew no other witches, and being married, I could not have attended the gatherings anyway. I had never felt I fit in any place my entire life anyhow, so not being part of a group did not feel strange to me. After suffering constant abuse for years, I was drawn to the power witchcraft offered. I thought if I could learn to do magick, I could change my life for the better. Throughout this time, my Mom interceded for the Lord to save me. She knew I was headed down the wrong road and tried many times to warn me, but in my youth and stubbornness, I refused to listen to her.

> *Jesus was not in the Church, and I didn't know where else to look for Him.*

Several times over the ten plus year period when Mom was interceding, the Lord drew me and I searched for Him. In my early twenties when the abuse in my marriage was at its worst, I felt Him draw me again. I began praying, reading whatever I could find, trying to find out more about Him. For a while, His presence was with me, though I didn't understand why or what it meant, or what to do about it. I just remember feeling very comforted whenever He was near, and I desperately needed comfort then.

Years later, I was again drawn to the Lord. At that time my husband and I lived in McKinney, Texas, and I began to attend a small church there, taking our two children with me. I found Christianity in that small church, but I never found Jesus. I never felt any repentance for my sins or any fear or awe of the Lord's mighty power. As a result, I still did not understand that Christianity was not about rules but about relationship, and eventually I fell away. Soon after, my younger brother committed suicide. Two months later, after nearly twelve years of marriage, I left my husband and fled to Oklahoma with the children.

It would be years before I sought the Lord again. After the divorce, all I wanted to do was have fun, to let the child in me come out and play as it had never been allowed to before, and I did. By my early thirties, I had returned to the occult. I didn't really believe in what I was doing, but I didn't really believe in anything else either, so it didn't matter to me. I was still searching for the truth.

After years of partying and doing whatever I felt like, I began to feel the Lord calling me again. After feeling the leading for weeks, I visited some churches, but I left each one filled with disappointment, and feeling even more lost than before. Whatever was in those churches, it did nothing to quell the longing I felt to find the real God. No one approached me and talked to me about salvation, or even seemed to care that I was there, and I didn't know enough about the God I was seeking to know what questions to ask of them. Not knowing where else to look, I returned to the world, and my life of partying and having fun. Jesus was not in the Church, and I didn't know where else to look for Him.

In the spring of 1996, I was working as a seismic permit agent when I was assigned to permit part of a 3D seismograph job in Chickasha, Oklahoma. The job was projected to last at least six months, and after much begging, I had persuaded the crew chief to allow me to rent a furnished apartment instead of another motel room.

A very interesting young girl in the complex whose parents were ordained ministers became friends with my son who occasionally stayed with me there. The young girl intrigued me. She was a pretty young girl with a friendly personality, but it was more than that. She was very open about her Christian faith, and I saw a peace and a joy in her I had never seen in a Christian before. I saw a conviction - she lived what she believed, and she did it joyfully. I had never seen anyone so young that was so strong and so joyful in their Christian beliefs.

One afternoon in early summer, the young girl came to visit, and found me at my dining room table reading my fortune with playing cards.

She paused for a few seconds, tilted her head slightly and asked, "You know it's wrong to do that, right?"

I smiled. *Here we go.*

I knew the drill. She was about to hit me with a lecture about how much of a sinner I was and how I should turn to her God to fix me. Boring. I hoped it wouldn't take long.

"I know the Bible you believe in says it's wrong, if that's what you mean," I answered, still looking at my cards.

"Okay, that's all I wanted to know," she said with a smile, and bounced off into the living room.

I stopped and thought about what she had said. I had been different my entire life. Basically, I had never fit in any place, so I was accustomed to others not approving of me, and had long since ceased caring about their opinions. It wasn't that I cared she said it was wrong, it was the *way* she had said it that intrigued me. She wasn't offensive. She didn't beat me over the head with her beliefs. She shared them in a way that was less condemning, and more like informing. I decided I liked her even more for allowing me to see the way Christians believed without degrading me for the way I did.

Her response made me curious about the Christian faith. I had tried it a few times before, and fallen away each time. The dry churches I had experienced in my young adulthood had been filled with older people of somber face who seemed like they were just doing time there to get good marks for attendance, waiting for the sweet by-and-by. I wanted no part of that dry, boring life, but this young girl had something else. She seemed happy about being a Christian.

Could there be a way to be happy and be a Christian, too? Was it possible to do right things and be happy about it? I had never seen joy before in a Christian like she had, or the peace I saw in her eyes, and I wanted it. No amount of whiskey and dancing had ever given me what she had, and I knew it.

In my heart, I prayed a silent prayer to the God I did not believe in. *If You're real, show me, and I'll follow You.*

On July 28th of that year on a quiet Sunday afternoon, there was a knock at the door, and it was the young girl. I was home with my live-in boyfriend at the time, just hanging out.

"I have a message from God for you," she stated, matter-of-factly.

My eyebrows shot up to my hairline. "Reeeeally?" I asked. *Is this some kind of a joke?* What could her God possibly want to say to me?

"Yes," she stated. "Come with me." With that she turned and began descending the stairs. It was obvious whatever it was, she did not want to say it in front of my boyfriend.

Oh well, I was bored anyway. Let's see what this is about. Closing the door behind me, I followed her out into the bright sunlight of the July afternoon, down the stairs and out into the parking lot. She walked a ways and then stopped, turning to face me.

"The Lord said to tell you that He has a plan for your life and the way you're living is not it," she stated, looking me in the eye.

I laughed. "Yeah, I can imagine it wouldn't be." For years I had lived a life of drinking, partying and chasing cowboys.

"He said to tell you that you have always known you were special, that you were not like everyone else. You have been out in the world playing for years. Now the time has come when you must choose. He has a very special work for you to do, but you only have a short time to decide whether you will accept it or not."

By this time, she had my full attention, and I wasn't laughing any more. My eyes widened with surprise and my jaw dropped. He was answering my silent prayer. And if He was answering, that meant *He was real!* ... and... *He was alive!!*

"He said to tell you that if you will accept this work, He will open up the windows of heaven and pour out all the blessings on you that He has held back all these years you've been living in sin."

He's real! He's real! And He answered me! He knows I'm here! He knows who I am! He answered me!

In that split second in my spirit, I saw a forked road. I knew the choice was mine and mine alone, and I felt that He would not force me to choose His way, or even be angry with me if I did not choose His. I also felt very strongly that, although I had the right to say no to His plan, I wouldn't be on planet earth very much longer if I chose that route.

As I thought back over the terrible emptiness and loneliness I had felt for years, and how nothing ever made me feel truly joyful, I knew I wanted to give His plan a try. I knew, in spite of the fact that I did whatever my flesh felt like doing, I wasn't nearly as happy as I appeared to be or as I tried to convince others I was.

"My plan isn't working out all that great anyway. I'll try His plan! - Lord. If you can do something with my life, You can have it!"

And that was the beginning of my real walk with God. Immediately, I began making changes. I told the boyfriend he had to move out. I bought a Bible, and I began listening to Bible teachings.

That night, I had a long talk with the Lord.

Lord, I can't promise You I'll never fall. We both know I have a lot of sin in my life. I know it won't all go away overnight. I am going to trust You to show me one sin at a time that You want me to let go of, and I will do my best to obey You. And I promise You that if You'll never give up on me, I'll never give up on You, and when I do fall, I promise You I'll always get back up and try again. I won't ever just give up again like I did in the past because now I know for sure You're real and You even made a plan for my life. You know me!

GETTING TO KNOW THE LORD

Not long after giving my life to the Lord, I asked Him for another job. I had heard contract permitting paid more than salaried permitting, and I wanted to try it. Having become familiar with researching land and mineral title in the courthouses, and seeking land and mineral owner permission for seismic activities while working with the seismic crew, I felt I had enough experience. I thought I would pray, and then research permit agent broker services, and make phone calls to see if anyone would hire me.

Okay, You're God so this should not be a problem for You. I want another job doing the same kind of work, but making twice the money for it. And I'd really like for it to be in Louisiana because I've never worked there. Oh, and I'll need a truck, because I don't have a vehicle. I want a GMC, or Dodge or Chevrolet; dark blue or black, extended cab, with a V6 engine because I'll be driving a lot and I want to save money on gas. You said, "Ask and you shall receive," so I'm asking, Lord.

I was challenging Him. If He really was God, then He could bring me the job I wanted, and a vehicle to go with it. *Show me what You got, Lord.*

He not only took the challenge, He shocked me with His response. Within a week, I had a job offer. When the man who offered me the job was talking about how much they would pay me, I began praying silently.

Is this it, Lord? Should I take it?

Silence.

"Can I think about your offer and get back with you?" I asked.

"Sure, no problem," he answered.

For days I prayed about whether to accept the man's offer, but the Lord never answered me, so I waited. A week later, he called again.

"That wasn't enough money, was it?" he asked as soon as I answered the phone.

"No, it wasn't," I said, not knowing what else to say. He raised his offer. Immediately, I heard the Lord speak to me. *Take it.*

When I hung up the phone, I began praising the Lord. He had just given me a job paying two and a half times what I was currently making. He not only took my challenge, He raised me! My first contract position would begin in South Louisiana two weeks later.

Immediately I called a dealership where I had previously purchased a pre-owned vehicle. "I need a GMC, dark blue or black, extended cab pickup with a V6 engine. You got anything like that on the lot there? I want a new one this time, not pre-owned."

The next day, my salesman called me back. He had my truck. Dark blue, extended cab Sierra, fuel injected V6 engine, just like I wanted.

"Okay," I said. "Run my credit and let me know how much I need to put down and I'll be down to sign papers on it."

Three days later he called again. "I've run your credit through six companies and no one will finance you because you've never borrowed that much money before," he said.

"Run it through some more. That's my truck. Someone's going to approve me," I answered and hung up.

The next day he called me back. A major bank had approved me and he was ready to prepare my paperwork. I had my truck! When I signed papers on the truck and picked it up days later, it actually had features I hadn't even known to ask for, having never purchased a new vehicle before. I was thrilled.

Within a month of giving my life to Christ I left Oklahoma for the contract job in Louisiana. I began spending as much time as possible listening to Bible teachings and in private prayer and worship.

CHAPTER 2 – THE SPIRITUAL HOUSE CLEANING BEGINS

EZEKIEL 36:25-27

*I WILL SPRINKLE CLEAN WATER ON YOU,
AND YOU SHALL BE CLEAN FROM ALL YOUR
UNCLEANNESSES, AND FROM ALL YOUR
IDOLS I WILL CLEANSE YOU. AND I WILL
GIVE YOU A NEW HEART, AND A NEW
SPIRIT I WILL PUT WITHIN YOU. AND I
WILL REMOVE THE HEART OF STONE FROM
YOUR FLESH AND GIVE YOU A HEART OF
FLESH. AND I WILL PUT MY SPIRIT WITHIN
YOU, AND CAUSE YOU TO WALK IN MY
STATUTES AND BE CAREFUL TO OBEY MY
RULES.*

For years, my walk was mostly me stumbling and falling down. I got into sin again and again, only to go back to the Lord and repent. I had been out in the world sinning for thirty-six years before turning my life over to Him, and a lot of the world had gotten into me in that time. Not having been raised in church meant I had to learn everything from scratch. I knew virtually nothing about God. I tried reading the Bible, but it made no sense to me in the beginning. I knew He heard me when I talked, so I poured out my heart to Him continually, and I believed at the right time, He would help me to learn more. One day, He spoke to me about journaling.

I want you to start writing down what I say to you and what I show you. You'll need it to tell the story.

Okay, Lord.

It never occurred to me to ask Him what story He meant, I just assumed He had a plan.

One hot June evening months later, I had moved to a job in another part of Louisiana where I had an apartment. I was at home cleaning when the Lord began to show me He wanted me to clean my spiritual house as well. He began to lead me to various objects in my home that were displeasing to Him. In my travels and over the years, I had collected various trinkets and souvenirs, as well as books and gifts from old lovers He did not find pleasing. I removed each one as He showed them to me, prayed over the lot of them, and removed them to the dumpster. When I walked back inside my apartment, His peace permeated the atmosphere more than ever before.

Any time the Lord asks you to give something up, it is always for your own benefit. The things we give up are the things He is trying to prune off us so that we might bear more fruit. As I would learn along the way, the Lord's nature is always to give back better things than we let go of. We cannot hope to have a good relationship with God, and still keep our sins and our pleasures. We must choose.

THE EXCHANGE

Not long after the spiritual house cleaning, the Lord began telling me He wanted me to give up smoking. At the time, I had been praying and asking Him to make me able to at least carry a tune when I sang in church so people wouldn't stare at me. I knew I was off-key and it was embarrassing. He began to deal with me about smoking. He showed me He would make an exchange with me. He would give me the ability to carry a tune for the cigarettes, and I had been arguing with Him for two weeks trying to change His mind. I was desperately hoping to hang onto my bad habit and give Him something else instead, but He hadn't budged. Cigarettes were my way of dealing with the stress of my job and other stresses in my life and I was reluctant to give them up.

Two weeks later, I was about to settle down on my bed to read the Word with a cigarette and a cup of coffee before bedtime. Suddenly, I felt Him point to my cigarette, and He spoke only one word.

Tonight.

Come on, Lord, I just bought a new carton!

Silence.

I knew His silence meant He was not going to change His mind.

I sighed.

Okay, I'll do it. Let me just smoke this last one and I'll give them up. But I'm not going to pretend I want to do it, because I don't. But I love You far more than I love smoking and I want to please You.

I smoked that last cigarette, then I went all over my house and out into my vehicle and collected every cigarette, every ash tray, every lighter, even the cigarette butts, and made a pile. I had tried on my own to quit many times in the last couple of years and I knew just how mean those cravings could be. I wasn't taking any chances. If I was going to quit, then I was going to give myself every possible chance to succeed at it. And that meant not leaving any cigarette butts to tempt me in a moment of weakness.

I got down on my knees. *Lord, You know I really don't want to do this. But You know I love You desperately and I will do anything to please You, so here they are. But please help me - You know I usually chain smoke a half a pack in the morning alone, and that we go outside at work and smoke every two hours, so I'm going to be around smoking constantly. Please help me with the cravings.*

I readied myself for bed, dreading the following morning when I knew the nicotine cravings would invade my every thought, but I was determined to obey Him no matter how bad the cravings were.

The cravings never came.

After years of smoking a pack and a half a day, He had set me free!

MY FIRST WILDERNESS WALK

One quiet afternoon when I was alone in my rented apartment, the Lord spoke to me in that still small voice He has.

I want you to get out of debt.

Okay, Lord.

The following payday, I began systematically paying down my credit cards. For a while, I paid extra on those and my truck loan, but nothing having happened and not feeling any urgency, I stopped after several months. *He probably just wants me to understand it's not good to be in debt*, I thought.

It is easy to ignore the small nudges of God, to stop doing what He has spoken to or led us to do before completing it, or before He has completed something in us in the process. It is easy to rationalize in our minds that He doesn't actually mean what He is saying in a literal sense, but it is dangerous ground for a Christian to do so, as I would soon learn.

By Easter Weekend 1998, I was finishing a job in South Texas, and I decided to go back to Western Oklahoma for a few weeks before reporting to my next job in Hattiesburg, Mississippi.

Extremely tired of staying in motel rooms, I rented a small house for my visits home and moved my things out of storage and into the small house.

After two weeks off and having set up the small house, I decided it was time to go back to work. I picked up the phone and began to dial the number of the person I would be reporting to, to find out where to show up the following Monday. In the midst of dialing, the Lord spoke to me.

Put down the phone.

Somehow I knew when He said that, exactly what He meant. Though it had never happened before, I knew in my spirit He did not want me to go on that job to Mississippi. What I didn't know was why.

Can we just talk about my bills for a minute, Lord?

Silence.

For a few minutes I protested, but understanding the importance of obedience, I knew to go against Him would only bring circumstances I did not want.

ISAIAH 1:19-20

IF YOU ARE WILLING AND OBEDIENT, YOU
SHALL EAT THE GOOD OF THE LAND; BUT
IF YOU REFUSE AND REBEL, YOU SHALL BE
EATEN BY THE SWORD; FOR THE MOUTH
OF THE LORD HAS SPOKEN.

So I obeyed, and my first walk into the wilderness began.

Maybe God had something for me to do in this town. I didn't feel I knew enough about Him to minister, but I was willing to share whatever I did know, if it could help someone else.

I continued unpacking the last of my things since it was obvious I was staying for awhile. As I unpacked one of my traveling tubs, I pulled out my stash of Crown Royal Bourbon.

Lord, I really need to deal with this. You've never asked me to stop, but I know it can't be pleasing to You for a lady to drink whiskey.

I thought back on my drinking years when I had lived for the next party and all my bad behavior back then. Though I hadn't taken a single drink in the weeks since I had come back from my latest job in South Texas, I knew at some point I would probably have a stressful day and want to. And if I had it on hand, it would be so easy to just unscrew the top and pour a glass...

Okay, Lord. I know alcohol impairs my judgment, and I know being drunk isn't something You want Your children doing. I'm afraid this could come between me and You, so I'm going to get rid of it. I'm going to pour this down the sink right now, and I'm going to believe You that I am not going to need it or want it any more. I need You to keep me in this. I started back once before, and I know this is something I like to do, but I'm offering it up to You. You are better than any drink ever was.

I then proceeded to pour two very expensive bottles of Crown Royal down my kitchen sink. I was determined never to drink again. Nothing was more important to me than my relationship with God.

HE SENT HIS WORD AND HEALED ME

One night late in April during my prayer time, the Lord gave me an open vision of Jesus on the Cross. Then the vision changed and it was me up on the cross. I didn't know much about God at that point but I knew enough to be afraid when I saw that vision. I was pretty sure it meant He planned to crucify my flesh. The only question was....*how?*

Without a job taking up my time, I began spending even more time getting to know the Lord, and I began attending services at a small local church. To my delight, I learned I could now suddenly carry a tune, so I began singing with some of the other women there. In my prayer times, the Lord began teaching me truths about myself. He also began leading me to fast for various periods of time.

One afternoon, one of the ladies I sang with in church dropped by my house to chat.

"I was praying for you this morning and the Lord told me to tell you that He has healed all the emotional effects of your marriage," she announced casually.

Was she kidding me? She could not have known the weight of what she was saying, she had said it so casually! *He has healed all the emotional effects of your marriage.*

Years earlier, I had gone to a counselor complaining of horrible recurring nightmares and flashbacks of the abuse in my marriage. I had been diagnosed with Post Traumatic Stress Syndrome and told there was no cure, and the only treatment was to be tranquilized, which to me meant walking through life like a zombie. Unwilling to walk through life being constantly medicated, I had continued to live with the effects. She was telling me He had healed me. No more nightmares and flashbacks! I knew if the Lord had set me free, I was truly free! The nightmares and flashbacks never returned after that day. God had sent His word and healed me.

PSALM 107:20

HE SENT OUT HIS WORD AND HEALED
THEM, AND DELIVERED THEM FROM
THEIR DESTRUCTION.

LIFE BEGINS COMING APART AT THE SEAMS

That summer, my eldest sister and father were both diagnosed terminally
ill within about a month's time. I remember the night I was called over to
my Mom's house and got the news about Dad having cancer. The doctors
gave him six months to a year and a half to live. I had begun waiting
tables part time at a nearby restaurant, and I had to be at work thirty
minutes after getting the news. I was working the graveyard shift that
night, and with no other waitress, I couldn't call in, though I didn't know
how I would get through my shift. I was devastated over Dad's illness.

Everything I knew suddenly seemed to start falling apart. My daughter
and her husband separated around the same time, and began divorce
proceedings. My Father and Sister were both dying. My son had his own
troubles during that time as well. My job did not pay enough for me to
survive once my savings ran out, and I wasn't sure why God was keeping
me in the small, dusty town. It seemed we were all struggling in one area
or another. I felt not only my own pain, but massive pain over the trials
my loved ones were walking through. I wanted to fix everything and for
life to be happy again, but there seemed no place to start. I couldn't even
fix my own life.

Alone at night, I stared at my computer screen, searching for the words to
describe what I was going through in my latest journal entry. I felt as if I
had entered some surreal state of being, blinking like the cursor on the
screen, waiting for direction. A nightmare of unforeseen events had
unfolded around me, and I was helpless to change any of them. I had no
idea what was happening to my life, or why. I knew God was in control,
and I knew I was where He wanted me...so why were all these terrible
things happening in my family? And why would He not let me get a real
job so I could provide for myself?

I had prayed and prayed, and He still said no. My savings were dwindling quickly, soon I would be living completely on my charge cards, something I did not want to do, and yet in my spirit I knew I was not supposed to seek full time employment. I had taken up a sideline selling to go along with the part-time job waitressing to help pay the bills. I covered my vehicle payment with cash drawn against a credit card. It was far from an ideal situation, but I didn't know any other way to pay everything. I knew God was doing something, having taken me out of my chosen career. I just wasn't sure what, or how else He planned for me to pay my bills.

All of these changes, coupled with the uncertainty of not having my regular paycheck put me in an extremely vulnerable and frightened state of mind, and I entered into a second marriage which turned out to be a complete mistake. He left me shortly after. The truth is, we did care for each other, but we were drawn together more because we were both scared and lonely, than for anything we felt. The marriage was totally wrong for both of us. He was going through life changes and missed his parents, and I had two family members who were now terminally ill. The feelings of failure I felt over having chosen a wrong mate added to my already burdened mental state.

I felt as if I had entered some surreal state of being, blinking like the cursor on the screen, waiting for direction. A nightmare of unforeseen events had unfolded around me, and I was helpless to change any of them.

Six months after entering my first wilderness walk, the restaurant where I worked cut my hours from three shifts a week to three hours a week with no notice. Suddenly, I had not only no husband, but I had no work and no money. Within a week, I could not even pay the $200 rent on my small house and bill collectors began calling me for charge card payments I could not keep up on my small earnings as a waitress.

A compassionate friend offered to pay for a motel room for a week for me while I figured out what to do, so I packed up and moved into the motel room where I spent hours weeping and pouring my heart out to God, asking Him for direction. I had no idea where to go next, or what He wanted me to do. I had thought the marriage was of Him, and I had put all my proverbial eggs in that basket, and I was wrong. Heartbroken, disappointed and broke, I felt very alone, and very frightened.

I tried not to think about the fact that I was now homeless. I didn't even have $50 to buy food, and all my bills were due. The brook had dried up, and I knew when the brook dried up, it meant God was moving me some place else.

I KINGS 17:5-7

SO HE WENT AND DID ACCORDING TO THE WORD OF THE LORD. HE WENT AND LIVED BY THE BROOK CHERITH THAT IS EAST OF THE JORDAN. AND THE RAVENS BROUGHT HIM BREAD AND MEAT IN THE MORNING, AND BREAD AND MEAT IN THE EVENING, AND HE DRANK FROM THE BROOK. AND AFTER A WHILE THE BROOK DRIED UP, BECAUSE THERE WAS NO RAIN IN THE LAND.

I would be happy to pack up my broken heart and move, but I dreaded leaving my family yet again. Driving through Elk City that evening, I was reminded of the late eighties when I had first come to it for refuge from my violent marriage. I had been twenty-seven and full of dreams. I dreamed of falling in love with a man who would love and cherish me, and living in a house I could call my own, one that didn't have white walls. I had grown up in rent houses and had been a renter my entire life, and my most cherished dream had always been to have a home of my own. Not a mansion, just a house. A house with trees the breeze ruffled nearby and a porch swing. Now here I was almost forty, unemployed, and broke, and feeling about eighty. Elk City had become a haunting reminder of broken dreams.

In all the years since I had divorced my husband, I had never been without finances. I had worked two jobs many times to keep the bills paid, sold cosmetics on the side, and cleaned houses to keep my children clothed and fed. It had been a tough road, but even then, I had not ever been without a house to live in and a job to put food on my own table. Now I had neither. I thanked God my children were grown and out of the house and that it was only me I had to provide for. To add to everything else, by the end of that week, my sister, who was in town with her husband on a job, was leaving town. She had been feeding me and I was down to a dollar and some change. My charge cards were getting dangerously close to being maxed out, and I was trying hard not to use what little credit I had left on them.

I didn't have the gas money to drive to Mom's one town over and eat, and I had no idea how I was going to make it. The wilderness was quickly moving from trying to survive on little in the faintly familiar to walking into the dark and forbidding unknown with nothing, and my emotions bounced back and forth between scared half to death, despairing, and trying to have faith. I felt as if I were in the middle of a dark bridge. I couldn't go back the way I came, and I couldn't yet see where I was going. And for once in my life, I had no Plan B. How could I make a Plan B? I had no home, no job, no nothing. I had nothing to make a Plan B out of. I was still trying to figure out what Plan A was.

I prayed again about trying to find work there but the Lord told me it would only prolong my time in the wilderness. That was the last thing I wanted to do. If I obeyed, He said I would come through it more quickly, so I began to pray and press in more to find out exactly what He wanted me to do. Surely He had a real job in mind and some place for me to go? Maybe He was going to let me travel again?

I bet that's it, I thought.

I began to make calls to oil and gas companies, searching for a job that needed a permit agent to permit ahead of seismograph crews. If I found work permitting for a seismic crew, I would be traveling again, and my living expenses would be mostly paid for. After days of calling, I had three possibilities and all of them wanted me there as soon as they had budgetary approval for the jobs they were planning.

Okay, Lord, where do I stay in the meantime? I have no money to pay for another week at this motel. I have no money for anything.

I prayed and prayed, beseeching the Lord for an answer.

Finally, worn out from the strain of the worry and completely at a loss, I decided to take a nap.

Lord, I am believing You will show me where to go while I wait on one of these jobs to come through. Please help me!

When I awoke, the first thought that came to me was to visit my Dad in Texas, who had been diagnosed with cancer that summer. My Dad and I had never been very close. Most of my memories of him were either of him being drunk and yelling at Mom or us kids, or of him with a hangover the next morning and Mom letting him have it over breakfast. Though we didn't have a lot in common, I did love him and I wanted to spend some time with him, so I called my brother and told him I was coming to visit Dad on my way to my next job on the road, and began packing up what I would need to take with me to my next job.

MY TIME WITH DAD

Leaving my Mom and grown children and my tiny grandson behind in Oklahoma was the toughest thing I had done in a long time. Not knowing where God was taking me next or when I would see them again broke my heart. I cried all the way to Texas.

Dad lived in a very small house on my brother's property in rural North Texas. The whole place probably wasn't four hundred square feet. His entire house would fit in some people's living rooms, but Dad's tastes were simple and he didn't need much to be happy.

Since Dad's diagnosis, my brother and his wife had been caring for him, driving him to doctor visits and chemotherapy treatments. I suspected they would welcome any help I could offer for a few days while I waited on a job call. Bill collector calls had become a daily thing and I was anxious to get back to work and catch up on my payments.

Dad was overjoyed when I surprised him with my visit. Since having part of one leg amputated, he was no longer able to go places by himself, and he was having a hard time dealing with being alone so much. My favorite trait about Dad was his sense of humor. He would often say things that were so funny, we would double over in laughter.

After spending the first night at Dad's house, I figured I could at least be earning gas money for the trip to whatever oil and gas job came through first. None of the three jobs I had located were nearby. One of them was in Louisiana, one in far West Texas, and the other was in California where I had never worked before. Whatever I could earn would put me that much ahead. I could use the money to pay on my charge cards and then use them for expenses until I got my first check.

I completed my paperwork at my favorite temporary employment agency in Dallas that afternoon, but was advised they had only temp-to-perm jobs, which were temporary jobs that went permanent after six weeks. Since I was certain I would be leaving for another job shortly, I asked them to look again for something that was just temporary fill-in or data entry, but they had only temp to perm. I began to pray silently.

Lord, I need to make some gas money while I'm here. Please give me some work.

They have another job that isn't in the computer yet. That's the one I have for you.

> *Everywhere I looked, it seemed as if all I had ever known was coming apart at the seams. It left me feeling scared, and confused.*

They continued to look and discuss among themselves. A few minutes later, a woman at a nearby desk turned around and said, "I do have one position that hasn't been entered into the computer yet, but it pays less than ten dollars an hour."

Less than ten dollars an hour wasn't a drop in the bucket to what I needed to meet my obligations, but it was still more than nothing, and I knew that was the job the Lord wanted me in. At least I had been able to extend the payment on my pickup. I had mailed a letter to the bank before leaving Oklahoma. That would buy me some time to get a paycheck coming in again. The woman continued, saying the temp job was working a switchboard job covering someone going on maternity leave. I immediately agreed to the job. It didn't matter how little it paid if it was His will, He had a plan.

I drove back to Dad's, looking forward to a hot shower and a quiet evening with him. That night at Dad's, I discovered the tiny five gallon hot water tank would not allow me a warm shower long enough to shave my legs, and the breaker tripped shutting off all the power in the house when I switched on my blow dryer. After that night, I accustomed myself as best I could to cool showers, and sat in front of a fan to dry my hair.

Never in all my almost forty years had my life felt like it was coming completely unraveled. Everywhere I looked, it seemed as if all I had ever known was coming apart at the seams. It left me feeling scared, and confused. I had given my life to Christ only two years before, and I had no idea how to handle what was happening, or why it was happening to me.

Every day I drove almost an hour to the temporary job, crying and praying, begging God to open up one of the oil and gas jobs for me, and to help me get my life back. I worked all day, then cried and prayed all the way home, trying to ignore the calls from bill collectors as I checked for the message I lived for, the one that would tell me I was going back to my work in the oilfield.

Over the next few weeks as I waited on one of the jobs to come through, I spent time with Dad, taking him out of the house on weekends to the flea market and second hand stores he loved, watching movies with him, and making his favorite dessert to encourage him to eat. I made him coffee in the mornings and ate dinner with him at night, usually brought over by my brother or his wife and left for us in plates in Dad's small kitchen. Dad was a private person, he didn't talk much about how he felt, so we didn't share a lot of feelings or emotions, but I knew my presence comforted him. He would always smile when he knew we were going out some place, and it brought me great joy to be able to do at least small things for him during such a trying time.

In the early hours each morning I put my makeup on sitting on the bed under a bare light bulb. Every inconvenience only added to my feeling of being far away from my old life, and made me feel as if I lived in a foreign country. I tried to hide my emotional turmoil from Dad, but inside I was in meltdown mode. I worried about Mom, my kids, my soon to be ex son-in-law. I worried about my grandson. I worried about my bills. I grieved that my Dad and my sister would be taken from us too soon. It seemed all I could do was cry. Everything hurt and comfort was nowhere to be found. I was a mess.

Going home every night to the small house after fighting rush hour traffic in Dallas, with the Jerry Springer Show blaring from the television only feet away from where I slept and having no privacy, my nerves were more than on edge. I wanted so much to be a help to Dad, but I was an emotional mess myself. I had always found peace in quietness and solitude, and the constant noise and strife from the television added to my already raging stress level. I quietly cried myself to sleep almost every night. Dad once told me he watched The Jerry Springer Show and The Ricki Lake Show because the people on the shows made him feel like his problems were small in comparison.

As the days passed and then the weeks, the oil companies still did not have budget approval for the jobs they were planning. I tried hard to have faith and not fear. Surely the Lord would deliver me out of the terrible mess I found myself in, and give me another job that paid well enough that I could pay my obligations and make my vehicle payments on time. There was no way I could support myself and pay everything on what I was making doing temp work. Every day the jobs did not come through, I got further behind on my bills, and my fight against fear became more difficult. The most frustrating part was my inability to change anything about what was happening to me.

Almost three weeks had passed since beginning the temporary switchboard job, and I was spending as much time with Dad as I could on the weekends, knowing I would soon be leaving for my next job. I was trying desperately to keep my payments up as well as I could in the meantime on my small paychecks. I had called many of the companies to arrange smaller payments, some agreed and others refused.

I missed my Mom and kids so much, and I missed my only grandson, who was growing up without me. I wanted to be in Oklahoma near them, but I had to work, and I knew the Lord had led me to visit Dad, He had even provided me some work while I was there, so even though my heart wanted to go back to Oklahoma, I stayed. Even if He hadn't led me there, I had no money to return home, and no place to live if I went back.

The homesickness worsened by the day. Often I would find myself driving to work and thinking of Mom or my grandson or one of my children, and tears would begin streaming down my face. Once, when I called Mom's house, my grandson was there. She put him on the phone and he said," Nana bye-bye!" and started crying. My heart shattered into a thousand pieces as tears filled my eyes. I felt the same way about being away from him.

As the weeks passed, I became increasingly uncomfortable staying at Dad's. Not only was there never a moment's peace from the blaring television, but he suddenly began asking where I was going, what I was doing, and who I was talking to on the telephone whenever I received a phone call. Though I was up at five o'clock a.m. every week day, he also insisted I be up at 8:00 a.m. on weekends. It seemed there was no comfort and no rest anywhere I looked.

I tried repeatedly to put my problems aside and concentrate on helping Dad and just spending time with him, but my failed marriage, low-wage job and the constant battering from bill collectors, plus all the problems my loved ones were suffering back home in Oklahoma made it impossible to do. I felt like a prisoner living in a tiny space with no privacy and no choices, being told what to do by everyone around me. I was desperate for even the tiniest glimmer of hope in the huge all encompassing darkness that had become my life.

Only a year before I had been living in a quiet apartment paid for by the company I was contracted to with hours of uninterrupted quiet every evening for praying and worshiping the Lord. Now the only quiet I had to pray in was the bumper-to-bumper traffic in Dallas on my hour plus commute to and from my very low paying job in a city where I did not wish to be.

Why had I not saved every extra penny when I was working before? Why had I not planned for the future? I felt that debt and careless living along with all those holiday shopping trips the December before had financed this sad vacation, and it filled it with remorse. Buying gifts for my family on credit was a way to deal with my loneliness in the barren West Texas town where I had spent the last several weeks of the previous year before moving on to South Texas for my next job in January. I had been seduced by the ease of shopping with plastic, even after months of working hard to pay down my debts earlier in the year. I knew no one in the town I had been sent to and the bright lights of the Christmas season had only increased my loneliness. Shopping brought happy thoughts of my family and gave me something to look forward to after working all week besides sitting alone in my motel room.

Thinking about the past didn't help, though. I was trying to spend as much time as possible with the Lord where I was, at Dad's. My morning commute time into Dallas became a time of intense prayer and worship. On the way to work each morning I would pray and praise God for all the good things I could find, in between bouts of begging and pleading with tears for Him to deliver me out of the mess I was in. On the way home I would pray and cry some more, before finally turning on worship music and worshiping Him. No matter where I was in my walk, He was still God, and He still deserved to be worshiped. The reward was sometimes the worship experience took me so deep that His presence would fill my vehicle, and I would be filled with joy. His presence wrapped around me like a warm blanket. Those times sustained me through all else, the times that allowed me to forget for just a few minutes how painful my life had become. His presence was the one thing I knew I could never live without.

I located a church in Princeton not far from Dad's and began attending, hoping to find encouragement there. I invited Dad but he had no interest in attending with me. One morning as I walked to the bathroom, Dad was sitting in his chair watching preaching on television. It was the first time I had ever seen my Dad pursue anything spiritually in my entire life, and I was greatly encouraged that he was at least interested in the Lord now. I had tried to talk about the Lord some with him, but Dad was very private. Whatever he believed, he wasn't interested in discussing it with me.

One evening I was driving home from work after receiving yet another bill collector call demanding money and the pressure was becoming increasingly hard to bear. I began thinking of my quiet life earlier that year in Oklahoma. I missed my family and my old life so much tears again began streaming down my face again. I had already decided to look for a second job to try to make more money. Maybe if I did that I could somehow keep my payments made on time while I waited for work in the oilfield to come through.

By the time I was a quarter of a mile from Dad's house I was weeping uncontrollably. I didn't want to upset Dad, so I pulled into the cemetery and parked near my younger brother's grave. Everything in my life was broken. I desperately wished my brother was still alive. Just the sight of his smile could cheer me. As I sat by his grave, I knew I was still mourning the loss of his life at such a young age, as well as the loss of my life as I knew it. I mourned for all my loved ones back in Oklahoma going through such hard times without me there to offer whatever comfort I could, though it seemed obvious I couldn't even run my own life well. I didn't understand what had happened or how it had all happened so fast.

Though I did not understand at the time what was happening, everything dear to me was being crucified; my ability to provide for myself financially, being near the family I loved so much, even holding on to my credit rating. My first walk through the desert had begun, and I was being stripped of all my flesh held dear. Like Job, I wondered if I had sinned and was being punished.

JOB 10:15

IF I AM GUILTY, WOE TO ME!

   IF I AM IN THE RIGHT, I CANNOT LIFT UP MY HEAD,

FOR I AM FILLED WITH DISGRACE

   AND LOOK ON MY AFFLICTION.

My life wasn't perfect, but it seemed to be going along okay and then everything just started coming apart at the seams. Now it all lay like shattered glass at my feet, fractured in so many places I could not hope to ever put it back the same again.

I want to go home, Lord! Please let me go home to where my family is. Please! I miss them so much!

I knew by blood my Dad and brother were also family, but we just were not close. All the family I was truly close to were back in Oklahoma.

As the weeks rolled by, Dad's questioning led me to feel as if I had worn out my welcome there. He did not like me talking on the phone or working late. I seemed to be getting on his nerves more than helping him. I prayed fervently that the oilfield job would come through soon. More pressure was the last thing I needed and my emotional state of mind was the last thing he needed as well.

Please, Lord! Please let me out of this place! Please help me!

CHAPTER 3 - DALLAS

One day not long after, it was my lunch hour and I walked out to my truck to once again to call my list of oil companies about the jobs we had discussed. I was praying one of them had a job that had been approved, and would tell me to report to it right away. No one did. I hung up the phone, more than disappointed. It had been weeks now, and no one had any work for me. Everything felt so hopeless. I was completely miserable, and I was trapped. I could not find a way out of my situation.

I hung my head and prayed, tears filling my eyes.

What's going on, Lord? I've always been able to work and make enough money to pay my bills on time, but now I can't. I'm virtually homeless and beyond miserable staying at Dad's. Please help me!

I didn't understand why none of the promised jobs were coming through after all those weeks. I knew all three companies wanted to hire me. Was it possible oil and gas was cycling down again? I hadn't checked the markets and I was out of touch with everyone I knew in the industry after taking the six month sabbatical.

Was it possible I was stuck here in Dallas? My blood ran cold at the thought. I knew I could not handle living at Dad's much longer and I was in no way prepared to live in a big city alone. I had no money, no way to rent an apartment and no hope of being able to rent one on the small wage I was earning. On top of that, all my furniture and household items were stored in Oklahoma and I had no money to go get them.

Suddenly I felt the witness in my spirit that staying in Dallas was God's will for me. My heart dropped and tears began to stream down my face. I wanted to go home to where my loved ones were, or at least back out into the oilfield, where I could be happy in my work. I knew then the call I had waited and waited for would never come. For a minute the fear hit me so hard, I thought I would be sick.

Why here, Lord? Why couldn't I stay in Oklahoma? Okay, so I wasn't doing great up there, but at least I was surrounded by people who loved me. At least I was near the oilfield work I want to do. Why did You bring me here to Dallas? What could possibly be the reason for this? I've never even lived in a big city before!

Silence.

Whatever the reason was for the Lord leading me to Dallas, He wasn't telling me about it. Tears streamed down my face. I was beyond miserable, and I had no place else to go. I couldn't go back the way I came, and I couldn't move forward either. There was nothing to do but keep putting one foot in front of the other, and trying to make some kind of life here while I figured out what the Lord wanted me to see or do in this place.

Just days later, with the atmosphere getting more and more tense at Dad's, I was advised the temporary switchboard job where I had been working was ending, and the manager of the office pleaded with me to interview with her boss whose administrative assistant had recently given notice. She had watched my work and seen the extra effort I put out and was sure I was exactly what he needed at his office. I had no place else to go so I agreed to interview and fill in temporarily.

I took the temp position on a fill-in basis, but it was further from Dad's house, making my commute almost an hour and a half each way, something I did not look forward to. I was already rising at 5:00 o'clock a.m. every day to get ready for work, and make the long commute through bumper-to-bumper traffic. The upside was my new manager was nice, professional and friendly. The office was small and more private. Only a few other people worked in it, so it was much quieter than the hustle bustle at the previous one, which was a balm to my jangled nerves. His young college age assistant was leaving for another position and it didn't take long to see he needed someone more mature and capable, who could be trusted when he was out of the office traveling, which was more of the time than not. I did not want to commute even further and I had no place else to live, but I agreed to at least work there while he looked for someone suitable for the position.

Not long after, my forwarded mail caught up with me and I received a letter from the bank where my truck was financed. To my horror, they had sent me papers to sign to extend my payment at my request and because of the delay in forwarding my mail to Texas, I received them two weeks too late. Consequently, my payment had not been extended and now they were threatening to repossess my truck. I sat there terrified, Ricki Lake blaring from Dad's television only feet away. Without my truck I would be trapped there at Dad's house - no way to work and no way to escape. No hope of ever escaping. I was almost sick with terror, my stomach felt as if it were filled with molten steel. I wanted to cry out to God but there was no place in Dad's tiny house to cry out. Inside me, my soul was screaming for Him to intervene in my situation.

I didn't feel comfortable talking to my brother or his wife about my situation, and they had their own difficulties to deal with anyway. My brother had missed many days of work taking Dad back and forth to doctor visits and they were playing catch-up themselves. They were obviously overjoyed

> *I was crossing the shaky bridge of brokenness, and not only did I not know where I was at, I had no idea where I was going. Would the problems ever end?*

someone else was there to help care for Dad for a few weeks, and I was doing my best to be a help to them. My brother was very close to Dad, so Dad's illness was even more difficult for him, and he didn't need my problems on top of his.

In the midst all of the madness, and although it made no sense, I still felt God's peace about the area I was in. Though everything around me looked dark and terrifying, though nothing that was happening made any sense at all to my mind, I knew when all else failed, if I stayed in the place where I felt God's peace that He would take care of me. At that point in my walk, I knew very little about God, but I did know His provision would be where He wanted me physically. Some days it was all I could do to just get through the next hour, but I continued putting one foot in front of the other and just taking the next step, doing the next thing I had to do. In my spirit, I could feel Jesus with His arms held out in love to me and I held on to the thought of His love with everything in me.

One morning in early November during a bumper-to-bumper commute from Dad's house to my new temp job, I was creeping along in traffic when the brakes in my truck started acting funny. I had driven enough old worn out cars when I was married and living in poverty to know when the brakes were going. I prayed I was wrong, and pumped the brake pedal to test it. It went all the way to the floor. I tried not to panic, I was stuck in multiple lanes of bumper-to-bumper rush hour traffic, and there was no place to pull off the road safely. I had an extended warranty but absolutely no idea where the nearest qualified mechanic was, so I kept going, albeit very slowly.

Over an hour later with my stomach in knots I finally arrived at work. I called a tow truck and had my truck towed to the nearest dealership. After checking it over, they told me the battery had somehow leaked onto the brake lines and eaten through, causing the brake fluid to leak out, and the master cylinder had failed completely. The dealership informed me not a drop of brake fluid was left in it when I brought it in. My extended warranty covered a rental car so I picked up a rental and returned to work. Two miles from home that night, the rental car had a flat. I pulled over into an abandoned driveway in total disbelief. I had so many problems it was becoming ridiculous at this point. My poor overworked brother had to come out in the cold that night to put the spare on for me so I could make it the rest of the way home.

The tire place I took the flat for repair the next day said the tire on the rental had a bubble in it and was just waiting to go flat. The rental car company informed me it was my problem since the car was rented to me when it happened. It was not a well known rental place and I would never rent from them again, but having to use one of my nearly maxed out charge cards to buy a tire for their car was just one more problem on my mountain of difficulties at the time.

Every day at work when things were quiet and I sat thinking over everything that was happening, I fought back tears. I was crossing the shaky bridge of brokenness, and not only did I not know where I was, I had no idea where I was going. Would the problems ever end? Was this what happened to people who made bad choices? Their lives fell apart and they could never put them back together?

Soon after the tire incident, I received a letter from my daughter. She had been writing regularly since my trip to Texas. She had gotten a job and was scraping by, sharing a small house with her best friend. At the time, her best friend was not covering her part of the bills and they were really struggling to make it. She had made an extra ten dollars, and she put five dollars of it in the envelope for me. Tears streamed down my face as I read her letter. She had so little, yet she was still trying to share with me.

On my way to Texas, my son had tried to give me his last fifteen dollars, and now this. My children were everything to me. We had been through so much together, and the bond between us was strong. I wanted to be the one helping them. It is very humbling in the wilderness times when those who help you often have even less than you do.

After starting the new temp job, I found a second job and decided to move to an extended stay motel in Dallas where at least I would have peace and privacy to pray and worship in the evenings. If I could go into God's presence, all the pain and fearful events would at least be manageable. Maybe then He would tell me why He had me in Dallas.

I wasn't doing Dad much good in the emotional state I was in. I walked in exhausted with tear-streaked makeup every night, and not knowing what was wrong made him anxious. There was no use in telling him all that was wrong, none of it was fixable. Not by him and not by me. Only God could help me now, and I prayed every hour of every day that He would answer my prayers. I wished with all my heart I could be more emotionally present for Dad. Why did I have to be going through so much when he needed my care?

In spite of my money struggles, I continued to tithe. Mom had taught me that giving ten percent to the Lord was His due, and the Word backed up what she said. The Lord had prospered me in my time out in the oilfield, and I believed Him to take care of me in Dallas as well. I had nothing to fall back on here, I had to make it, and the promise of the blessing from the tithe was what I was standing on. Paying for the extended stay motel on top of my other obligations out of my tiny paycheck left me very little money for food. I bought sparingly for my evening meals and I ate lunch on five dollars a week, but I was so overjoyed to have quiet in the evenings I was willing to give up almost anything.

I did not know it at the time, but just before going to Dallas, I had entered the wilderness. The wilderness is a dark and terrifying unknown time where life as you know it is stripped away; a time when God prunes what is not pleasing to Him so we can bear more fruit for His kingdom. For several months after going to Dallas, it seemed I heard sermon after sermon on Deuteronomy 8:2. I wondered what God was trying to tell me through that verse. I read it over and over. I thought maybe He was telling me to remember that He had saved me from my old life, and to be grateful and not forget, so I tried to thank Him often for saving me.

DEUTERONOMY 8:2

AND YOU SHALL REMEMBER THE WHOLE
WAY THAT THE LORD YOUR GOD HAS LED
YOU THESE FORTY YEARS IN THE
WILDERNESS, THAT HE MIGHT HUMBLE
YOU, TESTING YOU TO KNOW WHAT WAS
IN YOUR HEART, WHETHER YOU WOULD
KEEP HIS COMMANDMENTS OR NOT.

As I moved deeper into the wilderness experience, I tried to remind myself that even in the darkest of times we can find some small thing of beauty or goodness to concentrate on, to help us get through it. I remembered a time in the early eighties when I was married and the abuse became worse than ever before, branching out into new areas. I was working in an office in McKinney where I had no friends, and was not performing all that well on my job. At night I would go home to hours of horrible abuse in a rented mobile home that was sometimes so cold in the winter the inside of the back door would ice over. The economic recession left us without jobs on the Texas Gulf Coast, and we had sold everything we had just to get gas money to move further north. When we got there, we had to buy everything again. With low wage jobs that barely covered the rent and utilities, there was nothing left over for household needs, or to rent a nicer place.

We slept on an old mattress on the floor in one bedroom and the children slept on another one in the back bedroom. We didn't have enough blankets, so I made rag quilts from layers of rags and old clothes to help keep us all warm. By the time we got paid every Friday, we didn't have even two dollars left from the week before. We bought most of our clothes at thrift stores, and I cooked our meals in scraps of pans with no handles.

I remember once in the earlier years of our marriage, visiting a next door neighbor's house whose husband my husband had befriended. He and his wife were a young couple in their early twenties like us, who lived in the simple rent house next door. I was in awe of the beautiful pictures she had on her wall. I had never lived in a house that had walls that were decorated, and I wondered what it would be like to live in a house that actually felt like a home the way that one did.

Several years later, we had moved to a rent house in town. When my family came in for my brother's funeral, they were shocked by our living conditions. Unable to afford to turn on the gas due to an unpaid bill, we heated water by placing a two burner hot plate under the antique tub, and heated four inches of water to bathe in, adding hot water from the stove. Life had felt so hopeless back then. During one period of time, when the abuse was at its peak, the only thing I could find to cling to for hope was the colorful picture on my desk calendar at work. I would stare at whatever beautiful scene it offered me each morning and pray for help, hoping for brighter days. It was my one tiny spot of beauty in a life otherwise filled with constant pain. Focusing on that picture helped me to hang on to my sanity while I looked for a safe way out. In a hidden corner of my heart, I built a dream of a quiet little house somewhere safe, filled with love and laughter. Years later, during the toughest times in my life, I continued to use that method. I would find one small spot of beauty somewhere in my environment, and cling to it to help me get through.

After moving to the extended stay motel in Dallas, I began spending more and more time with the Lord, and though I was terrified living alone in a big city, I felt my strength beginning to come back. I took a small portable radio to work at the new office and when no one else was there, I listened to Bible teachings for encouragement. Any time I was in my truck, I listened to Bible teachings or worship music. When I was in my room at night, I was either listening to more teaching or I was in prayer or worship. Jesus was the rock I went to for strength. He was absolutely essential to my happiness, and I knew whether my life got better or continued to get worse, I could not make it through one day without Him. His presence was the one place I knew I could find comfort, no matter how bad my circumstances were.

Often when I would call Mom, she would tell me God had told her to pray for me during a particularly rough time. He had her praying frequently when I was staying at Dad's. Mom had been my prayer partner ever since I had given my life to the Lord, and we talked as often as I could afford to call her.

In the evenings driving back to the motel past neighborhoods of beautiful castle-like houses, I thought back to warm evenings after work in South Texas when I would take long walks just before dusk, enjoying the cool air. Late one evening I had walked past a lovely one story home surrounded by trees where the soft yellow light shone from the windows. Happy family sounds poured out into the evening air. A family was laughing together in this beautiful home. I stopped on the sidewalk, tears filling my eyes as longing rose up in my soul for a home of my own, and for happy family sounds to fill it with.

Like Mom, my only real dream was to own my own home. We both dreamed of a little farmhouse some place in the countryside filled with peace, God's presence, the smell of food cooking, and beautiful quilts. That was our idea of heaven on earth, to be able to lie in bed at night listening to the wind ruffling the leaves of the nearby trees without the jarring noise of traffic nearby. Some place where we could sit on the front porch late in the evening, enjoying the sunset, and praying.

All those terrible years of abuse, I held on tight to that one dream of escaping with my children and someday owning a home filled with peace and joy, and that dream kept me from giving up on all those mornings when I stood before my mirror, trying to cover the latest bruises with makeup or a scarf. Someplace quiet where no one was angry and yelling, where I could be at peace and my children could be children. I will never forget the look in my children's eyes as we waited for someone to answer the door at the women's shelter we escaped to in Oklahoma in 1987. They were only 9 and 11, but their eyes looked like the eyes of the very old who have suffered horribly for many years.

Now here I was, alone in a big city with no clue why I was there, starting over at nearly forty years old, broke and alone, my children and grandson far away going through some of the hardest times of their lives, with yet another failed marriage behind me and dealing with the impending deaths of two of my family members. I could not see how any happy ending could possibly come after so much tragedy.

Everything in my life felt so unstable. I was living in an extended-stay motel, working a low paying job far away from my family, and I was literally afraid every single day. I could no longer meet my obligations and at this point was just doing damage control, paying my vehicle payment, my storage, my motel, buying as little food as possible, and tithing. I refused to even consider not tithing. I knew well the promise of the tithe and I didn't care how many said it was Old Testament and not required, I had seen it carry my Mother through thick and through thin and it was the only insurance available to me in the wilderness. In my heart, I clung to it in those moments of intense fear, and it carried me. I had been eating lunch on five dollars a week and I would often run out of money by Friday, even being as careful as I could and eating off dollar menus. When I ran out of money, I would pray and ask the Lord to send someone to buy me lunch that day. I never told a soul around me I was

> *I had been eating lunch on five dollars a week, and I would often run out of money by Friday, even being as careful as I could and eating off dollar menus.*

doing that, and not once in all those months did He not answer that prayer. Not one single time did I go without lunch.

One morning in the motel, as I was praying and praising and getting ready for work, I had a flash vision. A flash vision is where you see a vision vividly in your spirit, but only for a few seconds. As the vision opened, I saw myself in a bright sunny apartment or house, and all my things were there with me. I could feel in the vision all my decor was hanging on my walls and that I was making enough money to pay my bills. And I was full of joy. I rejoiced – that vision was God's signal to me that I would indeed be happy again!

I clung to that vision. That vision meant brighter days and days of enough were coming. It meant that though I might not know where a place to live was that I could afford, God did. He did and He would get me there if I only believed Him to. I just had to hold on to my faith until then.

HEBREW 12:2

LOOKING TO JESUS, THE FOUNDER AND PERFECTER OF OUR FAITH, WHO FOR THE JOY THAT WAS SET BEFORE HIM ENDURED THE CROSS, DESPISING THE SHAME, AND IS SEATED AT THE RIGHT HAND OF THE THRONE OF GOD.

WINTER'S CHILL

Not long after the vision, the weather began to get very cold in Dallas. One evening, I was climbing the stairs to my room at the extended stay motel and the cold wind felt like it was cutting through my thin clothing.

Lord, I really need a warm coat!

The next evening, I drove to the grocery store to get food for that week. As I stood in line, I noticed a lady in line ahead of me wearing a beautiful trench coat with epaulette trim on the shoulders.

Lord, I would love to have a long coat like that, with epaulette trim, in a bright colored wool.

The manager at my second temp job had asked me every day for weeks if I would consider taking the position permanently. He was so kind and so pleasant, and I had no other plans, so I finally accepted a permanent position there. It did not pay much, but at least I could be happy working in the quiet office for someone who truly valued me as an employee.

One day near the middle of that first December, I was feeling particularly vulnerable. Things were not going well for my daughter back in Oklahoma and Mom missed me terribly, as did my son and grandson. I wanted more than anything to be near them, but I knew God had sent me to Dallas, and I could not disobey Him by leaving until He released me to. Night after night I longed for nothing more than to back my truck up to the motel door and throw everything I had in it, and just head back to Oklahoma, but I knew better. I believed in not moving until God moved me.

One particular morning my burdens felt so heavy, I felt so sad inside, and so homesick for my family. I sat at my desk and struggled to focus and do my work.

Where is my home, Lord? Why can't I make a home near my family in Oklahoma? Why don't I have a home of my own yet? I'm trying so hard to do everything You want, please help me understand.

Finally, filled with sadness, I called the prayer line of a ministry I gave to regularly and asked for prayer. The woman who took my call prayed so beautifully over me, my situation, and my family back in Oklahoma. Her prayer brought comfort and peace to my soul. I quickly hung up the phone a few moments later, when I heard my boss stirring. Seconds later, he came out of his office and laid a red suede pouch on my desk, and said, "'Merry Christmas." After he walked away, I opened the pouch. Inside was a beautiful pewter Christmas ornament. It was in the shape of a two-story house. Tears welled up in my eyes. I felt God saying *'Hang on, I know where home is and I'll get you there.'*

Thank You, Lord. Thank You for letting me know You're still there and You're watching over me. I really do believe You will give me a home.

My son was planning to come and stay with me in Dallas after I got an apartment. At that point, barely able to pay for my motel room and food, I wasn't sure when that would be. Unable to keep up my credit card payments, I wasn't even sure my credit would pass so that I could rent one. I planned to wait until I got my tax return and use that money to get my furniture out of storage in Oklahoma and move into an apartment. There was plenty of work to do a the office, and I was hoping to be able to work overtime and save the extra money.

That night as I prayed about trying to rent an apartment, wondering if I could even qualify for one, the Lord spoke again.

You are Mine. Your son is Mine. A place for you to live is My problem, not yours, because you belong to Me and he belongs to Me.

I had been delivered of anger, and I hadn't even been aware that spirit was on me. The Lord showed me later that anger had attached to me in my childhood and had been causing me to have anger outbursts ever since.

The next day during my lunch hour, the enemy began trying to plant fearful thoughts in my mind, telling me there was no way I would ever be able to move into an apartment of my own; I didn't make enough money, my credit wouldn't pass; blah, blah, blah. On and on he went, telling me I was stuck forever in an extended stay motel. I would never have a place of my own. Never!

I knew what God had told me the night before. I knew He had spoken to me, and anger at the enemy began to rise up in me. I had only recently gotten my hope back, and he was *not* going to take it from me! I decided to let him know it.

"The Word says my God shall supply ALL my needs, Satan, you're a liar! I rebuke you and I won't listen to any more of this nonsense! God will provide a place for me to live! He said so!"

Silence.

It worked!

On my last work day before the Christmas holidays, my boss laid a card on my desk and told me not to open it until I left the office. When I got back to my motel that evening, I opened the card. It contained a hundred dollar bill, and a note saying things at the office had really improved since I had been working there. The Lord had led me to a job where I was not only happy, but appreciated and rewarded. I had the best boss ever. I used the money to buy gas for a quick trip to Oklahoma to visit my loved ones over the Christmas holiday.

One Saturday right after the first of the year, I was at a laundromat doing my laundry. I had been praying and asking the Lord to lead me to a church – a real church where I would be fed spiritually. A pleasant older lady at the laundromat struck up a conversation with me about a magazine I was reading. Though I never mentioned I wanted to go to a church, she invited me to go to church with her at The Potter's House in South Dallas. I was very familiar with T.D. Jakes' preaching, he was one of my favorite television preachers. I was delighted. We made arrangements to meet early the next morning to go to the second service. I really felt this was a divine appointment and that I would hear from God at church the next morning, and I longed to hear from Him as often as possible. His words sustained me like manna from heaven in that wilderness place.

The next morning as I got into my friend's car, the wind felt like it was blowing right through my dress. My friend's car heater did not make the car very warm until we were almost to church a half hour later and I was trying to hide the fact that I was shivering in the cold. I began to pray silently.

Lord, Monday I'm going to the Goodwill near the office and look for a coat. Please, please let there be one there I can buy for five dollars. I'll take peanut butter sandwiches for lunch all week, but I really need a coat. This wind is so cold!

That morning at The Potter's House, T.D. Jakes preached a wonderful sermon, and as we all held our tithes and offerings up to the Lord for a blessing, he prayed that everyone in the house would have the spirit of anger broken off of their lives. When he prayed that, I felt something leave my body, and then a hollow feeling where it had been. I had been delivered of anger, and I hadn't even been aware that spirit was on me. The Lord showed me later that anger had attached to me in my childhood and had been causing me to have anger outbursts ever since.

Driving back from church that morning, my friend and I were discussing how wonderful the sermon was when she must have noticed me shivering.

"Do you by any chance need a coat?"

"Yes, I actually do need one," I answered.

"I don't want to offend you, but if you want it, I have one I no longer use and you're welcome to it," she offered.

I wasn't offended, I was cold!

"I would love to have it, thank you!"

When we arrived back to our area of Dallas, she drove to her house. There in a hall closet hung a coat covered in plastic wrap from Lord & Taylor's Department Store. She said the coat no longer fit her, and she had been looking for someone who could use it. My eyes lit up when she pulled the plastic off. Not only was it my size, it was a long coat made of bright red wool with epaulette trim on the shoulders. My mouth dropped open. I was thrilled - God had answered my prayer!

For days afterwards, I would look at that beautiful red coat, and think of how loving and merciful God was. In spite of the many times since beginning my walk I had gotten into sin, He still provided for me, still took care of me. I would have been happy with any decent looking coat that fit even marginally well, but He had sent me something so much better than that. He sent specifically what I had prayed for, the kind of coat I would have purchased if I had been able to buy what I wanted. I thanked Him each time I wore my beautiful red coat. It was long and so warm against the freezing winter wind, and I was overjoyed that after praying just a simple prayer and asking for something I needed, He had supplied my need so perfectly. Every time I looked at that coat, I saw my Father's love for me.

> *Every time I looked at that coat, I saw my Father's love for me.*

I told my Mom and daughter about the wonderful miracle of my new coat. Not long after the coat incident, the enemy launched an attack on me which started physically, then he attacked me with increased fear, and then the financial pressures increased. It went on for weeks. At that time, I was only beginning to learn about attacks from the enemy.

MIRACLE DEPOSIT

In February, I began to look for an apartment. I would drive to nearby apartment complexes during my lunch hour, then rush back to work. Each one was nice, new and fully equipped, but none of them felt right. Each time, I would pray. *This one, Lord? Is this where You want me?*

And I would only get silence. After weeks of searching, one of the managers at the office where I worked drove me to a complex where she had lived for years while raising her children. It was much further from work than I had planned on moving, and it wasn't new like the others, but as we pulled into the parking lot, I read the name - *Royal Arms*. That sounded so much like God. Royal Arms - *His* royal arms. It was an older property, but I didn't care, I wasn't into prestige. I just wanted a safe, decent place to live.

We parked and I stepped out of the car. As soon as my foot touched the ground, I knew I was in the right place. The apartment I looked at was sunny and spacious, three bedrooms and two full baths plus a balcony, with big trees outside the master bedroom window in the back. When I saw the light in it, I remembered my flash vision, and I felt it was the place I had seen. I picked up an application and asked about pricing.

My heart dropped at what I was told. The apartment was more expensive than those I had been looking at, and the deposit was two hundred dollars, a fortune to me. The good news was, I had just discovered I got paid for overtime at work, so it was at least possible. Maybe if I worked extra hours every week, I could live there. But I would need the deposit as well as the first month's rent, and deposits for the utilities. How could I possibly come up with that much money? I decided to just believe for the deposit to start. The whole amount would be well over a thousand dollars, and that didn't include the money to rent a truck and go get my things out of storage in Oklahoma. I didn't think I had enough faith to believe for the whole amount. I would have to do it in pieces.

Okay, Lord, I feel strongly this is where You are leading me to live. I feel Your peace in this place. If that is true, please bring me the deposit. I have no other way of getting two hundred dollars and this beautiful apartment won't stay empty long.

Two days later, a friend I had worked with in Louisiana was in town, and met me at church to see what the services were like after hearing me rave about it. After church, he handed me an envelope with a note inside. He told me not to open it until I got back to my motel room, but I opened it in the car as my friend drove out of the parking lot. Inside was a check for $200 and a note saying "The Lord told me to give this to you." My friend and I rejoiced and praised God all the way back to her house.

My visiting friend knew nothing about the apartment or the deposit I needed. God had provided yet again. I was sure it was confirmation that I had found the right apartment, and that I would be approved. Soon, I could move out of the motel and into my own place. The apartment was so spacious and so full of light and I couldn't wait to live there, to fill the balcony with potted plants, to decorate the walls, to wake up there every day!

That week, I scheduled a moving truck and friends in Oklahoma to help me load and move, along with some vacation time so I could drive to Oklahoma and get my things out of storage.

I left the motel late one evening to do my weekly grocery shopping and returned to find the light on my phone blinking. Since I could no longer afford a cell phone, I had to receive calls at the motel. My daughter had left a message that my Dad had taken ill and to call her. The switchboard had already closed and I had no idea where any payphones were in the area, so I waited. The next morning I called my brother and learned Dad had suffered a full blown seizure. The x-rays showed the cancer had spread from his lungs to his brain. I had no idea the cancer had gotten that bad. When I talked to Dad on the phone, he hadn't said anything, but maybe he hadn't known. I got the hospital room number and headed to McKinney.

My family did not know how broke I was, they only knew I was living in Dallas and had found work there, and that they did not hear from me much. Only my children and my Mom knew I was barely getting by, and even they did not know just how close to the line I was really running. I knew if I bought gas to go to McKinney that something would go unpaid, because I had already bought food, but I had to see Dad.

When I walked into the room, Dad was in terrible pain. As soon as I walked into his room, I felt the presence of an angel on the left side of the room, but I didn't know what it meant. As I stood by Dad's bedside, he kept staring at that spot in the wall, and trying to raise up in bed and look at whatever he was seeing there. I tried to comfort him, and to tell him to call on the name of Jesus for help with the pain and that Jesus would take care of him.

"I hope so," he said.

"He will, Dad. I promise He will."

I stood by his bed, holding his hand and trying to think of how to comfort him. I had never sat with anyone who was terminally ill and I had no idea what to do. *Please, Lord, if Dad isn't saved, please save him!*

When my brother and one of my sisters found out I had no gas money to come back, each one had pressed a bill into my hand so I would have money. None of us were very close at that point. Years earlier when our other brother was alive, we had been closer, but we had each gone on with our lives.

I returned to Dad's hospital room for each of the next several evenings after work. I would talk to him and stand at his bedside, stroking his hair, and just try to comfort him. I had never sat with anyone who was terminally ill so I wasn't sure what I should do. I just did what I could.

On Thursday the doctors were talking about nursing care at home for Dad. I was scheduled to leave for Oklahoma the next day to move everything out of storage and bring it back to Dallas to move into my new apartment. I told Dad I would be gone for a few days to move from Oklahoma back to Texas and I would come see him as soon as I got back. Everything was reserved for moving and I was picking up my son along the way to help me move. I kissed him and drove back to my motel room.

The next day I got an early start for Oklahoma. I was so happy to be leaving that motel, and that I was going to see Mom, my grandson and my kids. That night I stayed at my daughter's house. The next morning the call came that Dad had passed away.

I was in shock. His doctor had been talking about care for him after he got home. I never thought he would die while I was in Oklahoma. His funeral was set for two days later, the day we would be driving back. I realized then the angel I felt in his room must have been a death angel, waiting to take his soul when it left his body. No one knew for sure if Dad had been saved, though we all prayed he was.

The moving truck was paid for and the apartment had already been rented. I didn't know what else to do but keep loading and then head south. There was no one else to move everything and I could not possibly come up with the money to rent the truck again, it had taken all my tax return money plus months of overtime to get enough to do it once and even with that, I barely had enough.

It seems at every funeral there is one person who completely falls apart, but before that it had never been me. This time it was. I did okay until it was over and we were passing for the last viewing. When I saw my little sweet Mom bend over Dad's casket and kiss him goodbye with tears streaming down her face, I completely lost it and almost had to be carried back to the sitting area.

When they got me to a chair, everyone kept telling me I had to stop crying, that I had to be strong, but I was so tired of being strong. I couldn't bear seeing Mom say goodbye to Dad, the one love of her life. She had lost so much already, it seemed all life had ever dealt her was pain and disappointment. Why couldn't they just leave me alone and let me cry? I was so torn and so tired and sad inside. Finally we headed out to the graveside service. Grief had left me unable to drive, and my aunt drove Mom and I in my truck, my son having taken the moving truck on to the new apartment to unload.

When it was over, I skipped the meal after and got back into the moving truck. I really didn't think anyone other than Mom would care whether I was there or not, and I didn't feel up to being around anyone. I was so grateful when Mom gave me her blessing to pass on the gathering. I could not spend one more minute acting strong. I just wanted to go home.

Within a few months of moving into my new apartment, I was out of my first wilderness experience and greatly relieved. The Lord had taught me about His faithfulness to provide. I had also learned not to underestimate the importance of that still, small voice when it said something like *I want you to get out of debt.*

CHAPTER 4 - BEAUTY FOR ASHES

In the early part of June 1999, the Lord spoke to me and told me He wanted me to give myself to prayer, so I began getting up an hour earlier every morning to pray, and set aside two to three hours each evening to pray and worship Him.

One night later that month, I went into worship and the worship just got deeper and deeper. The deeper I went with the Lord, the longer I wanted to stay in the sweetness of His presence. As it grew more intense, a vision opened up before me and I saw myself lay a box at His feet. I could not see His face, I just knew those were His feet. I saw that I was dressed in filthy rags. The box I had laid there was full of ashes and I knew in the spirit that the ashes represented my life. The Lord then blessed the box of ashes and a beautiful vine sprang up covered with fragrant roses. I saw a beautiful fragrance of some kind rise up before Him from the box. He kept touching the vine and each time He touched it, it would grow more fragrant and more beautiful. This process seemed to please Him very much. I was reminded of Isaiah 61:3. In the King James Version of the Bible that I read, that verse said God gives us beauty for ashes.

Autumn found us busy at the mortgage office in the bank. When the winter logo product catalog arrived, I poured over it in my break time. Inside I stared at a beautiful Kenneth Cole watch with the bank's logo on it.

Lord, I really want one of these watches.

That payday found me writing out my tithe and offering checks. I was still barely scraping by, but the overtime made me at least able to cover rent and utilities and my son had found work, so I felt sure things would be getting better soon. Regardless, I continued to tithe into God's work. As I was writing out the checks, the Lord spoke to me.

Give an extra $7 this time.

Yes, Lord.

The only place to get the $7 the Lord told me to give was out of my $35 grocery money, but He said give, so I gave.

As I began to press in to learn more of the Word, the Lord continued to show me simple truths through visions and words He would speak to me.

VISION OF THE POWER OF THE WORD OF GOD

One night during prayer around the end of October that year, in a vision I saw a line of doors, each having a label on it. Some of the doors I saw were sickness, poverty, depression and debt. Then I saw a mountain of a man, big and burly looking, with huge muscles bulging out everywhere, with a huge jutting chest and powerful legs. I watched as he crashed through each door one by one, without so much as lifting his hand to push on it.

Immediately after the last one, he looked around with a look on his face as if to say, *'Where's the challenge?'* He was so strong, nothing seemed to be even the slightest challenge to him. Then he turned towards me and I saw his shirt. On it were the words *'Power of God.'*

What does this mean, Lord? How can I use that power?

Then the Lord showed me my faith in the spirit mixing with His word - the man walked towards me, then he walked right into my body, and became a part of me. Next I saw the muscle man start operating through me. The Lord showed me that if I would learn His word, and mix my faith with it, the enemy's tactics would have no power against me.

JEREMIAH 33:3

CALL TO ME AND I WILL ANSWER YOU,
AND WILL TELL YOU GREAT AND HIDDEN
THINGS THAT YOU HAVE NOT KNOWN.

As the word says in Jeremiah 33:3, if we call upon the Lord, He will answer us and show us what we do not know.

Throughout this time of intense daily prayer and worship, the Lord continued to bless me in ways that delighted me. The revelations and visions were blessing enough, but He always goes above and beyond what we expect, it seems. The Lord loves to delight His children. If I saw a restaurant I particularly wanted to try, He would move on someone's heart to take me there for lunch. Once when I was wishing for more money to eat out during the week, I won a business card drawing for a free lunch. Often I had no idea where my provision would come from, but it did always show up, and it always exceeded my expectations.

One morning in early December, my boss walked out of his office and laid a box on my desk.

"Merry Christmas," he said, smiling, and he walked away.

I opened the box. Inside was the beautiful Kenneth Cole watch I had looked at so many times in the company logo catalog. God had answered another prayer!

Later that month, I had my first performance review. My boss gave me high ratings and I received a raise of 7%. I knew it wasn't a coincidence the Lord had me plant an extra $7 in offerings a few weeks earlier.

One day that summer, it was payday again and I was writing my tithe and offering checks.

Give $20 extra on your offering.

Yes, Lord.

One day around lunch time, a pretty Filipino woman came walking into my office asking directions for a business where she had an appointment that afternoon. In the course of giving her directions and chatting, we discovered we were both Christians. She asked for my card, and soon we were talking on the phone every day.

Not long after meeting my new friend, my truck broke down. The garage told me my extended warranty would only cover half the cost of the repairs. I had done some database work from home after hours for a friend, and had managed to save up a few hundred dollars, but now the repairs to my truck would take it all. The news was depressing, and I took the last hour of the day off and went home early.

I walked into my bedroom and kicked off my shoes in disgust. Would we never get ahead? Was life always going to be so difficult? I was so discouraged. I decided to watch some TV to take my mind off everything. I just felt like crying. There was never any money to spare, even when I worked evenings and weekends on the side. After a little while, I fell asleep.

When I awoke and remembered what was happening, I decided to go into the Lord's presence for a while, knowing His presence always made me feel better about whatever was happening. As I began to worship, I gave the financial problems to the Lord.

It's only money, Lord. Help me remember none of my problems are too big for You.

Two days later, things were looking up again. My son had moved into a higher paying job that provided great training in a field he wanted to learn and the Lord spoke to my new friend to sow a gift of $200 cash to me out of the blue. I had worshiped and God had brought the blessing!

GOD'S POWER TO DELIVER FROM ADDICTION

In July of that year, all the mortgage company's branch managers came to town for a meeting with my boss. My boss insisted I attend a dinner with everyone that evening, in spite of my attempts to be excluded. I was terrified of being anywhere near alcohol. I had stopped drinking once before in the early nineties and one night when I was out, someone had innocently shoved a glass of liquor under my nose, and I had begun drinking again. I was more than a little afraid of that scene repeating itself, and I took great pains to avoid any situation where alcohol might be served to be sure it didn't. This time it could not be avoided.

At the dinner, I chatted with a few of the branch managers who were also abstaining from alcohol, but my fear was never far from my mind. Near the end of the dinner, one manager who sat nearby became concerned that because I was not drinking, I was not enjoying the gathering as much as others were. I tried to tell him I did not need alcohol to enjoy everyone's company, but in the end he would not be put off. While I was chatting with one of the managers, he suddenly shoved a glass of cognac right under my nose. I jumped back from the glass, but it was too late, I had smelled the alcohol. I gasped - my worst fear had come true.

Then..... Nothing happened.

No craving, no weak moment....nothing!

The dinner ended not long after and all the way back to my apartment, all I could do was praise God for His mighty power in keeping me. He had helped me not to fall back into that earlier weakness. Tears streamed down my face as I praised Him on the drive home. I was so full of joy I could not stop praising Him. Then He spoke to me.

This night have I delivered you from the power of alcohol. You need never fear it again!

I was free!

JOHN 8:36

SO IF THE SON SETS YOU FREE, YOU WILL
BE FREE INDEED.

Around the end of July, a branch manager who had left the bank to work at another business came by the office and told me she had a job position she felt I would be perfect for. It sounded like a great job, but I wasn't interested in leaving my boss at the bank. It also paid several thousand less than my base salary did, not to mention I would lose all my overtime pay.

"I know you would never leave your boss here, but if anything happens to make you decide differently, give me a call. I think you would be a perfect fit for this job." She laid her card on my desk and left.

Early in August, a merger took place at the bank and 13,000 employees were let go. My boss was one of the first employees whose job would be cut. Everyone in the office was heartbroken, especially me.

Please bless him, Lord. He has blessed me in so many ways. Please help him get through this. He didn't deserve to be cut. He worked so hard for them. He doesn't want to leave. It seems so unfair!

My eyes filled with tears.

You are released from here.

I am? Am I supposed to take the job that was offered to me last week then?

I knew that had to be why the offer came a week earlier. The Lord knew what was coming and as the word says before we call, He answers.

ISAIAH 65:24

BEFORE THEY CALL I WILL ANSWER;
WHILE THEY ARE YET SPEAKING I WILL
HEAR.

I had received other offers in the past year, including one company in a nearby office that had begged me to interview for an Administrative Assistant position in the tech industry they said would pay a minimum of $50,000 a year – far more than I was making, but I loved working for my boss. Money was nice to have, but knowing I could work for someone with integrity who treated me with respect was better, at least to me.

That evening I called the manager who had offered me the position and scheduled an interview.

The following week the new manager installed himself in my old boss's office. He was a nice enough man and seemed very competent, a large, soft spoken man. I suddenly seemed unable to do anything right on my job. It was obvious the anointing was no longer on me to be there.

After interviewing for the other position, I was offered the job and gave my notice at the mortgage company. I found out soon after that the new manager was already making plans to move the office to downtown Dallas. God had seen what was coming and gotten me out of there just in time. I had no desire to work in a downtown office, especially in a skyscraper. I was terrified of heights.

GOD'S POWER TO HEAL THROUGH DELIVERANCE

One Sunday not long after, my new friend picked me up to go to South Dallas to pray for a woman she had talked to on the phone earlier that week who had terrible crippling arthritis. She lived with severe pain, and had been on full disability for eight years. I talked to her for a while to get a feel for where she was in her walk. She was obviously a believer, and also a kind and compassionate woman, and I liked her immediately. After about half an hour, I stood in front of her and laid my hands on her and listened for the Lord to tell me what to pray.

It's a spirit of infirmity. Cast it out.

I immediately commanded the spirit of infirmity to leave the woman and never return. I prayed for her body to be healed, and I asked God to bless her.

When we left, I prayed silently for God to answer my prayer for the woman. I had felt absolutely nothing as I prayed that short prayer for her and I fervently hoped we had not raised false hope in her.

Three days after the prayer visit, my friend called and told me the woman I had prayed for was completely healed, and was going back to work full time for her church. We rejoiced together at God's mighty power to deliver his people.

I started my new job right away, and began making friends quickly. The new office had many employees, and lots of people to talk to, quite a change from the quiet of my previous office. I also had my own office at the new company, which was a bonus.

One morning not long after I started, I was near the front desk and I overheard one of my coworkers discussing religion with the receptionist in front of some of the other employees. The receptionist was a very classy older woman that I really enjoyed talking to. I heard them agree that the Bible was just a guide, a set of guidelines to live a good life by. I began praying silently for both of them right away.

Lord, please help them see You are real and You are alive. If You can use me in this place, please do. I'll do whatever You want.

The next morning, I walked to the front desk with some paperwork for the receptionist. She was crying, and had apparently just received some bad news about someone she loved. She seemed to want to be left alone to try to regain her composure. I had made friends with another coworker who was also a believer, and I motioned to her. We went aside into a conference room, and quietly prayed for the Holy Spirit to comfort the receptionist and to bless her, and returned to our desks.

The next day, the receptionist asked me if we had prayed for her the day before.

"Yes," I answered quietly, wondering how much trouble I was in, and whether I would have to find a new one already.

"A few moments after the two of you walked away, this great peace suddenly just surrounded me," she said in awe. "I've never felt anything like that before!"

She had never been a believer.

"We prayed that the Holy Spirit of God would comfort you," I said. "What you felt was the presence of God wrapping you in His love."

Her eyes filled with tears. It was obvious this beautiful, poised older woman had never felt the presence of God before in her entire life. She thanked me over and over again. I smiled and walked back to my desk, silently lifting praises up to my God. The next day I took her a book by Jesse Duplantis on his visit to heaven. She read almost the entire book the first day she had it. I soon began bringing her CD's by my favorite Bible preachers, and we began to discuss the revelations we had gotten from them on a daily basis. I never saw her without a smile after she became a believer.

> *Her eyes filled with tears. It was obvious this beautiful, poised older woman had never felt the presence of God before in her entire life.*

As weeks passed, the workload in my new job increased and I felt increasingly uncomfortable in my new environment. Most of the people who worked there were focused on wealth and materialism, and it was difficult for me to relate to them, or them to me. I had made a few friends I really liked – the receptionist, a man named John W. Morgan, and a few others. Outside of that, my job was truly work, and the pay was definitely nothing to smile about. I could barely pay my bills and buy food.

My times of worship intensified as I continued to press in night after night. I began to experience something even deeper than before, it was as if during worship the Lord's face were before me. Not in the sense that I could see it or had a vision of it, but as if I felt it there. And I could feel His love coming back to me. I was overjoyed.

It was six days before Christmas that year and I was nearly broke. My new job paid a flat salary, unlike my job at the bank where I had been paid for overtime, and there were no bonuses. I had figured up my bills and I would have $75 in the bank after I paid them. That was all the money I would have to buy food and gas for two weeks, and I wouldn't get paid again until New Year's Eve. My new lower salary made it impossible to do much of anything outside of work, and I had no money to set aside for emergencies.

My Mom and daughter were begging me to come to Oklahoma and spend Christmas with them, but I had no gas money to go. Most of my check would go to pay rent on the first of January, and that could not be delayed, so there was no way I could hope to spend Christmas in with them.

As I prayed about my situation, and about my increasing misery at my new job, I decided to increase my tithe. I figured if I increased my seed, then my harvest would be increased. I decided to begin tithing on my gross pay, not just my net as I had been, and I decided to increase my offerings on top of my tithe. I told the Lord I wanted to go to Oklahoma for Christmas and I would go if He would bring me enough money for gas.

Lord, Your word says if I give, it will be given back to me, good measure, pressed down, shaken together and running over shall men give into my bosom. I'm believing You for that. You and I both know I don't have the money to do this, but I believe Your word is true and it says to prove You, so I'm going to do that.

As I wrote out my bills and my tithe and offering checks, the Lord spoke to me.

I will perform that which I have spoken.

Thank You, Lord! I know Your word is true!

The gas money for my trip to Oklahoma wasn't long in coming, but it came through a very unexpected source. My ex-husband gave my daughter money to send me to come and visit.

Going through Oklahoma City on the way back, I was caught in a terrible winter storm. Vehicles were sliding off the freeway right in front of my eyes. I kept going, but slowly and carefully. Clearly, I should have left earlier in the day, or maybe not at all. This storm was really bad. I had traveled for years with the oil and gas industry, and thought I could drive through it, but the roads were much worse than I expected. When I turned south on I-35 and came to a slight incline, my single axle drive pickup wouldn't go up the hill. I tried for ten minutes but the tires would only spin. It was after dark and the roads were really icy.

A wet snow was falling and I was stuck three and a half hours from home with only enough money for gas back and my rent money. There wasn't even a shoulder I could pull off on. I got out of my vehicle and climbed an embankment to call a tow truck. I had the truck towed to the nearest motel, where I rented a room with part of my rent money. I no longer had any charge cards, so cash was my only option. I had no idea what else to do.

For three days I was snowed in at that motel room. I ate only once a day, choosing the least expensive items on the menu at the family restaurant next to the motel. I was trying to conserve as much of the rent money as possible because I knew

> *Do not fear. This is My hand.*

I had no way to replace it if I spent it. I made one long distance call to my friend John Morgan and asked him to call in to my job and tell them I was iced in, and to let my kids know I was okay. I prayed constantly.

Lord, I don't know how I'm going to pay the rent when I get home. Please help me!

As it turned out later, the Lord had been protecting me that night. Others who tried to drive back in the dark on the same icy highway never made it back to Dallas.

GOD'S MIRACLE PROVISION

When the snow finally melted enough I could drive home, I prayed all the way for the Lord to help me replace the part of the rent money I had used for the motel and to eat once a day while I was there.

Two hours after I arrived home, my boss called from work and told me she had cleaned out my desk and that I needed to come and pick up my personal items.

My mouth dropped open. *What did she just say? Did she just fire me?*

She proceeded to tell me she did not believe I was unable to make it back on the highway, that she knew others who had gotten back safely.

Did I just hear her right? She thought I should risk my life to avoid missing one day of work? Was she serious?

I hung up the phone in shock. Not only was I very unaccustomed to being fired, I was in shock she actually believed I should have risked my life to avoid her being inconvenienced by my absence.

As I began to pray about it, the Lord spoke to me.

Do not fear. This is My hand.

Okay, Lord. I didn't like that job anyway, but I need You to bring me money to cover the part of my rent I spent on that motel.

Twenty minutes later, my phone rang again. It was a woman I knew from my previous job. She had never called me at home before. She asked how I was. I told her I had just been fired from my job.

"I called you because the Lord told me to call you, and to pay your rent," she said.

My mouth dropped open. *Did she just say pay my rent?*

"Can you meet me in Plano?" she asked, "I'm about to leave my office now."

"Yes!"

She didn't even ask how much it was.

I drove to meet her. She wrote a check for the full amount of my rent, and then handed me a twenty dollar bill as a bonus. I didn't know what to say.

In the days that followed being dismissed from my job, I received phone calls from coworker after coworker whose lives I had touched while working at that office, thanking me for making a difference in their lives. Some had gone to great lengths to get my home phone number in order to thank me and I was beyond moved by their words. I was so grateful to know I had touched the lives of others in my short time there and happy to hear from my friends. The job had not been a pleasant one, but God had used my time there to enrich the lives of others to His glory, and that made it worthwhile.

OBEDIENCE BRINGS INCREASE

Not long after that, I was in my friend's office at the mortgage office where I had gone to help her with her paperwork. She was talking on the phone when I glanced up to look at something, and the Lord showed me several angels in her office. Each one was carrying white bags tied with a gold band and they were coming and going, placing the bags on her floor. He told me all she had to do was speak to claim them.

The next day I was back helping her in the office again and I began feeling under the weather. As I got ready to leave, she handed me a check. I had volunteered to help her, and was not expecting payment of any kind. She said the Lord had told her to give it to me, and had even given her the amount, and that it was a strange one. I looked at it and it was the amount of my vehicle payment. It wasn't even due for another week!

God always knows how much our bills are. He knew I was concerned about not having a paycheck, and being able to make my vehicle payments on time, and He had graciously provided for me ahead of time. I constantly prayed for my friend to be blessed and increased for her obedience in giving to me at His word. I knew He would not let her go unrewarded.

I began talking to her about designing a marketing program for her to increase her sales. She was really excited at the idea of having help, so I had her choose which products she wanted to promote and I began designing it. I wanted so much to do something to bless her back for her sacrificial giving to me.

Within a few hours, I had designed a flier and marketing push that I believed would bring in a good amount of business for her, and I began compiling a list of mailing addresses to use for the mass mail marketing campaign.

Within weeks of the first mailing, her phone lines were jammed, and extra help had to be hired to process the loans the marketing campaign had brought her. God was indeed bringing the blessing, and I could not have been happier for her. She became so busy with the business the marketing push brought her, that she had to increase her part time helper's hours to full time to handle all the loans it generated.

Over the following weeks and months, word spread over her success, and she was interviewed by local new channels and newspapers, and even national publications. Within two years, God made her a millionaire. He had indeed rewarded her obedience in giving.

Over the next week, the Lord began showing me that my faith was lacking. He did not seem to be leading me to find another job, but I wasn't sure what it was He did want me to do. I decided to work on my faith while I waited. I would need faith to believe Him for provision if He led me not to work anyway, which I felt in my spirit was what He was doing. Matthew 6:28 had always been a favorite scripture of mine....*consider the lilies of the field...*

MATTHEW 6:28

AND WHY ARE YOU ANXIOUS ABOUT
CLOTHING? CONSIDER THE LILIES OF THE
FIELD, HOW THEY GROW: THEY NEITHER
TOIL NOR SPIN,

And the Lord showed me as I meditated on it that the lilies did not toil away their days, nor did they worry. It seemed I was always worrying about how I was going to pay the rent, my truck payment, or the next bill that came in.

After cleaning houses to make money to pay my bills for several months, my body had begun to ache in more places than I could count. Each night after working all day, it screamed with pain that no amount of painkillers would take away. I began to pray for a job.

Lord, can I just go back to the oilfield long enough to pay off my truck? If I didn't have this vehicle payment, it would be a lot easier to pay everything.

Hoping that God would answer my prayer, I called up my old broker to inquire whether they had any work. They did, and it was only an hour away from me. I set up an interview.

It seemed God had answered my prayer, and within two weeks, I was back in the oilfield, commuting back and forth. I worked through the summer and into the fall locally before taking another job in South Louisiana.

Days after I arrived in Lafayette, strange things began happening. Only a few days after setting up the new office, I noticed a man scoping out the building in a way that made me feel uncomfortable. I was rarely ever afraid of anyone, so it made me really nervous. I saw him there watching our office on several occasions.

I was only a few weeks into the job when one evening, I returned to my room just after dusk, something I usually did not do. My rule was always be in the room before dark and don't go back out when traveling alone. But this particular evening, I had wanted a particular fast food that was nearby and I thought I could make it through the drive-through and get back to my room before dark. I was wrong. Upon arriving back, I got out of my vehicle and as I unlocked my motel room door and opened it, a man tried to follow me in. I was able to close the door in his face and lock it before he could push in, but I was really frightened. I pushed a chair

> *Upon arriving back, I got out of my vehicle and as I unlocked my motel room door and opened it, a man tried to follow me in.*

under the door knob and prayed for protection. Nothing like that had ever happened to me before in all my years of traveling.

Something was wrong. I had traveled for years before with my work and never once had I ever been frightened or felt truly threatened. I was feeling threatened now.

What is going on, Lord? I've never felt I was in danger before when I traveled.

It is not My will for you to be here.

I was out of His will! No wonder I felt unsafe. I suddenly realized I had not felt at peace since arriving in Lafayette, but I had thought I was just tired. I would pack that night and leave in the morning. If He didn't want me there, I wasn't staying.

Within two hours, my room and all my computer equipment were packed and ready to load first thing in the morning. It was Thanksgiving week and I didn't want to disturb my boss and his new wife on their holiday, so I did not let them know I was leaving. They got so little time away from the job, I couldn't bear the thought of ruining their holiday. There wasn't much to do yet on the job anyway, they could get someone out on Monday of the next week. No one else had been assigned to the job except a map maker who was going home to his family for the holiday, so there weren't any agents I needed to be there to supervise.

In the morning, I filled up my vehicle and headed north. Arriving back home in Dallas late that night, I felt His peace again which confirmed I was in the right place. I wasn't sure how I was going to pay the bills, but I

knew I was where He wanted me, and I believed strongly in the saying *'Where God guides, He always provides.'*

A week or so later, the Lord spoke to me just as I was waking up one morning.

You are hard-hearted, prideful and presumptuous. We cannot move forward until I get that out of you. I have a wonderful job for you and you will love everything about it except you will have to learn how to submit. I want you to learn to submit without back talking, backbiting or thinking bad thoughts. I will also not allow you to pretend you submit and then secretly go do things your own way.

Immediately I felt conviction. I knew in my heart that I was supposed to do that on my previous job an hour from home, but I had refused and insisted on doing everything my own way. My pride would not let me submit to someone I did not like, especially someone I knew was dishonest, and I hadn't. I decided to begin a study on pride. I knew whatever He had planned was not going to be fun for me. I might as well get a head start on finding the scriptures I would need to beat my flesh into submission.

By mid-December, I had run through all the money in my bank account and was waiting on my last check from the job in Louisiana. It would only be for two weeks, but it would keep the bills paid a little longer. It was after the September 11th attacks in 2001, and the economy was suffering terribly. My son had been laid off from his job, so I was carrying the bills at the time. When I emailed my broker on December 14th to check on the status of being paid, I was met with silence.

> *It was clear my faith was in my circumstances, and it was taking me further into debt instead of bringing me out. The Lord showed me that by believing in the power of my circumstances, I had empowered them.*

My friend John W. Morgan felt strongly a spirit of fear was holding back my finances. He prayed over me and bound it up. I received an email response only hours later. It was a hostile response, but at least someone was answering me. The owner's wife was extremely angry that I had not contacted them Thanksgiving week so they could get a replacement on the job in a timely manner. I tried to explain in my email back to her that I hadn't wanted to disturb their holiday, but it was clear she did not believe me.

Her response back to me left me unsure I would be paid my last check at all. I pushed down the panic I felt rising in my spirit. I had no more savings and no unemployment.

On top of that, I had injured my back trying to work out, and now had a huge purple and blue lump on one side of the middle of my spine. I wasn't sure what happened, but whatever it was, it hurt really bad. That alone would probably take weeks to heal. I certainly had no money for a doctor visit.

How would we survive with neither of us working? Fear and doubt assaulted me from every side. By December 20th, I was terrified of not having any way to pay the next month's rent. I spent my days lying in bed trying to receive healing for my back. Many times I could not walk and had to crawl to reach the bathroom, and the pain was intense.

During that time, I saw a beautiful angel statue on a television commercial of the archangel Michael with his foot on Satan's neck being offered by a Christian television network for a pledge of a certain amount. I had no money to pledge and didn't know when I would, so I had no hope of getting the statue, but I prayed anyway.

Lord, I really want one of those statues, but You know I have no money to pledge. Will You please bring me one?

In an attempt to step into my calling to minister to prisoners, I had begun a colorful Christian newsletter to send into prisons three weeks earlier, and started pen paling with various prisoners, using a post office box as my address. I was terribly lonely as well as concerned about my situation, and the letters I received from prisoners became the bright spot in my days. If I thought I had problems, I had only to think of what they had to live with to forget my own. Though I knew they had committed crimes to be where they were, I never asked them or wanted to know about the crimes. I only wanted to show them Jesus was there for them.

Our electric bill and phone bill were both two months behind and I was expecting to receive cut-off notices any day. I had never had a utility disconnected for non-payment since getting divorced from my first husband, and I prayed it would not happen now that I was walking alone. None of my close family had a lot of money, I didn't know what we would do if God did not come through for us.

Christmas was sad and lonely and there was no money for gifts. It grieved my heart not to be able to give to the people I loved. I counted the days until it would be over.

I had thought I was doing my boss and his wife a favor when I did not interrupt their Thanksgiving to tell them I was leaving my job post. But as it turned out, I realized later that I had acted hastily, and put them in a bad position. I had simply thought it would be easy to replace me on the job and that they would be glad I did not interrupt their rare holiday away from work. In the future, I would remember that there is a right way and a wrong way even for leaving a place when you discover you are out of God's will. When the Lord showed me my error, I wrote and asked them to forgive me.

In the meantime, I was praying God would take care of us. I felt we were extremely close to going under. I still did not know how I was going to make rent or buy food. We had eaten almost nothing but beans for four weeks straight, alternating types to add variety, and we didn't mind, but if no money showed up, pretty soon we would not have even those.

Something has to change, and soon.

Lord. I have heard preachers talk about using faith like a tool. I need You to teach me how to have faith like that, and how to use it. It was clear from the scriptures that we were given a measure of faith, so it had to be working somewhere in my life. The question was, where was it working?

How can I know where my faith is now, Lord? How does this all work?

Suddenly I saw it. He showed me in my spirit that our circumstances program our faith unless we have renewed our minds in His word. It is up to us to change where our measure of faith is working in our lives.

It was clear my faith was in my circumstances, and it was taking me further into debt instead of bringing me out. The Lord showed me that by believing in the power of my circumstances, I had empowered them. Instead of putting my faith in the power of lack in my circumstances, He wanted my faith in His power to overcome my lack.

That night I went to work on my faith. I began confessing that my needs were met, that wherever God guided, He did provide and no devil in hell could stop Him from doing so. I laid hands on the past due bills and declared them paid in the Name of Jesus based on the fact that I was a serious believer, a faithful giver and tither and God's word said to prove Him if He would not open the windows of heaven and pour me out a blessing.

Around the third of January, I was beginning to become really concerned. I did not have the rent money, and there was still no sign of my last check. I told the apartment complex manager I had a check coming and would be down to pay the rent as soon as it arrived. Since I had always paid on time, she was allowing me some leeway, but I knew her patience would not last forever.

Please help us, Lord! If You don't come through for us, we'll sink for sure!

The night of January 3rd, I prayed hard and decided to try confessing out loud to encourage my faith. Speaking fear and negativity over my situation to anyone who would listen to me was certainly not getting me anywhere, I had nothing to lose. Starting the next morning, all during the day as I thought of it and in my prayer time, I confessed the check had arrived and my bills were paid.

I walked through the next few days trying hard to believe but ending up fearing instead. My circumstances seemed so overwhelming. I was sure I was where God wanted me, but there was no provision in sight. I felt He wanted me to minister and I was attempting to the best I knew how, but I wasn't sure how He was going to provide for us while I did it.

What if He was punishing me for some sin I committed? I didn't know how to be perfect, I just kept trying to be better. What if He wouldn't help me because I wasn't perfect? I wasn't sure what was going to happen, and the fear just kept growing.

CHAPTER 5 - BACK INTO THE DESERT

My mind was constantly filled with images of cut-off notices and past due bills. I was afraid God wouldn't come through in time. I prayed often, and hard. During one of my prayer times, the Lord spoke.

You are already familiar with your circumstances. Stop studying your mess and look into My word and see what I have provided for you as a way out!

So I began studying the word more. I have always loved Ephesians 3:20, where the Word talks about God doing exceedingly, abundantly above and beyond anything we can ask or think, according to the power that works in us, but I didn't see anything above and beyond going on in my circumstances, so I decided to ask Him about it.

EPHESIANS 3:20

NOW TO HIM WHO IS ABLE TO DO
EXCEEDINGLY ABUNDANTLY ABOVE ALL
THAT WE ASK OR THINK, ACCORDING TO
THE POWER THAT WORKS IN US, (NKJV™)

Lord, what does 'according to the power that works in us' in that scripture mean?

The power that works in you will be equivalent to the depth of understanding you have of the promise in My word you are standing on.

My understanding was very shallow. No wonder then that I did not see any exceedingly, abundantly above and beyond blessings in my life! I needed to pray for understanding. God wanted to give me a breakthrough, but first He would have to break through my unbelief.

Lord, please tell me Your plan - I don't see how this is going to work out at all. No one here knows me. I have no church to preach at, even if I knew how to preach, though I know You have called me to minister, and I don't understand at all what You want me to be doing. Please help me understand!

Where was the job He said He had for me? I had no idea where to start looking or what He expected of me. I felt as if I was standing on a dark highway - I couldn't see to go back and I couldn't see what was ahead of me either.

THE LADDER VISION

On January 5th, I was given a powerful dream vision. In the vision, I was in a white room, and in front of me was a ladder. I was dressed in ragged looking clothes, and I stepped on to the first rung of the ladder. I watched as big black bands fell off my ankles. I felt the shackles were bondages from my past life.

When I stepped onto the next rung, my shoes fell off, which I felt symbolized following my own path. On the next rung, all my jewelry fell away, which I thought might symbolize wealth or prestige or any attraction I had to it. On the next, my makeup fell away, which I felt symbolized vanity, and I was left with a bare face. On the next rung, I could feel I had taken up humility and was truly and honestly seeking the Lord with all my heart. As I stepped on to the next rung, a huge face of Satan breathing fire came at me, roaring. Suddenly a sword appeared in my hand and I whacked him on the head with it and he fell away. I stepped up another rung, and armor appeared on my body. The next rung up, a lovely wind began blowing on me, which I think may represent the Holy Spirit and maybe the gifts of the Spirit. On the next rung up, beautiful white clothing with purple embroidery on it appeared underneath my armor. All that was above the last rung was clouds. I prayed and asked the Lord what the dream vision meant.

To go to the next level, look in your life for what you are still holding on to. Every time you lay something down, you go up a step.

On January 7th, the check I had waited over a month for finally arrived in my mailbox. It was dated December 19th. It was postmarked January 4th.

The Lord showed me in my spirit that when my friend John had bound up the spirit of fear, and I had stopped being fearful, it had been released to me, but when I got back into fear and doubt just after that, it became held up again. On January 4th when I stopped speaking lack and negativity and began confessing that the check had arrived, the check was actually sent on its way to me.

Our words are so much more powerful than we believe. One of the most difficult aspects of every wilderness walk I have entered has been learning to just shut up, and believe God will do what He said He will do.

> *To go to the next level, look in your life for what you are still holding on to. Every time you lay something down, you go up a step.*

It is human nature when we are scared or hurting to want to tell someone about it. Staring at your negative circumstances and speaking about them only gives the enemy power to manifest them in your life. We need to stop thinking and talking about how powerful our bad circumstances are, and start thinking and talking about how big our God is.

The Lord had shown me that I could stand in fear, or I could stand in faith, but I couldn't stand in both at the same time. I had to choose a side.

It was discomfiting to be so dependent on God for everything. I had been independent for years and had learned if I wasn't making enough money, I could always pick up another job, work longer hours, or pick up a sideline. Now I wasn't sure what to do. I didn't want to go against the will of God, but I really needed a steady income. I had my resume out on all the job sites, but nothing was happening.

I had laid down everything in my old life and put all my hopes and dreams in Christ and whatever His plan was for my life, but I could not see where He was leading me, and the uncertainty was terrifying. Being an organizer and a planner by nature, I preferred the security of a plan I could see on paper, and a paycheck I could see as well, but my need for security still took a back seat to my love for Him. That left me dangling somewhere between worldly security and heavenly faith and I didn't know what was going to happen next from one day to the next.

My friend John was also going through financial challenges trying to build his business. One day we pooled what few dollars we had and bought books by a prosperity teacher hoping to find some revelation to bring us out of our current dilemmas. We took turns reading the books and applied the principles but it seemed God wanted something more from us, because nothing seemed to change. It wasn't that either of us was seeking after wealth, we weren't. Neither of us is at all materialistic, but if you are sick, you study healing. If you are in poverty and lack, you study prosperity. You study what you feel you need to learn. We were just trying to come out of the land of Not Enough into the land of I Can Pay My Bills On Time.

One day as I was reading Mark 10:25 about the camel and the eye of the needle, the Lord spoke something. I had heard somewhere that there were short gates which camels had to kneel down to enter. I did not know whether it was true or not, but it seemed at the very least it meant entering through a narrow passage of some sort, or entering in an unusual way.

MARK 10:25

IT IS EASIER FOR A CAMEL TO GO
THROUGH THE EYE OF A NEEDLE THAN
FOR A RICH PERSON TO ENTER THE
KINGDOM OF GOD.

As I meditated on this passage, the Lord spoke to me.

When you are kneeling, you are not walking in your own way.

I was doing everything I knew to submit to the Lord and let Him do His work in me. I watched Bible teaching constantly, and listened to teaching tapes. Every night I prayed and beseeched God to let me in on His plan, to reassure me that everything was going to work out. In the meantime, I prayed He would send a financial miracle to meet my needs.

Something was going to have to happen soon or I was in big trouble.

In Deuteronomy 8:18, The Lord showed me something else.

DEUTERONOMY 8:18

YOU SHALL REMEMBER THE LORD YOUR
GOD, FOR IT IS HE WHO GIVES YOU POWER
TO GET WEALTH, THAT HE MAY CONFIRM
HIS COVENANT THAT HE SWORE TO YOUR
FATHERS, AS IT IS THIS DAY.

The Lord showed me that although He does do miracles, He doesn't want us to have to depend on them to get our needs met. He wants to teach us to walk in His ways so our needs are met at all times. That's why He gives us the 'power to get wealth,' not just a miracle of money. He gives us the power to walk in enough, because He does not want us to be constantly afraid of not having rent money or money to pay our light bills. It is not about being wealthy, living in a mansion, and driving a Mercedes, it is about His promises to provide so we are not without.

One night the emotional pain and uncertainty was really getting to me. Bills kept coming in the mail and I had no paycheck to assure me I was going to be able to pay them. On my knees, I cried out over and over, and the Lord began to answer me.

He began to show me how those who truly desire to minister to the lost and broken of the world must first be schooled in pain and brokenness themselves.

He showed me how it is our part to submit to Him as the Great Physician. The Great

> *Staring at your negative circumstances and speaking about them only gives the enemy power to manifest them in your life. We need to stop thinking and talking about how powerful our bad circumstances are, and start thinking and talking about how big our God is.*

Physician knows what is wrong inside us and how to heal it. But before a physician can heal you, before he can cut out the cancer that is killing you, he must first cut you and make you bleed. I saw in the spirit that it was the only process by which a physician could get the bad stuff out and bring healing, but that when we are cut, the blood rushes to the wound and healing comes.

I was in the process of being humbled. He showed me that the more a believer asked Him for, the more he or she would be humbled. I had asked to be able to bring the news of the gospel and healing to very broken people. I would first have to experience brokenness and healing before I could do that. Then He led me to Isaiah 48:10, about being refined, and my eyes were opened. I remembered, many are called but few are chosen.

The King James Version says "I have chosen thee in the furnace of affliction..." In my spirit, the Lord showed me that it is those who are willing to submit to Him in the furnace of affliction that become His chosen.

Many are called, but few will honestly submit and surrender all that needs to be laid down. And there were times when I had trouble laying things down as well. Lots of them. At that time, I was struggling with laying my independence down. I had not depended on anyone but myself for many years. I had built a wall and I stayed safely behind it where there was no abusive husband who could throw me out into the snowy morning in a strange place with nowhere to go, or force me out of the car on a dark night. I was terrified of being dependent again, and yet He had shown me clearly that where He guided, He would always provide.

PSALM 23:1

THE LORD IS MY SHEPHERD; I SHALL NOT WANT.

A shepherd guides his sheep, so according to Psalm 23:1, if I let Him be my shepherd by going where He guided me, then I would not be in want. I stood in faith on that scripture, and I declared often to the Lord that where He guided, I believed He would also provide and that I was counting on Him to do that, though everything around me looked as barren of provision as the Sahara Desert.

FRUIT THOUGHTS

It was the first week of February 2002, and I still had not been able to pay the rent for the month. I was searching frantically for work but so far nothing had turned up, and I was struggling not to panic. God would take care of us, surely. I was doing everything in my power to be in His will and to serve Him. Surely He would not let me just fall flat on my face....would He?

That night I prayed.

Lord, what am I doing wrong? I am doing Your work, writing and doing the newsletter for You, witnessing to anyone and everyone I can witness to, studying Your word, spending time in prayer and in Your presence. I don't understand why Your provision isn't here. What am I doing wrong? Please tell me!

Fruit. Thoughts.

Fruit thoughts? Lord, I know I think too much about food...

No.

Fruit. Thoughts. Faith without works is dead.

I grabbed my Bible and quickly found James 2:26.

> JAMES 2:26
>
> FOR AS THE BODY APART FROM THE SPIRIT IS DEAD, SO ALSO FAITH APART FROM WORKS IS DEAD.

Show me, Lord. What are You telling me?

Suddenly He illuminated my spirit. I saw that my words were confessing provision, but the screen of my mind was showing me lack. I constantly imagined past due bills and my utilities being cut off. I saw myself not being able to pay my rent and having nowhere to go. He showed me that whatever I saw on the screen of my mind was what I *truly* believed and that until that changed, my words would produce nothing.

The fact that my faith was not working was trying to tell me I had dead faith. I had thoughts of lack and they were producing the fruit of lack in my life. *Faith without works is dead*, I thought. I rolled it over and over in my mind. *He's trying to tell me I have dead faith even though my words say I am believing for provision!* The screen of my mind was the report of my spirit, and there was no faith there. All I saw was unpaid bills and scary circumstances on that screen.

Not even half way into February, my truck developed leaks and suddenly needed a thousand dollars worth of repairs, and that news came the day after I learned a close friend of the family had been arrested on serious drug charges. My emotions swung back and forth between terrified and devastated. I was a mess.

As the weeks passed, my hairdresser offered to do my hair for free every month if I would clean her house for her. When I went to have my hair trimmed that month, she told me of other clients she had that were searching for a reliable housekeeper. I prayed silently as I listened to her, and the Lord spoke to me.

Take the houses.

Okay, Lord.

SOWING AND REAPING

Only months into my faith walk, I was cleaning a couple of houses every week, but the bills were coming in faster than my meager earnings could cover them.

Lord, I am $1,000 short on the bills I need to pay this week. I don't know how to get them paid, but I believe Your word is true. I believe that You guided me to this place. You told me that losing that job was Your hand and I believe I am in Your will. I need You to provide this money for me. I believe in the spiritual law of sowing and I am going to sow a $10 seed and believe You to multiply it back to me so I can pay my bills on time. I praise You ahead of time because I know You are always faithful to provide for Your children. Thank You, Lord. By the way, Lord, where should I plant the seed?

He named a ministry I gave to often.

Okay, Lord.

He also spoke to me to help my friend again with her marketing tasks and sow that as a seed.

Okay, Lord.

I sowed my $10 seed and drove to my friend's office to help her. Working for a few hours would help me not think about all the bills I couldn't pay anyway. I welcomed the opportunity to distract myself.

I worked all evening again helping my friend with her marketing plans. I never said a word about not having enough money to pay my bills, or what I had prayed that morning and the seed I had sown.

When it was time for me to go home, my friend called me into her office. She handed me a check.

"I don't know what's going on, but the Lord told me to give this to you," she said, smiling.

I saw that my words were confessing provision, but the screen of my mind was showing me lack. I constantly imagined past due bills and my utilities being cut off.

I glanced down at the check, and my eyes grew wide. It was a check for $1,000. He had provided again!

God is so faithful to provide for His children, if only we will believe and not doubt. I had no choice but to believe Him - I had no place else to turn for that amount of money. I knew I was where God wanted me to be, I believed I was doing what He wanted me to do at that time and I had been faithful to tithe and to give offerings, and to help the poor whenever I saw a need, giving extra offerings any time He led me to. Because I had obeyed, I believed that He would supply my every need, and He was.

I was really weary of believing for every bill to be paid, and I began praying harder the Lord would send me a job. Even though He came through again and again, each time was a fight between faith and fear, and it was exhausting.

Lord, I need a job now.

When my next hair trim came up, I mentioned to my hairdresser that I had begun searching for a job, in case she knew of any openings. As it turned out, she had a client who was searching for office help. Within a week, I had accepted a new position, for a business not far from where I lived. The first month I worked there, I knew the job I had accepted would be a test on love being patient and kind.

Keeping accounting records was part of my job there, and that in itself was not so bad, though I had never done it before. What was bad was trying to do it in the midst of an insane amount of noise and activity. The chatter-filled, high pressure environment I had entered was like nothing I had ever worked in, the hours were longer than normal days, and I hated every minute I was there, but I feared being without a job again, so I stayed.

In the evenings when I was home, I would call my friends and complain about my awful situation, and gossip about my boss and a mean spirited coworker. I was miserable, and really wanted someone to sympathize with my miserable state of being. To add to my trouble, I barely made enough to keep my rent and utilities paid. I was scraping by, and there seemed to be no jobs to be had any place else at that time.

THE POWER OF OUR WORDS

One night I was praying for someone I knew who had been a faithful Christian since childhood, asking the Lord why she had tithed and served Him faithfully for so many years, and yet she did not seem to be very blessed.

Suddenly, a vision opened before me. I saw the woman sitting in her favorite chair, and across the room there was a stairway. She lived in a small apartment that had no stairway in the natural. She was smiling, and I saw in the spirit her faith has been stirred up, and she had been praying and believing God for something. I saw angels coming down the stairway carrying bags. I knew the bags contained blessings for her. Suddenly she opened her mouth and spoke something negative, and the words spewed out like poisonous smoke, filling much of the room. The smoke I saw made me think of sulphur for some reason. As soon as the negative words were out of her mouth, I saw the angels hang their heads in disappointment, and they turned around and started back up the stairs, taking her blessings with them. As I watched, the Lord spoke to me.

Yes, she has been faithful for many years and I do desire to bless her, but her words turn away My blessings.

The vision made me think more about how much negativity I had been speaking over my job situation. Our words have not only the power to help us receive from God, they also have the power to send back what we have asked for.

MALACHI 3:13

YOUR WORDS HAVE BEEN HARD AGAINST ME, SAYS THE LORD. BUT YOU SAY, 'HOW HAVE WE SPOKEN AGAINST YOU?'

VISION OF THE WALL OF PRIDE

I continued going to work every day in the noisy environment and trying to make the best of it. At least I had a steady paycheck. I really had no choice since it was the job the Lord had sent me and I had no other income to fall back on. In the meantime, I prayed constantly.

Lord, I am trying hard to do everything You tell me to do. I'm studying Your word, I'm tithing, I give when You tell me to give and I'm working the job I believe You sent me even though I hate it. Why am I still barely getting by? I'm not asking for wealth, but a little more than enough would sure be nice. Please show me what is holding back my finances.

Early in March, I was praying one night and the Lord gave me a vision. In the vision, I saw a large clear wall. I was standing on one side of it and on the other side piled as high as I could see, was currency. He showed me that the wall was pride, and that if I lined up my actions with His word and if I had the word working in me, that wall would melt like ice in summer and all that abundance would spill over into my life. I thought of all the people I would be able to help if I had such abundance. People like the young single mom who lived next door to me with three small daughters. People like my Mom, struggling to survive on a small monthly check and not even owning her own home. After that night, I tried harder to resist the stubborn pridefulness inside me that wanted to fight against my unkind boss and mean-spirited coworker. I tried to cast down harsh thoughts I knew should not be in my mind. It was a constant struggle trying to even recognize the thoughts, since before I had just let them roam freely through my mind.

In the wilderness, we need to be constantly aware of our atmosphere, especially the atmosphere we are setting if we get into fear or complaining. We need to look for ways to set an atmosphere of faith, being in constant prayer, but not commenting on what is going wrong. We need to remember that just because we are in a hard place, it does not mean that is where we are going to stay. It is just where we are right now.

Sometimes we want to leave a place, but God delays our departure because He knows we are going to run into a storm that will destroy us on down the road and something inside us is not ready to face the storm.

I was reminded of a visit to my sister in Amarillo in 1995. It was late spring and I had been working a job in Quanah, Texas. When I got ready to leave, my sister told me she had had a terrible dream that I was in some kind of accident in a certain town on the way back. She pleaded with me to take an alternate route, and I promised her I would. When I arrived in Quanah that evening, I saw on the news that a devastating tornado had hit the town my sister dreamed about. I was not aware there was a storm system anywhere nearby, but God was. I would have been driving through that town on my way back had my sister not warned me.

GOD DELIGHTS EVEN IN GIVING US OUR DESIRES

One Saturday, I received a catalog in the mail from a clothing store that I really liked but could no longer afford to buy anything from it. As I looked at the pages, I really wished my salary were large enough that I could go there and buy even a few pretty feminine things to wear, having worn the same clothes for so long, but I knew it was hopeless. Barely scraping by for so long had left little money for even necessities, and the thought of a fun shopping trip was a distant dream from my current vantage point of barely being able to pay the bills. Still, I was grateful to have any job at all. As I closed it and tossed it into the wastebasket, I voiced my longing to the Lord.

Lord, I pray some day You bring me enough money I can just walk into that store and buy whatever I want.

It wasn't that I was materialistic or vain, I was just so weary of never having any extra money and being able only to look at pretty things in store windows, never able to buy them. I walked off into the other room to begin my chores.

Not long after, a friend I had worked with years before was coming to town and came by to visit. When he arrived, he told me he had just ended a relationship with a woman he had been seeing for a while and had hoped to marry. He had purchased a number of surprise gifts for her, and since she had moved out of state and he had not given them to her, he wondered if I would like to have them, suggesting maybe I could take them back to the store for credit if I could not wear them myself. He then proceeded to give me almost a thousand dollars worth of clothing *from the very store I had prayed about two months earlier,* with the tags still attached. I was beyond overjoyed.

When I returned the new merchandise for credit, I was able to buy every single thing in the store I liked, plus some. Though I had prayed that prayer only one time, I had prayed it from my heart and really believed the Lord would make it come true at some point. I had never doubted, in fact I had forgotten about it. I had only believed.

One day in April, my friend John called me and said he had a small gift for me. He asked if he could drop it off at my apartment. I told him I would be gone, but he could set the box outside the door because I would only be gone a few minutes. When I arrived home, I carried the box inside and opened it. Inside was the angel statue I had longed for so many times the previous December as I lay in bed in pain watching preaching on television! Along with it was a note that said, *I got this for me, but the Lord told me to give it to you.*

I had never told a single soul I wanted that angel, not even my friend John. Though I often did share with him things I prayed for, the angel seemed inconsequential at the time. It was such a small and unimportant thing in light of everything else that was going on, but it had not been small to God. He had seen how much I wanted it and He had sent it.

Lord, it's the angel statue I prayed for! Thank You! You remembered!

I never forget a prayer!

Our prayers are that important to the Lord that He never forgets even one of them!

LEARNING TO SUBMIT

My job had become an extension of my wilderness. Every day at this job was beginning to seem like a replay of the same nightmare. One day, it got even worse. My boss threw some papers in front of me and instructed me to do something I felt would be dishonest, and walked away. There was no question in my mind about how I was going to respond.

I picked up the papers, carried them over to his desk and laid them down. I calmly informed him I could not do what he asked because I felt it would be against my Christian beliefs. I turned, walked back to my desk and sat down, waiting for him to fire me.

All afternoon I waited. Nothing happened.

Driving home, I prayed even harder about my job. I hated what I did and I hated where I worked to do it. I longed for a quiet atmosphere and some sense of sanity in my work environment. Even as I prayed, I knew I was stuck there until God had accomplished whatever it was He wanted to accomplish in me. I decided to try harder to work with Him.

Okay, Lord, You said I was prideful, so I am going to work on humility. I am going to try harder to serve, and to not complain or gossip about my misery so much. I am believing if I can pass this test that You will open a door for me to get out of there into a better job, with better pay.

That night, I began to bombard the gates of heaven praying for the Lord to bless my boss and bless my work place. The next day, I prayed all the way to work, and when I got there, I began to look for ways to serve. I saw that my boss drank coffee so I began making fresh coffee several times a day and serving him. I wasn't sure of any other way to serve that I wasn't already doing, but I did every little thing I could find. I showed respect for his authority at all times, though in my heart I did not respect him. I could submit to his position even if I could not submit to him as a person.

> *I showed respect for his authority at all times, though in my heart I did not respect him. I could submit to his position even if I could not submit to him as a person.*

The first time I set coffee in front of him, he looked up in surprise. "Thank you," he said, smiling.

At least he appreciated the effort I made, and that was at least a tiny glimmer of light in that very dark place. The environment was constant stress and not at all pleasant. Often I saw the strain on coworkers faces as well, but we all needed our jobs. Every evening, I continued to pray prayer after prayer for my boss to blessed, and for the Lord to bless my work place. The job did not change, but I felt the atmosphere lighten slightly as I continued to pray day after day after day, and as I continued to just submit, and to serve while I was there.

One blazing hot evening in July, I was driving home from work when my cell phone rang. An old acquaintance I had worked with had recommended me for a new job opening. The person knew nothing about my current situation, as it had been months since we had made contact. I nearly shouted with joy when I was offered a position to work in a nice office as a new manager's assistant. At last I would be free from the noise, confusion and low salary where I worked! God had answered my prayers!

I was thrilled to be able to give notice at my current job and I had high hopes about my new one. With great joy I wrapped up the last of my work in my present job just weeks later and headed out the door. That was one job I knew I would never miss, though I would miss some of the good-hearted coworkers there. My heart broke for them being stuck in that high pressure environment and I prayed for them for months afterwards.

LORD, WHY ARE YOU SILENT?

Within weeks of beginning my new job, it was clear things would not be quite as rosy as I had imagined, but I knew the Lord had opened the door for me to exit the other job and I was determined to make the best of it. With the tech bust and 9/11, there were few jobs available anywhere. Everyone was clinging to whatever job they had for dear life, and I was no exception. I had no desire to be without income again in such a dark and gloomy time.

> *I began to feel I had been abandoned in the middle of the blistering desert. I prayed and cried out to God every night, but He was silent much of the time. I learned later that the teacher is always silent during the test.*

I had no favor with my new boss who was extremely driven and believed in working very long hours. Driving home emotionally drained from the high pressure sales atmosphere late at night was not my idea of fun, but I needed the work.

The new job was like a pressure cooker. It seemed no matter how hard I worked, more tasks were piled on me, and I received even more criticism about how I handled them. Why was nothing I did ever enough? I constantly fought the desire to speak my mind, trying to submit. Sometimes I won the battle, and sometimes I lost it. At night I would drive home, complaining to whoever would listen to me on my cell phone. At work, I would rebel against my boss, and the unceasing demands I felt were put on me every day. My emotions constantly went back and forth between anger at the situations I was placed in, and despair that I could not seem to come out of the wilderness.

As the pressure continued to build over the following months, I began to lose interest in activities I normally enjoyed. It took every ounce of energy I had just to keep going. I began to feel I had been abandoned in the middle of the blistering desert. I prayed and cried out to God every night, but He was silent much of the time.

> *He showed me I was trying to fight the prideful spirit I thought was in my boss at work, and He wanted me to fight the one working in me.*

Lord, why won't You talk to me? Why are You silent?

Silence.

I learned later that the teacher is always silent during the test.

In His silence, it seemed He did not want me to ask Him for answers so much as to search my own heart for anything within me that might not be pleasing to Him. I needed to meditate on what I knew about God to help me connect the dots about why I was still in the fiery place I found myself in. Was I working with Him to destroy the prideful spirit in me, or was I pretending to submit while doing things my own way? He had warned me about that, had I listened?

I had read many scriptures about how displeasing pride was to God. Having lived under years of abuse and having someone else's will forced on me, I struggled with unkind authority figures in my life. Still, I knew His word said submit. Was I submitting, or was I clutching that prideful spirit close to my bosom, refusing to let Him crucify it?

Every day I struggled as the demands placed on me continued to increase. Within months, I literally had to fight every hour to not pick up my purse and run away from my job. Only two things stopped me, the first being I knew God would calmly put me in another job just like that one, just as difficult, just as miserable, because He was trying to work humility in me. The other was, I needed the paycheck.

My new job at least paid more than the one before it, thanks to many hours of overtime I was working. I hated the constant emotional turmoil I worked in, and the fear of losing my job, and I wasn't sure how much more strain I could take. Nevertheless, God had opened the door and that's where I was, so I dug in my heels and stayed put, constantly confessing I was going to stay the course and be done with the pride test – once and for all, even if it killed me, and the way it felt, I was pretty sure it was going to do just that.

One Saturday early in November, I arose early to pray. As I began praying and asking God to deal with my workplace problems and get me through the wilderness test He currently had me in, He suddenly showed me something that shocked me. He showed me I was trying to fight the prideful spirit I thought was in my boss at work, and He wanted me to fight the one working in me.

The enemy will always try to turn our attention to someone else's sin or perceived sin to keep us from seeing the sin in ourselves. I decided to press in and try harder to fight my own pridefulness, instead of trying to show someone else where they were wrong. Maybe if I did that, the Lord would let me out of the desert.

JUST SAY THE WORDS

One day after listening to a sermon, my life had so little joy in it any more, that I decided I would begin confessing "This is the day that the Lord has made, I will rejoice and be glad in it." I heard in the sermon that if I confessed that, something happy would happen to me that day. It was worth a try, because I definitely needed something to be happy about. My attitude was so terrible, I could barely even stand myself.

Each day on my drive to work, I began confessing it over and over. One morning soon after, I woke up feeling so weary and so discouraged. The long months of struggle had left me beaten down.

> *If you'll say the words, I'll back them up.*

Every day I was dealing with the constant fight at work against the unreasonable demands, and the constant battle going on inside me at the same time to try to make my flesh submit to authority. It was the age old battle between good and evil, between pride and humility, and I didn't think I had the strength to confess it that day. While I was lying there thinking it over, the Lord spoke to me.

If you'll say the words, I'll back them up.

It never failed after that - if I confessed that even a few times, my day contained at least some small bit of hope that helped me cope, and I seemed to have more grace to walk through it. The Lord told me during that time to just do the opposite of whatever my flesh wanted to do and it would break the power of whatever evil spirit was working through it. He also reminded me that in submitting to authority, I was not submitting to that person, but to Him through that person. That made it much easier for me because I had no problem submitting to my Lord.

I began looking for opportunities to serve the office supervisor there that I was having problems with. If she got caught in a barrage of phone calls, I would take her fresh coffee or hot chocolate. If it was near lunch time, I would make her soup and crackers, or take her some kind of snack to sustain her until she could get to lunch. Though she seemed to appreciate the gestures, she continued to put more pressure on me to work harder. Everything I did seemed to fall short of what she wanted. I am a hard worker by nature anyway, and it was difficult to take the criticism without fighting back, but I knew that was what the Lord wanted me to do, so I kept trying to make my flesh behave.

Early one afternoon in late November, one of my nieces called from Amarillo to say that my sister was getting worse and had begun asking why I wasn't there. I broke down in tears. When I hung up I informed my coworkers I was leaving for Amarillo. They were shocked I was not going to wait for permission, but if I lost that job because my dying sister had asked for me, then I lost it. My sister was far more important to me than my supervisor's opinion of my actions.

My supervisor called me as I drove north towards Amarillo, insisting on knowing when I would return to my duties. When I did return, my life was not made any easier by the fact that I had defied her authority.

CRYING OUT IN PAIN

One night in prayer, I was crying out to God about the intensity of the pain I was walking through, when a vision opened up before me. He showed me a vision of a child's wound being cleaned and operated on. The child was crying out in pain. He showed me that just as I wouldn't blame the child for crying out, He doesn't blame us when we cry out either. The Lord is so merciful towards us!

As I continued to pray about being able to submit to my demanding boss, the Lord spoke to me.

You don't even need to have an opinion about anything she says or does, or tells you to do.

After that night, I began practicing trying not to have an opinion.

I was completely miserable at my job. Though I worked in a nice area of Dallas and made more money than I had since leaving the oil and gas industry, the office environment I worked in was horribly stressful and I hated every minute I had to spend there. Forced overtime required me to exit the building late at night through a dark deserted parking garage which also terrified me, after having narrowly missed being attacked in one in my early twenties.

Everything in me wanted out of that job. My emotions screamed constantly, I worried about my sister and the rest of my family far away and I didn't understand why nothing God had promised me was happening.

Where are You in all this, Lord? Please help me understand!

A health problem I had been struggling with had not been improving. For over two years, my doctor had advised me to have surgery,

You don't even need to have an opinion about anything she says or does, or tells you to do.

and I had put it off. As it worsened, I decided to go ahead with it. I was so unhappy in my job that major surgery was beginning to look like a vacation anyway. The office environment was one of intensity and deadlines, and I could find no peace from the constant anguish that had taken over my mind.

My boss protested loudly about me taking off to have surgery, and tried to convince me to postpone it for another six months. Knowing the doctor told me I would not get better any other way, I refused and scheduled the surgery, enduring the verbal onslaught I caught in return.

Three weeks after the surgery, I fell into a deep depression, plagued with nightmares about my boss, my job and my sister dying. Overwhelmed by so many circumstances outside of my control, I felt as if I was falling off a cliff and there was no place to grab hold to save myself. I began to sleep more and more. My body was healing from the surgery, but my mind seemed headed the other way. I could not face the thought of returning to the job I was so completely miserable in, but I didn't know what else I would do when my allotted recovery time was up.

Please help me, Lord. I don't know what to do and I don't understand why I am not seeing Your promises come to pass in my life.

I looked down at my Bible as it fell open to Malachi 3:13.

MALACHI 3:13

"YOUR WORDS HAVE BEEN HARD AGAINST
ME, SAYS THE LORD. BUT YOU SAY, 'HOW
HAVE WE SPOKEN AGAINST YOU?'

Even though I hadn't been playing Bible Bingo, I knew immediately the Lord was speaking to me, because my spirit bore witness to His words. I wondered which of my words had stopped my blessings. I had been so horribly miserable for so many months there were probably many words charged against me at that point. I knew I had a tendency to mouth my misery, in spite of the fact many declared the power of our words was great. I again determined to put a guard over the door of my lips.

I'm sorry, Lord. I'll try to do better. Please help me. Please don't make me go back to that job!

In early March, I received a call my sister's condition was worsening. I quickly packed a bag and headed for Amarillo, stopping in Oklahoma to pick up my daughter. I pulled up at my sister's house just in time to see her body being loaded into the back of the funeral home's van. Though I was happy her pain and suffering had finally ended, I was heartbroken I had not had the chance to say goodbye to her.

When my time off for the surgery ended, I filed for temporary disability through my job because the depression was not lifting, and was approved. A second doctor prescribed me medication to help get it under control, saying I was suffering from "situational depression," or depression brought on by situations occurring in my life. I felt as a Christian I should not be suffering from depression at all, but I could not seem to affect the terrible sadness in my soul. I set about praying and doing everything I could to help myself get better. I took long walks through a beautiful park nearby, tried to exercise, spent hours sitting in the early spring sunshine, and wrote in my journal.

One afternoon the next month, I called Mom to check on her.

"How are you doing, Mom?"

"Not so good," she said.

"What's wrong?"

"I think I'm having a heart attack."

"Mom, that's not funny!"

"I'm not joking."

I quickly got off the phone and called an ambulance for Mom, while throwing things into a bag and running out the door to my truck to head to Oklahoma. It turned out the chest pains were caused by something else, and Mom was okay. I spent the night in Oklahoma and returned to Dallas.

CHAPTER 6 – LEARNING ABOUT HUMILITY

I knew from what the Lord had spoken to me months earlier that I was in the wilderness season because of being prideful and hard-hearted and I began to work harder on learning about humility so I could fully submit. I wanted out of the wilderness, and I wanted out badly. I didn't know how much more I could take of the test I was in. One night, knowing the Lord wanted to work humility in me, I began to pray.

Lord, I really want to understand. What is Your definition of humility?

Humility is the absence of self in all you think, say and do.

Inside, I felt myself breaking, and becoming more open to the Lord's commands. He was showing me day by day that if I did not humble myself, He could and would do the humbling for me. I had gained a newfound respect for the willingness of the Lord to help me to walk in His ways and I began watching myself much more closely. If humility meant not thinking about myself, then I needed to learn how to do that. I knew it would probably never come naturally to me, but I began putting as much effort as I knew how into obeying Him and walking in humility.

The second week of May arrived and I still had not paid the rent that was due on the 1st. My son had been laid off again, and was looking frantically for a position. My temporary disability had ended. I prayed constantly, trying to understand why so many bad things were happening at once, trying to find God's purpose in all of it, and trying to keep going and not give up.

Just after mid-May, I received a phone call telling me my nephew had died suddenly of an asthma attack, just a week or so before what would have been his eighteenth birthday. I was heartbroken. I had looked for him my last trip to Oklahoma and hadn't been able to find where he was living. I drove back to Oklahoma for the funeral, and cried all the way back to Dallas.

Why, Lord? Why so much pain and sadness? Will this ever end? And why him, Lord? I'm not questioning Your sovereignty, but please help me understand! He was a believer, Lord, with such a sweet, gentle spirit.

The company I was employed with insisted they had no position for me other than the one I was currently in. Soon after my nephew's death, while searching the internet, I found other positions open I qualified for within the company. I applied for one of them in another branch of the company and began pressing them to transfer me. I would do anything to avoid returning to that office and going back through that terrible darkness again. I was beginning to emerge from the black cloud of depression I had been living under ever so slightly and I knew if I had to return to work in my old position, it would throw me right back down into the abyss. Who knew how long it would take the next time to begin climbing out again.

> *Humility is the absence of self in all you think, say and do.*

As I grieved over my sister and nephew, and worried over Mom, the stress never seemed to lessen. I felt so broken inside, so devastated by one loss after another, and there was not one thing I could do to change any of what was happening.

As I walked through day after day of fear and grief, I felt something inside me beginning to give up hope that anything was ever going to get better. I knew I could not hang on much longer, everything inside me just wanted to give up. I grieved every minute of every day, I didn't know how to pay my bills and all my hopes were gone. I struggled to hang on, to find a dream somewhere deep inside to keep me going, but the pain was too deep and the grief too intense. Many days I wondered if I would ever even be able to function at work again. I kept praying, hoping the Lord would rescue me from the terrible ocean of sadness that had become my life.

My son had gotten engaged and was planning to get his own apartment. As he began getting ready to start his life as a married man, I began losing peace about staying in the apartment where we lived. I felt that was a sign I would be moving soon.

As I walked through day after day of fear and grief, I felt something inside me beginning to give up hope that anything was ever going to get better.

Please, Lord. Please grant me this one thing – give me this other job and help me move. I can't go back there to that office, Lord. Please, I'm not that strong!

Only days after returning to Dallas from my nephew's funeral, my truck broke down and stranded me at almost the exact time I got hired for the new position I had applied for at the other branch.

Help, Lord! Now I have a job but no way to get to it! Please help!

An uncle I had not seen in decades but had spoken to recently helped me get the truck to his apartment where we could work on it and offered to help me repair it.

I called around and found an apartment near my new job with a move-in special of only $100. I didn't have the $100, but I believed God would make a way for me. I felt strongly the anointing had moved off of where I was living and to the new city where my new position was. I had prayed and prayed over it, and I felt peace about moving, but not about staying where I was, so I went to stay at my uncle's house.

The truck problem turned out to be my fault. In my stressed out state of mind, trying to maintain my vehicle, I had accidentally poured power steering fluid down the brake line prior to driving to Oklahoma for my nephew's funeral

Thank You, Lord, for not letting me break down on that trip! I wouldn't have even had money to tow it off the highway!

All the brake lines had to be redone, along with the master cylinder, and the water pump.

It turned out to be quite a job. In the evenings, I would climb under the truck or under the hood with my uncle, doing whatever he showed me to do as we began the repairs. By the end of the evening, I would have grease all over me. Each morning, I would walk out the door in a suit and heels, double checking my nails for grease before getting into my uncle's old truck to drive to my new job.

Within a few weeks I had gotten paid and moved into my new apartment. I quickly began making friends at the complex, and at my new job. My new place of work was a happy environment, so unlike the last few places I had worked where I had felt only darkness. Almost every day, a group of us had lunch together at some cheery place, and laughter was often heard in the office. Everyone worked hard, but the spirit was positive and uplifting, so no one minded. For the first time in years, I had friends I truly enjoyed, both at work and at home around me.

HE SHALL SUPPLY ALL YOUR NEED

As I began to hang my wall décor and arrange my furniture in the living room of my new place, I realized I needed an entertainment center to put my television and VCR player on, but I had no money at all to buy one with. It would take me over a month just to catch up on my past due bills.

Lord, I really need an entertainment center for right there, and I have no money. Your word says You will supply all my needs. Will You send me one?

The next afternoon I was talking to a new friend on the phone. Suddenly, she asked, "Hey, you don't know anyone who needs an entertainment center, do you? I have one I need to get rid of."

I drove straight to her apartment and got the entertainment center and took it home. It was a perfect fit for my space.

Thank You, Lord! Thank You for caring even about the small things in my life!

One evening about a week later, still unpacking and arranging my things in my new smaller apartment, I realized I had a large empty spot where a dining room table should be.

Lord, I need a dining room table and chairs that will fit right there but I don't have the money to buy one. I'm a tither and a giver and I believe you will supply all my needs according to Your word. Will You send me one?

The next morning a friend called. "Hey, I have a friend who has a friend who's moving to Poland. She has a dining room set she needs to get rid of – by any chance do you need one or know someone who does?"

We arrived at the woman's apartment a few hours later, and my mouth dropped open as we rounded the corner into her dining room. It was a large dark wood table with lion's claw feet and six chairs. We loaded it up and took it to my apartment. It fit perfectly in my space.

Thank You, Lord! It's more beautiful than any I've ever owned!

The depression had lifted and life was finally good again. It seemed I was out of the wilderness at last.

> *The Lord had taught me that whenever my pain was great, His love was still greater, and He would be there to console me.*

It had been a long hard walk through the desert that time, but I had walked out with more knowledge than ever before, knowledge that could only be gotten one way. I had spent many months in the dark valleys this time, but the Lord had taught me that whenever my pain was great, His love was still greater, and He would be there to console me. He had taught me, too, that a prideful attitude was not acceptable to Him, and that I would do well to avoid pride in all I did.

CHAPTER 7 - THE WINDS OF CHANGE

I had come out of the wilderness in the fall of 2003 and, other than some very trying emotional times, I had for the most part stayed out. When 2008 rolled around, I had been working in the Oklahoma oilfield again for almost four years. I had been back in the oilfield and living out of motel rooms since the beginning of 2005 this time, and I was feeling pretty burned out when the Lord spoke to me that spring that my job would be coming to an end soon. I was so tired that it was not altogether bad news, except I wasn't sure how I was going to support myself. My job ending meant I would need to rent a house or apartment some place and find another job, and I had no idea where home even was any more. Since I had spent most of the last three years in Oklahoma, I felt more at home there than in Texas, but there was little work in my part of Oklahoma when oil wasn't booming. God already had a plan, though, and it wasn't long before He began to let me know it.

The leaves were just beginning to change to rich autumn hues, and the air beginning to turn crisp one afternoon in September during my latest oil and gas job. I was sitting in front of my computer preparing a lease when I began to sense very strongly in my spirit that work was about to cycle down. In the oil and gas industry, work comes in cycles and work availability depends heavily on current supply and demand. When oil prices go high, work is plentiful and many jobs are available, creating a boom cycle. When the supply increases and the price of oil falls to a certain point, projects are canceled and workers are suddenly laid off. Formerly booming oilfield towns become like ghost towns practically overnight as crews of workers pack up and head home to find other work.

Everyone in my group had just been told we had at least two years of work ahead of us on the current project, but I had worked in the oilfield long enough to know that was subject to change on any given day depending on market prices. Companies approved budgets for jobs and made plans, but if supplies suddenly increased from foreign sources and prices dropped in the U.S. as a result, those plans would be shelved or in some cases abandoned altogether. One day you had work, the next day you were packing up your motel room and heading for home hoping you could find a job in some other field of work.

I said nothing to anyone else about what I felt, but I quietly began to cut back on unnecessary spending. On October 1st, our project manager called everyone together in a meeting and announced our prospect had been canceled. They expected to have work in far away states for a few who could travel, but almost nothing in Oklahoma. I welcomed a break from work in my own life, I just wasn't sure what I was going to do after the oilfield this time.

Over the next week, Woodward, Oklahoma went from a bustling oilfield city to a ghost town. Where I once heard the constant whir of traffic, I now heard an eerie silence that echoed my own thoughts back to me. In my heart I was certain better days were ahead as, over the following weeks, I proceeded to wrap up the last of the oil and gas leases I had taken, and pack up all my files. Having been the title manager for my area, I was the last to leave. Everyone else had already packed up and left town.

One evening, I was listening to a Bible teaching about the winds of change while finalizing some leases when the Lord began to speak a message to me for a ministry group headed by my former mentors. The Great Recession had begun, and they were struggling financially because the people they ministered to had tightened their purse strings.

ECCLESIASTES 11:4

HE WHO OBSERVES THE WIND WILL NOT
SOW, AND HE WHO REGARDS THE CLOUDS
WILL NOT REAP.

The Lord led me to Ecclesiastes 11:4 and began to show me what happens when we get into fear in hard times and stop giving.

In my spirit, I saw people holding on to their money tightly, afraid to give, and they looked worried as they watched the wind blowing everything around.

Giving is an act of worship. Are they going to stop worshiping Me when the winds of change blow? Then they should not stop giving either.

> *Tell them, according to their faith, it shall be done unto them.*

They are staring at the winds of change, afraid in their hearts. They clutch tightly to their purses because they are not believing the promises in My holy word. They do not believe in My goodness to provide for them. They dishonor Me by believing the lies of the enemy over My word and lacking faith that they will have enough.

At the time, the Great Recession was in full bloom and job losses and massive layoffs were almost a daily occurrence in the news. The failing economy was all anyone talked about, and it became more difficult by the day to be optimistic among so much negativity.

I desire they would step up boldly and stand on My promise to provide for them. I desire they would give boldly while proclaiming their faith, and prove Me in this. If they will give in the face of lack, I will provide supernaturally for them, and they will not lack any good thing in this time. If they choose to believe the enemy's lies, that they will be in lack, and fear, they will instead reap a harvest of fear and lack. That is what he desires for them. All I have belongs to My people, but they fail to claim it as theirs and lay hold of it. They become afraid in hard times and do not give into My work and this dishonors Me greatly. I desire to bless them, but their faith is in the enemy's ability to bring lack, and not in My ability to provide for them.

Tell them, My daughter. Tell My people I desire they would believe Me for good things. I desire they would know I am a good and loving Father, and I take care of My children who trust Me to provide for them. It is not My will that they live lives of lack, fear, and worry.

Tell them, according to their faith, it shall be done unto them.

He showed me their fear would also keep them from being able to hear His voice, something I myself had experienced before. You cannot hear the voice of faith when you're listening to the voice of fear. That night during worship, He spoke again.

There is nothing you can ever need that was not covered by Jesus' work on the cross.

Come to Me nightly in worship, My daughter, for the time is indeed short, and there is much for Me to impart to you and the others I have called to My last days army. If you fail Me in this, you will not be able to survive what is yet to come, for the earth shall indeed become a terrible place, but that is as it should be and as it has been foretold in My word. I am about to arise terribly and shake the earth. Everything is changing, and it is changing quickly, so you must be ready at all times to do whatever I command you to do, and some of it will sound like insanity, yet you must obey My voice, or I cannot keep you safe.

ELECTION DAY 2008

On Election Day 2008, the Lord began to speak to me about the changes that were blowing in my own life. Little did I know just how much it really was about to change when He spoke this.

Each level will require more faith, more trust in Me and My plan over your natural instincts. I will stretch your faith to its limits for I want your testimony to be grand. Winds of change have indeed blown into your life, My child, and it is time for the manifestation of the fullness of My spirit in all My children now and you, being one of them, shall soon see My gifts take on a stronger anointing in your own life. Know that everything you do, say or think affects My anointing, and guard your heart, mind and lips accordingly. Tell all who will listen for the harvest is indeed white, and I will call My children home to be with Me very soon indeed. There is still time for more to be saved – it is not too late, but they cannot believe unless they hear. Believe – Trust – Obey.

Do not question My ways or methods of answering your prayers to Me. Just believe I am able to do all you have asked of Me, and so much more. Keep believing Me even when what you ask appears impossible, for I AM the God of the Impossible! Never lose your faith in Me, or let it waiver in any way. I will instruct you on what you are to do each step of the way.

I will require you to sacrifice the desires of your flesh, fleshly pleasures and indulgences you have oft used in the past to comfort yourself in times of mourning, sadness or grief, for I alone am to be your Comforter, and I will show you there is none other but Me.

I will require that you sacrifice time in prayer to intercede for the hurting and the unsaved. These are the sacrifices of the righteous, My child, and I shall require every one of them from you. I want you to lay down the distractions of each day and wait in My presence for a

> *I will require you to sacrifice the desires of your flesh, fleshly pleasures and indulgences you have oft used in the past to comfort yourself in times of mourning, sadness or grief, for I alone am to be your Comforter, and I will show you there is none other but Me.*

time, that you may clearly hear My instructions to you for that day. Each day you do not do this, you lose something – some blessing, some leading, some enhancement or revelation for your life, some move of My hand. Many times they are unseen movements giving to you, moving on your behalf or holding back something bad from you or your loved ones. Each day you ignore Me or neglect your time with Me, it costs you, so neglect it not, My child, for I desire that your life be greatly blessed.

Your heart weeps over this blood soaked land because I have called you to intercede for Me, that I may have mercy on it– that I may show mercy to you and your family. This is the seed I require to answer that prayer, Daughter, to keep your family from the worst of what is to come – intercede for Me.

Pray, intercede for this nation, and for the lost of all peoples for they are all precious to Me!

Be my mouthpiece in the earth for time is short, and I have called you as a bold witness to My glory, My mercy, My grace, My salvation. There are many books you will write for and about Me, and the first is coming soon. You have known this for some time. You will know when it is time to write it, it shall come easily to you.

Fear not, for there is nothing in this plan to fear. I do not desire you fear anything, but Me only.

VISIONS OF FAMINE COMING TO AMERICA

On December 1st, I delivered the last of the project files to my broker's office in Oklahoma City and drove back to Woodward. Around midnight that night, I was standing in the kitchen heating some beans in the microwave when without warning, it felt as if a giant wall of wind slammed into me, and suddenly I was no longer there in my kitchen.

I found myself looking down into a restaurant size soup pot that was boiling. It held almost all water, with not even a handful of beans, as if the beans were only for flavor. All around me, I felt famine, and I knew in my spirit that everyone was starving. I also knew I was in America, and that what I saw was happening here.

> *I will never forget what I saw in her eyes. In them was a mixture of desperation, and madness.*

I was then standing in front of a white cupboard, and when I opened it, there were only a few spices left – no food of any kind. Then I was back in my kitchen, standing by the microwave, completely in shock at what I had just seen. The power of the visions left me faint and dizzy. I had been experiencing open visions since my twenties, but I had never seen anything like a famine in any of them. Suddenly I felt very sad for America, as well as a strong urgency to get ready for what was coming.

Please show me more, Lord, even though it's hard to see. I need to understand what is coming. Please grant me more visions so I can prepare.

The next night, I was sitting on my couch eating again when the Lord opened another vision before me, and what I saw was much worse than the first one.

I was standing somewhere inside a town and it was very dusty. I saw some people across from where I was cooking things in pots and there was a woman who looked to be in her forties or fifties with dark disheveled hair cooking something in a big pot over an open fire. She looked very excited and I knew in my spirit she was excited to have something to eat. She was stirring the pot with a stick. I also knew in my spirit that she was cooking dog entrails. All the smells coming from the pots were horrible, really disgusting, yet they all were so excited that they had something to eat. They must have all been hungry for a very long time to want to eat anything that smelled so terrible. All their eyes and their faces looked so desperate, and so full of hardship that it broke my heart to watch them. Then I looked at the woman and she looked back at me. I will never forget what I saw in her eyes. In them was a mixture of desperation, and madness.

I felt that I was in some kind of protected area, shaped like an arc. I wasn't sure what was protecting me, if I was in a different geographical area, or if something had happened to part of the country and the rest of it spared, or what. There weren't heaps of rubble where I was, just total misery and starvation. I could feel that no food was growing anywhere, but I wasn't sure why. When I tried to see what had caused the terrible famine, the only thing I sensed was a giant iron block of some sort. I wasn't sure what the iron block meant, but I felt it could not be overpowered. It was strong and immovable.

> *Warn My people this is coming so they can prepare and be ready. Tell them I said to get ready to help those who are unsaved, for the end is very near now.*

I saw people walking along the road, and their clothing looked worn, and dusty. There were people dying along the streets and roadsides of starvation and disease. I saw they would just drop dead where they were stumbling along and people would walk right past them. Everyone kind of shuffled along hopelessly. They seemed to be in shock like whatever had happened had come upon them very suddenly. I saw no animals other than small creatures, and very, very few of them. I could tell they were starving too, and people were trying to catch them to eat them. I saw large open sores on people's skin but did not see what caused them. I saw no small children at all. The youngest I saw was a girl with straight blonde hair who looked to be eleven or twelve years old.

I sensed in the vision that there was no television or entertainment of any kind going on anywhere near. I saw no sunshine and no rain. It was very gray, and I felt it was cold. I wondered if maybe it was the aftermath of a nuclear attack, but it didn't seem exceedingly cold; only cold enough that the people were wearing light jackets and sweaters. The woman stirring the pot of entrails had been wearing long sleeves and more than one layer of clothing. No one seemed to be carrying anything – no bags or luggage or sacks of anything, but I wasn't shown why. They walked along in groups of two or three, and some were alone. I heard no laughter at all, and the only smiles I saw were the smiles of those who had cooking pots.

There was terrible desperation in the eyes of those starving people, and it was heartbreaking to look at. America, once so plentiful, so strong and so proud, had been reduced to look like a third world country. People starving and dying in the streets like the commercials I had seen on television to solicit donations for starving children in Africa and other places where there wasn't enough food. But this was America!

Father, why am I being shown such terrible things?

Tell My people, daughter. Warn My people this is coming so they can prepare and be ready. Tell them I said to get ready to help those who are unsaved for the end is very near now. Tell them to cling not to their own lives, but be willing to lay them down for a higher glory, for My glory. Tell them to give all even when they themselves are in need for many will die and go to hell in that time and those left behind will experience a fate even worse than that. The Beast, the False Prophet – all that was foretold in Revelations is about to come true. Tell them, My child, though you know many will not listen. Many hard-hearted ones will perish in that time but others will listen I will open the hearts of those who have ears to hear and those who are being interceded for. Tell My people I said to pray diligently for those you love so they will not be lost in that time, for many will want to take the Mark of the Beast and if they do there is no turning back for them. Tell them!

I am about to reveal to you many truths in My word that have not yet been revealed because you are in the last of the last days. The harvest is bright white with My glory and I am coming to take My children home! Be diligent in all you do for Me. I will provide for you from this time forward so that you may do this work for Me.

Every day souls are being lost to the enemy because of those of My children who have not obeyed Me in all I said to do. Angels will protect My chosen ones in this time of spreading the message of hope to the last ones to be saved. No evil will befall any of you except that which is part of My plan for you. You will hear My voice speaking louder and clearer in this time than ever before – that is because I am coming closer and closer and the end is nearer and nearer.

I could not tell anything about how far off the events I was shown are and so far I have not been shown what causes the famine, or the terrible disease those people seemed to have.

Before, the open visions I received usually happened during times of deep prayer and worship, but in early 2008, they began happening during the course of my day when I was relaxed and performing ordinary tasks such as walking across a room or preparing food in the kitchen. They came with no warning and took over all my senses. Whenever one started, I became completely unaware of the present moment or my surroundings. My sight was filled with the image of the vision and the power of them would nearly knock the breath out of me. This happened over and over again as the Lord began to show me things to come, and things I needed to know about those near to me that were coming in the future. Many of the visions made me fear what lie ahead, and grieve for the many souls that would be lost in that time. Some of the visions were physically painful, full of grief, and with those the pain was so severe I was glad they lasted only seconds or minutes because I was sure I could not have stood them for much longer.

MOVING SOME PLACE NEW

It was January, 2009, and the end times visions I had begun seeing were never far from my mind. I was sitting on the old worn sofa drinking my morning coffee in the furnished house I had rented six months earlier when the Lord began speaking to me about my next move. I had stayed where I was in Woodward after my work ended, awaiting His instructions. I put out resumes for work, but I knew the Lord planned to provide for me and already had a plan and would let me know when it was time for me to start on it. He did.

I will be moving you soon to a new place in order to position you. Fear not when I speak to you to move because I have already ordained the move and spoken your provision there, and if you remain when I am telling you to move, your provision in this place will dry up as you know. You will not be unhappy where I am moving you to, though at first you may want to doubt Me.

The recession was still all over the news in America and the news media was reporting that more jobs were lost the last several months of 2008 than after the September 11th attacks. Voters had pinned their hopes on President Obama, who now had the unenviable position of rescuing America from a complete financial meltdown. Everyone was clutching tightly to their money, and buckling down to watch how things developed while they waited out the economic storm.

Being middle age and suffering chronic back pain, plus having only a few months of unemployment would normally have terrified me, but after having come through some wilderness experiences already, knowing God had a plan gave me great hope. Whatever His plan was, I knew it would succeed as long as I submitted and obeyed everything He spoke to me.

As I prayed about my future, the Lord showed me in my spirit that He would block any wrong path I tried to take as well as remove any wrong person I became involved with as long as I was submitted to Him completely. I felt in my spirit that time was getting very short. I didn't have any sense of how short, but it was comforting to know He would guide me back onto His path if I got off the correct path at any point.

I had no idea where God was moving me, but wherever it was, I knew it would be in my best interest to go there. He gave me no clue about where I might be going, but He continued to speak more to me in my prayer times. I bounced back and forth between being certain the move was something great, and being fearful of not having a job in such a terrible economy. How would I rent another place to live with no job? What if He moved me some place I didn't like? I didn't mind change, but I hated uncertainty. I liked to plan

> *I liked to plan my work, and then work my plan. There was less chance of failing with a plan, but God was not interested in my need to plan, He was teaching me to trust Him.*

my work, and then work my plan. There was less chance of failing with a plan, but God was not interested in my need to plan, He was teaching me to trust Him.

I hoped the move was to a familiar place. Maybe He would move me nearer Mom so I could visit her more than just on weekends, near my family again. Or maybe He would send me back to Texas to the Dallas area, though I had only a few friends there. Or maybe He was taking me some place new where there were opportunities to witness or minister.

My daughter, I am not setting you up to fail, but to prosper - to grow great in Me, and in My word, in My ways. Do not fear, for you discredit My name when you fear what I am doing, like you think I will not provide for you. Have I not always provided for you in the past? Repent of your unbelief and stop fretting. The new place will indeed bring changes, but they are good ones. You are in a season of rest right now. I am getting you ready to do My will. Concentrate on My word – saturate your being with My word. You should be meditating on and speaking My word out of your mouth for victory! Would you ever desert your child or send them some place where there was no provision? No. How much greater is My love for you? How can you think I would?

Do not waste time giving heed to the enemy's lies that I will not provide for you and care for you, for have I not always? Speak My word to the enemy when he comes at you like a flood with his lies and deception! Stir up your most holy faith and remind yourself as David did – remind yourself of all the times I proved Myself faithful to you!

I know the exact dollar amount you will need to live on each month and I have already ordained it to be there for you as long as you do not turn from My ways. I want you to spend your days reading My word and receiving your healing.

Only a day or so later, I was talking with a friend on the phone about my upcoming move when I saw a vision flash in my spirit of a small, humble looking little house. I grabbed my journal and sketched it just in case it was important.

It is time for the next change to come into your life, My daughter. You know I do nothing without great purpose behind it so trust Me. Trust Me and know that I am acting in your best interest, and I have the interests of the Kingdom at heart.

You're scaring me, Lord.

It is more necessary that the interests of the entire Kingdom be served than those of one person, My child. Those who are truly chosen must give up much to serve Me, but the rewards are greater than you know. Trust Me and just obey whatever I say to you and all shall be well. I shall turn everything you see as negative to your great benefit, and to the benefit of those to whom I have called you.

I want you to fast for Me now. Fast solid food and believe Me to heal you. Fast television and movies. You must be in My word in order to receive it. As you fast for Me, think on My names. Think on My names and all they mean to you. Think on these things, not your future and not your present state of affairs for these are only temporary matters.

I have so much ahead for you, but your compliance is necessary in order that I may release it to you. I cannot give you that which could destroy you. You must prove yourself to Me now. You will do it now, or you fail, and you forfeit the call to another who studies and shows themselves approved.

The blessings will no longer be yours now if you do not obey Me starting now. I tell you the truth, I will take them away – those I have planned for your future, and I will make the ones you have now of no effect if you do not obey what I have this day commanded you to do. Do not fail and live a life of regrets, My Child, for your life is meant to be full and joyous.

*Remember the ladder? You must take off one more layer in order to go up
to the next rung. That is what I am asking you to do for Me. Take off that
last fleshly layer, lay it at the foot of the Cross, and climb up higher with Me.*

GO TO THE LAND I WILL SHOW YOU

Within a week, I had begun packing in earnest.

GENESIS 12:1

NOW THE LORD SAID TO ABRAM, "GO
FROM YOUR COUNTRY AND YOUR KINDRED
AND YOUR FATHER'S HOUSE TO THE LAND
THAT I WILL SHOW YOU.

The Lord continued to speak to me about what was to come.

*The place I am taking you to is a place of new beginnings for you. You will
delight to see each one arrive. Do not fear for anything. If it appears there is
no provision, it is only because I am going to do a miracle of provision to
surprise you there. Only believe Me. Many of My other children need to
learn this lesson to help them believe in Me, and how I can and will provide
for them, and you shall teach them. Your story shall go far and wide, and
many shall read of your trials, and how My mighty hand rescued you from
every one of them. You have been faithful to keep the record as I
commanded you, and you will be very glad of it, for it shall become a book
to witness to others of your testimony, and My mighty power to save and
deliver all who will call upon My name. Your husband awaits you in the new
place. The greatest times of your life lay just ahead for you, and I delight to
give them all to you.*

That Saturday afternoon found me at the care home visiting Mom. We
drank coffee and ate cookies, and talked of happy times. I always felt sad
to leave her, wishing we lived closer and I could see her more often. I had
not told her of the move, I knew she would fear for me, and spend many
sleepless nights worrying about me not having a job or enough savings.
My heart broke at the thought God might be taking me far from her, but
maybe He was moving me closer. He had not said yet, so that was still a

possibility. I hated keeping things from her, but I could not bear the thought of her worrying day after day over my welfare, when I knew God would take care of me in the end.

Day after day, I sat on a plastic tub in my storage stall sorting through boxes of belongings, trying to pare down what I owned enough to fit it into a U-Haul trailer. There had been no time for cleaning out in the years since I had gone back to oilfield work. Work in the oilfield is often demanding. Because the work is cyclical, there is an urgency to do as much as possible as fast as possible while the work is available. Deadlines and budgets loom, and those who cannot meet them are quickly released from their duties. That thought was never far from my mind.

As wind whipped around the dusty stall, I remembered so many mornings when the constant travel and stress of my job became too much, and I would come there with my coffee, anxious to escape the dim motel room with its manufactured art and heavy air freshener smells. I would sit in my rocking chair in the dusty storage stall in the midst of all my boxes, talking to the Lord. I longed so much for a place to call home. Sometimes I spent hours there, staring sadly at all the dusty boxes I had packed my life away into. I wanted nothing more than to have a house where I could unpack it all, and live a life that consisted of something besides just my job.

Day after day, I returned there where I cleaned, sorted and packed the most important of my belongings into boxes and labeled them for moving until the pain and stiffness in my back would let me pack no longer, then I would return to the house and pack some more there.

One night in the midst of packing that month, I dreamt the glory of God came down into my bedroom. I could see the angels in the glory cloud. Each night as I would lay down to go to sleep, I could feel the presence of angels in my room. Never before had I felt angels like that in the house with me.

About a week into packing, I was praying in the spirit one evening when all was still and quiet in my small house. Suddenly, a new voice rose up in me, and, though I was still praying in the spirit, I could feel I was decreeing something, into existence, and my tone of voice became very commanding. I felt utter sureness rise up within me, as if the Lord had suddenly released a huge measure of faith in me. I felt in my spirit I was declaring my provision and open doors to minister in the new place. I have no idea how long I prayed that way. Suddenly I saw a beautiful white mist descend into the room, like a fog of some kind, and I felt God's pleasure at the faith going forth in those prayers.

CHAPTER 8 - TEXAS

When I arose on the morning of March 1ˢᵗ, I knew I was packing the very last of my things and I would be ready to leave that day. I prayed fervently in my morning prayer time for direction.

Lord, please tell me where I am going. I don't even know which direction to point my truck when I leave. Am I going to where Mom is? Are you moving me closer to Mom so I can visit her more often? Back to Dallas? To some new place? I need to know which direction to drive, I will finish loading today.

Texas.

Texas? Can I know the town I'm going to?

Silence. I waited. Nothing.

Okay, Lord, I will just head south when I finish loading then. I know You will tell me more when I need to know.

Later that evening with friends and my son helping, everything was finally loaded into my U-Haul trailer. A typical Oklahoma spring day, the wind had blown hard all day long as we tried to load the last of the boxes. By the time it was all done, it was 9:00 p.m. that night. I wanted nothing so much as a hot shower and a comfortable bed. I sat in my truck and looked at my empty house as my son did a last check of everything. I had already returned the keys to my landlord, there was no turning back now. I had never moved at night before and it felt strange to me. Every part of my body ached and my mind was exhausted from the emotions of saying goodbye to all my friends and leaving my family, and my life as I knew it, and having no idea what I was going to.

As my son did the last check, he discovered some of the lights on the trailer did not work. As he worked on the lights in the cold wind, the physical and mental exhaustion overcame me, and tears began streaming down my face. It was 9:00 o'clock at night, and there would be no place open to get parts to fix the lights if he could not make them work. There was no strength left in me to face any more problems. We could not go back into the house to spend the night, and I didn't know what to do. As it turned out, he was able to get them working, but we had to stop every so often on the dark highway, whenever they stopped along the way.

I decided to try to get as far as I could, and then find a motel for the night. Even a couple of hours up the road would get the leaving part over with, and tomorrow was a new day. I was driving towards my place of new beginnings, wherever it was. I slowly pulled out onto the highway and headed for Oklahoma City. My son had talked to an old friend who had a job for him in the Dallas area, and he had agreed to help me move since I was going that way. He was excited to be leaving Oklahoma and getting a new start as well. He would move me into a house, then start his new job and get an apartment of his own. I was thrilled he would have work as jobs were almost impossible to come by with a recession in full swing.

As the truck sped over the dark highway, I thought of Mom. How would I tell her I was moving hundreds of miles away from her when she counted on my weekly visits? I would miss her bright smiles so much, her laughter, all the funny things she said. I would miss being able to hug her and see her, and know she was okay.

Lord, please take care of Mom. I won't be here to get her the things she needs and I don't want her to do without anything. Please, Lord, take extra good care of Mom. Her life has been filled with heartbreak and disappointment. I can't bear to think of her needing something and me not being here to get it for her. Please watch over her.

That night, I made it as far as Ardmore. I was exhausted beyond reason and felt in danger of collapsing by the time the motel clerk checked me in and handed me the keys to our rooms. The next morning, getting dressed in my motel room, reality tried to crowd into my thoughts.

I just loaded my entire life into a 6x12' U-Haul trailer based on what I think I heard from God. This move will either ruin me or redeem me, and at this point, I'm really not sure which one it will be.

I grabbed a stale sweet roll and paper cup of coffee on my way out the front door, and pulled out of the parking lot. I began praying in earnest as I pulled onto the interstate.

Okay, Lord. I obeyed You. I packed my entire life into a trailer, and I'm heading to Texas on Your word. I believe this is like when you told Abraham to go and You would tell him where he was going on the way. I'm on the way now, so can I please know what town I am going to?

I waited a few seconds. Suddenly, in the spirit I saw a map, and an oval shape highlighted in northeast Texas. I knew that area well, I had lived in it when I was married. I was going to live near Dallas again!

GENESIS 12:1

NOW THE LORD SAID TO ABRAM, "GO
FROM YOUR COUNTRY AND YOUR KINDRED
AND YOUR FATHER'S HOUSE TO THE LAND
THAT I WILL SHOW YOU.

As my truck sped over the interstate on that sunny day in March towards the area the Lord had shown me in my spirit, I prayed for the name of the town.

Silence.

I was sure He would tell me the town when I got closer. Late that afternoon, I was inside the oval shaped area He had shown me. I kept praying for the name of the town.

Silence.

Okay, Lord, I don't know what's up, but since You haven't given me a city yet, I will go to McKinney and get a motel room and wait for You to speak.

The next morning, I felt a combination of relief that the packing and driving were over, and uncertainty because I was still not home yet. The Lord's silence about the town was unnerving, but maybe He just wanted me to rest for the night before He told me. Physically I was drained, and emotionally I was completely spent. Later that afternoon, I went out driving in the area He had shown me on the map in my spirit, praying as I went. Maybe He would reveal the town to me as I drove.

Is this the town, Lord? How about this one? .... This one?

That night I prayed harder, while fighting the temptation of the smell of food cooking in the hallway, having already fasted all solid food for a month. I had no idea how long He would have me fast, and it never mattered to me, I just wanted to obey.

Okay, Lord. I really need to know where You want me so I can get that U-Haul trailer unloaded and turned back in. Please tell me which town my house is in so I can go rent it. I'm trying my best to do everything You told me to do.

Silence.

I continued praying, and praising and worshiping and reading the Word. Finally, I fell into bed, drained and too exhausted to press in any longer.

I went out again the next day and drove the roads, praying in the spirit and talking to the Lord.

Lord, those two rooms at that motel are costing a lot of money, and the U-Haul is already overdue and costing me late fees every day. I really need to know where You want me. Please tell me the name of the town You are sending me to.

Silence.

Please, Lord. You told me to come here and I did. Why won't You tell me where I'm going to live? I can't stay in that motel forever. I'll run out of money!

I only need one day.

Oh. That's right. You're God. You do just need one day. I'm sorry, Lord. I'll just go back to praying then.

Those first several mornings, I prayed and read the Word, and then prayed some more. The fast of all solid food was beginning to take its toll, especially on days when I was physically tired, but I continued to fast in spite of it. I knew if I ever stopped a fast for any reason, the enemy would be sure to try the same thing every time I fasted.

I kept driving and praying in the spirit each day, trying not to panic as I thought about the fees I was racking up on the U-Haul trailer and how much it would cost me to rent two motel rooms for a second week if His silence continued for the rest of the week. I drove for miles, alternating prayer for the towns I drove through while fervently begging the Lord to show me where I was supposed to go.

One morning as I begged and pleaded, the Lord spoke again.

I have arranged every detail for your arrival in the new town and I shall direct you to it soon. Concern yourself only with being in My word, and following My lead for all has already been prepared for your arrival there.

You shall know the place when you find it beyond any shadow of a doubt. You shall know it is I who have prepared it for you and sent you there. Do you think I would not guide you to where I wish for you to be? I lead My children!

Walk forth and be as a beacon of light in a world that becomes darker by the moment. Be my representative in a new place where I desire to do miracle after miracle and many signs and wonders to show the people My mighty power. I only need one person to fully obey Me and I can save thousands who would otherwise end up in hell. Go forth and watch My mighty hand move!

I tried to rest that night in what He had said, but I could not just sit at the motel and watch my tiny savings dwindling away. I would try to rest and fear would plague my rest. Why was nothing happening? Had I truly heard from Him or was I just deluding myself?

TERRIFIED

My days and nights since arriving at the motel were a constant battle with fear. The enemy tormented me with things like, *What are you going to do? You have no place to live. Everyone thinks you're crazy. You didn't hear from God, you only heard from yourself! You're going to end up homeless!*

I had no place to live and I was spending money every day on two motel rooms and food. I rebuked him over and over.

One evening, worn out from fasting and trying to hang on to my shaky faith, I awoke in a state of terrible fear. *What am I doing here? Why didn't I just stay in Woodward where I had a nice comfortable house? What will I do if God never tells me where I'm supposed to live? What if I didn't hear Him at all?*

Suddenly I began to shake violently as the fear overwhelmed me. I knew the enemy was trying to take what little faith I still had. I got up from the bed, and began walking around the room praying.

Please help me, Lord. I'm trying so hard to believe what You spoke to me. Please show me something so I will know I really heard from You! And please help me with this fear – it's attacking me constantly!

Knowing fear was a spirit from II Timothy 1:7, I began doing warfare against the spirit itself.

"Fear, I cast you out in the name of Jesus! Go now!" I commanded.

I continued to shake as minutes passed, as I rebuked it again and again. I wondered if the other guests in the motel heard me battling demons in my room.

The fear continued to increase until it felt as if it would overtake me.

Lord, I told it to go! It has to obey the name of Jesus – why isn't it leaving?

It's not Fear. It's Terror.

"Terror, in the Name of Jesus, I command you to leave me NOW!!"

Immediately it left, and I stopped shaking.

Thank You, Lord! I didn't even know terror was a spirit!

The wilderness experience is one where you often feel alone, and one thing I found very helpful was soliciting the prayers of others to strengthen me so I could keep walking. I had a few friends back in Oklahoma and also my sister praying for the success of my faith walk. I also had a powerfully anointed woman of God, my mentor, Beverly Willhoite.

I first met Beverly in 2004 when I was checking records on an oil and gas job in the courthouse in Anadarko, Oklahoma when she was mayor of the town. She is a woman of the very highest integrity and someone I deeply respected. A powerful prophetess as well as a wise and attentive mentor, I considered myself doubly blessed when the Lord had appointed her as my mentor and told me to begin tithing to her. She was faithful to cover me in prayer at all times, but especially when she knew I was in crisis. That night she called me to see how I was doing.

I poured out my heart to her.

"Beverly, I just want to go back home. It scares me because if I don't make it and I go back to Woodward, I know I will never have the faith to do a faith walk like this again!"

"Yes, I can see where that would be a challenge," she said.

"My week is up here Monday. I don't know what to do. I can just pay day by day but I don't understand why God sent me here and now He won't tell me where I'm supposed to go! I'm watching what little savings I have dwindle away."

"I have a knowing in my spirit that you are where He sent you. Just hang on. God is not slack concerning His promises, He will tell you. I will lift you up tonight when I pray," she said.

She prayed a powerful prayer over me before getting off the phone.

Thank You, Lord, for Beverly. I don't know what I would do without her right now! She has so much wisdom and she is always patient with me.

Every day at the motel, I received an auto-text from U-Haul telling me the rented trailer packed full of my belongings was overdue to be turned in, and I was reminded of yet more of my savings dwindling away. On Friday morning less than a week after arriving at the motel, I felt the doubt creeping in again. Still physically fatigued and fighting hunger and weakness on the fast, I decided it was time to call for more backup prayer, so I called Kenneth Copeland Ministries. Their prayer line is one of the few I have found I can always get through on, and the only one I've ever known that actually calls you back if you try to call, and end up hanging up before you reach a prayer warrior.

I reached a soft spoken lady and briefly explained my situation, told her that I believed the Lord had sent me to Texas, but now I was sitting at a motel with no job and no idea where I was supposed to be, and that I was trying hard not to freak out and run back to Oklahoma and blow the whole plan. She prayed a powerful prayer over me and we agreed in prayer the Lord would quickly show me where He wanted me to be. Then I told her I believed strongly in the prophetic anointing and if the Lord showed her anything to feel free to release it, because I desperately needed to hear from Him right then. She went silent for a minute and then began to speak.

"Are you married?"

"No M'aam," I answered.

"Are you believing for a mate?"

> *He had sent me, I had His proof. My evidence was that indescribable peace I had inside, and I wasn't leaving until I had done whatever He had sent me there for.*

"Yes, I am in fact believing for a godly mate," I answered.

"He's in the town where the Lord is sending you. He is physically and spiritually strong. He's a faith giant and the two of you are going to touch thousands for Christ!" she said.

"Yes! Thank you for that confirmation, Lord!"

I was overjoyed! The Lord had shown the woman what He had already told me, that my husband was in the town where He was sending me. I was sure I would not be alone much longer.

I continued to pray and worship, every day and every night, though I did not understand why it was taking the Lord so long to reveal the name of the town where I was moving to me. A strong feeling about the date March 11th began coming up in my spirit, but I wasn't sure why. I looked at the calendar. March 11th was the 40th day of my fast of all solid food. Maybe God was going to tell me I could eat again that day.

On the morning of March 8th, I decided to visit a church one of my cousins occasionally attended in nearby Princeton. During the worship service, I saw an opening in the heavenly realm in the spirit. I wondered if it was the door the Lord told me about the previous year, and what it meant.

That afternoon, tormented by smells of cooking food wafting into my motel room, I called Kenneth Copeland Ministries for prayer again. A lady answered my call and I quickly told her my situation, and that I was open to anything she received prophetically. She immediately said "Sent Forth. You have been sent forth." She prayed for me and agreed with me in prayer that God would move expediently on my behalf and show me where I belonged. We were sure it couldn't be much longer.

MELTDOWN

That evening, missing my friends back home terribly and thinking of my Mom and daughter and grandchildren, I went into meltdown mode. I was so tired emotionally, and I felt my faith had been stretched past its limits. As I prayed, I cried out to God to end my misery.

Please, Lord, I just want to go back home! If You want me here, why aren't You showing me where I belong? I can't keep staying here and paying all this money with no direction! Please help me! I can't hold on much longer, Lord. I'm strong, but not this strong!

Friends called that night. Some urged me to turn around and go back home, some prayed for me and urged me to keep walking forward, and some told me they had secretly thought all along I was making a big mistake, and that any thought I had of a grand future in the Lord for my life were just wishful thinking on my part. It was easy to see which ones truly believed I had heard from God and which had their doubts.

Through all of it, my sister was one of my strongest supporters, and I thanked God again and again for her. She and I were as close as best friends, and she had watched as many of the things the Lord spoken to me had come to pass in the last few years. I knew she regularly lifted me up in prayer. My mentor also stood with me and continued praying for me.

The combination of the fasting and the stress were beginning to scatter my thoughts, and I was finding it more and more difficult to keep everything straight. At times, I would wake up and think, *What am I doing here? Why did I just pack up my whole life and drive to this place with no plan? Have I lost my mind?*

In spite of everything, though, I had peace in my spirit, and even in my weak moments, I knew that peace could only be coming from God. It certainly was not coming from my circumstances.

PHILIPPIANS 4:7

AND THE PEACE OF GOD, WHICH
SURPASSES ALL UNDERSTANDING, WILL
GUARD YOUR HEARTS AND YOUR MINDS IN
CHRIST JESUS.

I knew if I had not heard from the Lord to go there, I would not have that
incredible peace that passes understanding, so I stayed put and kept
praying. I kept fighting doubt and fear. I rebuked the thoughts that I was
just insane and hearing things, and I continued to press in. I prayed
longer, worshiped more deeply. I refused to back down, because I knew
there was no way I would ever step out in faith again if I turned and ran
this time.

All I knew to do was continue going out in the afternoons and driving the
area the Lord had shown me, and praying in the spirit. I continued fasting
and clung to every scrap of faith I could muster as I forced myself to keep
my eyes on Jesus. He had sent me, I had His proof. My evidence was that
indescribable peace I had inside, and I wasn't leaving until I had done
whatever He had sent me there for. He would guide me, I just had to
hang on until He did. It would turn out to be almost an hourly battle.

PRINCETON

On March 8th, I was feeling afraid again. I had left Woodward on the night
of March 1st, and I still had no idea what town I was supposed to be going
to. I went out and drove the roads again, pleading with the Lord for an
answer, but got only silence. When I got back to the motel, the last scrap
of faith was almost gone as I had to pay for additional days for the two
rooms I had rented there.

I told my son I was thinking of going back to Oklahoma. He felt I had
nothing there to go back to, and offered to go with me the following day
to help me find a house. True to his word, he went with me the following
morning, writing down landlord information and making phone calls as I
drove. It had been over a week of exhausting days of praying and
pleading, and I had given up caring which town I lived in, I just wanted a
house to offload the trailer to. I was getting low on money and I had to

find a place and find one quick, or I wouldn't need a house because I would be sleeping in my truck.

In Princeton, we drove past a tiny white house I had passed several times in my daily rounds. It sat down in a depression and looked like it was sinking into the ground. With a scraggly lawn and leaning carport, it wasn't much to see. The sign showed a rent amount higher than I was willing to pay for a house that size and I had never given it a second thought because of the price.

My son insisted I stop and look at it, even though I told him I thought the rent was too high for a house that small. I noticed someone was at the house this time. He continued to insist I check out every house thoroughly just in case, so I stopped.

The house was tiny - it only had one bedroom plus a tiny partial room in the back that amounted to half or less of a small bedroom. It sat on a corner and had driveways in the front and at the back as well. It had only 110 air conditioning and one small gas heater to provide heat for the entire house. I knew how brutal the Texas summers were, and was reluctant to rent anything that did not have central heat and air, but as the days had worn on, I had become less picky, too. It wasn't the worst I had ever seen, and I was so very tired of looking every day, and of fighting fear in the motel every night. In addition, I really liked the friendly landlord. He was finishing up some last minute painting and floor work, and the house was almost ready to rent out.

I wasn't sure it was the house, but I was so weary, I wasn't sure I could go on caring either. When the landlord offered to drop the rent by $50 a month and give me the rest of the month free if I would do the initial cleaning of it, I felt that was a sign of God's favor, so I filled out an application.

The following morning, he told me I had passed the background check. When I went to take the rent and deposit money to him, I parked in the back drive instead of the front one. As soon as I walked in the back door, I knew I was in the right house. The Lord showed me in my spirit I had found home. I realized as I looked closer that the kitchen appliances and flooring matched my decor, and the bedroom paint matched all my bedroom stuff. On the outside, it was the least attractive of all the rentals I had looked at, but inside it was as if God had prepared it just for me.

On March 11th, we backed the U-Haul trailer up to the back door of the house and began carrying in belongings in the cold rain, fighting the March wind. I didn't care how cold it was though, I had a house! I had no furniture at all, not even a mattress to sleep on, but I didn't care. At least the fear of waiting every day at that motel was finally over.

A week later, I decided to visit the church I had gone to again. I prayed hard while getting ready to go visit a nearby church that the Lord would speak something to me while I was at church. He answered.

During worship, an older woman I later learned was Sister Margaret, who was worshiping beside me suddenly turned and began prophesying over me: *"You shall travel the highways and the byways. God has anointed your mouth. You shall lay hands and the lame shall walk, blind eyes shall be opened, the captives shall be set free! There is no struggle to it. As you obey Me, you shall see Me, says the Lord. Walk through the doors as I open them. This day the Lord says to you, I have chosen you because you have chosen Me and the things of Me. You will go into prisons. He will walk before you. Do not worry for the money for He will provide everything. He calls you faithful!"*

Later that month, I was still fasting, and I began experiencing the Lord's presence very strongly in my little house. Even in Louisiana early in my walk with Him, I had never felt His presence so strongly. Sometimes His presence would be so palpable I was sure I should be able to see Him, but I could not.

Soon after, the enemy began attacking my prayer time and my time in the Word. The Lord would lead me to intercede for someone in prayer or I would begin reading the Word, and my phone would begin ringing or something would come up that had to be done right then. As it happened again and again, I began to pray about it.

The distractions are aimed at keeping you out of My word, My daughter, for the enemy knows there is tremendous revelation power in My word, and he does not want you to have it, or to use its miracle working power. Fight him on this. Set aside a period of time each day for your writing and My word.

The world around you is filled with distractions. Many of My children do not spend time with Me at all, but the cost to them will be great in the days coming for I shall pour out My judgment upon all those who do not seek to know Me or My Will for their lives. No longer shall I look on as they go their own way following their own plans...

The Lord continued speaking what at the time I did not realize was a prophetic word for His people and which, to me, sounded pretty frightening for those who were not seeking Him.

I quickly grew weary of sleeping on an air mattress on the floor. I had held back from spending what little was left of my tiny savings on furniture, since I didn't want to have two sets of everything when my husband showed up, but at my age getting up and down off the floor was more than a little painful.

Lord, I need some bedroom furniture. I would really love for You to send me a four-poster bed and a dresser. A solid wood one. I could use a couch, too, but it needs to be really cheap because I don't want to spend what little money is left in my savings.

As March turned into April, I continued to fast and pray, and to study the Word, but everything in my life seemed strangely quiet otherwise.

One day in early April, I began praying about why nothing was happening yet.

Lord, why are none of Your promises manifesting? Where is my husband? Where is the ministry You've been telling me we will do here in Princeton? Am I doing something wrong? Please tell me how to handle this fear and doubt, Lord. I don't want to doubt You.

Declare those things I have promised you into the atmosphere!

Okay, Lord, I'll start declaring. Thank You. You know, Lord, when I prayed years ago and asked You for a year to rest and study Your word before You put me out into ministering full time, I thought I would have a husband to provide for me.

You have a husband - Me.

Oh, right. Sorry, Lord.

On the 68th day of my fast and I was finishing my morning coffee when my cousin, a local minister I sometimes helped with correspondence, called and asked if I would like to ride with him to pick up some boxes of donated books. I agreed.

We drove to a rural area not far from town where an elderly man lived in a trailer with several canine companions. As we were loading the books, I saw he had many other items in his yard, and I mentioned to him I was looking for some used furniture. He pointed behind me and when I turned and looked I nearly jumped for joy. There, on the back of a trailer, were pieces to a full size, four poster bed and a matching dresser. I seriously doubted I could afford what he would ask for the solid wood set, but I asked anyway. When he quoted me a price, I couldn't believe my ears – forty dollars for the bed and dresser? *Was he kidding?* I immediately agreed to take it, and when he showed me the two matching wooden nightstands, I bought those and a very old chest of drawers from another set as well.

Afterwards he referred me to a friend who sold me a decent couch for twenty dollars.

> *Spiritual journeys are like staircases. You can't take four steps at a time. You must climb each step as you get to it.*

Thank You, Lord! I just bought everything I needed for just over a hundred dollars! I have furniture now!

I began spending my days watching the headlines, and reading the Word. I was still praying, but I had put aside my regular prayer times. I was discouraged that nothing the Lord had told me was happening, I was ill, and I was handling what felt like a million distractions every day. Surely God wouldn't mind in light of everything that was going on.

By the time the fast ended, I had fasted solid food for 75 days. By that time, the upper respiratory infection I had was worsening, and I was hoping the food would strengthen me so I would not need to return to the clinic for more antibiotics.

The latest headlines on the internet were frightening. Some strange and deadly strain of flu had hit Mexico, and it appeared to be killing people rapidly. Texas bordered Mexico, and I knew it would not be long before it spread here.

Great, that's just what I need with my immune system like it is. Help, Lord!

I was praying one day soon after the news of the flu broke about why none of God's promises were manifesting in my life yet, and the Lord began to speak to me.

Spiritual journeys are like staircases. You can't take four steps at a time. You must climb each step as you get to it.

What do You mean, Lord? What about all the things You told me were going to happen here? I moved here at Your word.

Silence.

The following month, I was praying late one night when the Lord spoke to me about a battle that was coming.

Do not be concerned with provision, your provision is already ordained. You moved here on My authorization. I am Jehovah Jireh and My children do not lack any good thing when they believe Me! Honor Me by believing Me.

Instead of believing Me for so little, you need to put your faith in Me for more. You have seeded well, but you fail to call forth your mighty harvest. Call it in and I shall send the angels of heaven to deliver that which you so desire. Receive all I have for you that My name might be glorified! Receive by speaking to Me what you desire in prayer and then receiving in your mind thoughts that it is there instead of thoughts of lack and 'what will I do if...' If you will only believe this way as you have believed in the past, I will grant you many treasures!

You must believe, however, in order for us to move forward. I am willing, you must be also – willing to trust Me for everything, and know that I will not let you down no matter how things look in the natural. You must not listen to other voices that try to sway you off the path I have prepared for you – the path you know I have spoken to you to follow.

Study My word, labor to be in My word both day and night, for the issues of life are contained therein. Eat of My word and you shall grow full and rich in it. Take it in like fresh air and sunshine and it will refresh you when you are weary, it will uphold you when you are weak, it will feed you when you are hungry. Read it day and night. As you read it you will be with Me, and more and more found in My image, conformed more and more to My ways, transformed from glory to glory to glory! Beware of the enemy who seeks to take you from My presence and separate you from your sword and allow him not!

VISION OF THE PROVING THREAD

I was reading in Deuteronomy chapter 8 one day not long after the Lord spoke that word to me. I was struggling with not being able to hear the Lord speak as often as I was accustomed to. I tried not to think about it, but I had less than two months before packed my few possessions into a U-Haul trailer and left the only residence I had for unknown parts based on His word to me, and His promises. I had expected to see much more happen after arriving in the new place, and I was beginning to feel really confused. Not only was nothing happening, but He wasn't telling me why.

DEUTERONOMY 8:2

AND YOU SHALL REMEMBER THE WHOLE
WAY THAT THE LORD YOUR GOD HAS LED
YOU THESE FORTY YEARS IN THE
WILDERNESS, THAT HE MIGHT HUMBLE
YOU, TESTING YOU TO KNOW WHAT WAS
IN YOUR HEART, WHETHER YOU WOULD
KEEP HIS COMMANDMENTS OR NOT.

As I was reading *"to prove you, to know what was in your heart..."* in the King James Version of this same scripture, I saw a flash vision of a seamstress testing a piece of thread by pulling it taut between her hands. Being an amateur seamstress myself, I knew testing the thread like that was something you did to be sure the thread will be strong enough for the intended purpose, and that it won't break, causing all your work to unravel. He was showing me that in the desert places, we are being proved, tested...to see whether we are strong enough for our intended purpose, or whether we will break, causing all His work to unravel.

I could still hear God speak to me through His word, even if He wasn't speaking to me the other way very often. I had learned in earlier treks through the desert that the teacher is always silent during the test, so obviously this was some kind of test. Instead of coming to Texas to receive the fulfillment of so many promises, could it be I was about to be tested again? The thought terrified me. Having been through the wilderness experience several times already, it was not a place I wanted to enter in to again, especially in middle age with no job to even sustain me financially.

One thing I did know about the wilderness was you had to keep standing. You had to keep walking forward, to continue putting one foot in front of the other and taking the next step. If you refused to lay down your faith, and you kept walking one step at a time, I knew you always eventually walk out of that desert place, but it was often a long and trying journey before you did.

The Lord had told me more than once I would write a book about His ways. Could it be the book was to be about the wilderness experience? He seemed to take me back to the desert over and over again. Either it was to teach me more about it, more about Him, or I was just extremely disobedient and needed a lot of chastisement. I wasn't sure which one it was, it also did not escape my notice that if a thread did not pass the proving test, a seamstress will cast that one aside and use another thread instead. If I was being proved, I prayed I would prove to be strong enough for my intended purpose so I could be used.

As the days ticked slowly by, and I did not see a single promise of the Lord manifesting, doubt assailed me more and more. Had I truly heard from God about the move to Texas? Had I really heard the promises He spoke to me or had I fallen into some kind of hallucination of wishful thinking?

> *He was showing me that in the desert places, we are being proved, tested...to see whether we are strong enough for our intended purpose, or whether we will break, causing all His work to unravel.*

He had spoken things to me before and they happened. He had told me to pray for people and I had seen miraculous healings take place when I obeyed. Just before leaving Oklahoma, He had me lay my hand on the stomach of a barren friend and command her womb to open. A month later, after years of trying to conceive, she suddenly became pregnant. But if I knew His voice and if I had heard from Him, why weren't any of the things He promised me coming to pass yet? My unemployment check was not enough to pay my rent and utilities and buy food every month. I began to press into prayer and pray long, pray hard, pray more fervently for an answer from Him. Finally, He spoke.

Did I not say I shall supply all your needs? That you shall not do without any good thing in this place if you obeyed My voice and followed My will and plan? And so you have done, now I shall keep My part of our agreement and provide bountifully for you.

Can I not part seas and bring water forth from rocks for you as I did for My other children? Do you think Me weak and old? That I have forgotten how? Ask and you shall receive whatever you desire in this time, My child. Your mistake is you are having difficulty believing even for your rent and truck payment when the truth is, I want to give you far more than that. Did I say you were in the land of barely-get-by? Did I say you would have nothing to spare? Nay, I said abundance and more than enough!

Did I not send the children of Israel more than enough manna for each day and more than enough water from the rock? Did I not give them favor for raiment and silver and gold? The spoils of their enemies, when they defeated them?

Why do you expect so little from such a mighty God? Would you not expect more from even an earthly husband?

Stop trying to reason everything out, for My ways are much higher than your ways, and My thoughts higher than your thoughts, but I will come through for you.

I hung my head. My faith was so small and I wanted it to be so big. I would believe big for a few days and then thoughts planted by the enemy would assault my mind and I would bounce back to fear again. I began keeping my regular prayer times again, asking the Lord to help me understand. So many friends had said to me that they did not hear Him speak as often, and it made me doubt whether I was hearing Him as well. Who was I to hear Him more than they did? Listening to those outside voices instead of only His voice threw me again and again into the battle with doubt and fear.

MY WORD IS LIKE A CONTRACT

The Lord began speaking to me more and more about how to receive my provision from Him.

You do well to buckle down to My word as the authority in your life. That is what I desire for all of My children to do. I watch over My word to perform it, so any time I hear the voice of faith speaking it, I grant that request. Remember that. Remember the treasure of My word contains everything you need to live, all that you need to fully prosper as My servant Abraham did. Every treasure under heaven is yours through My precious word. There is nothing I have not granted you through My word, and the finished work of My precious Son Jesus if only you will walk in My ways and claim and receive what is already yours.

Lord, I don't understand how to receive it.

To receive is to state you own it, it is your right, and not back down from it. Like the clause of a contract, My word delivers. It is enforceable for I Myself back its promises! In order to know your entitlement as My child and heir to My kingdom, you need only read the contract and then claim the promises I have made you. The angels will be dispatched to aid you in receiving all that has been granted to you.

The enemy will always speak lies to defeat your walk unless you stop him, Daughter, but you have My contract, signed in the Blood of My Son, to back your every need and desire.

Your heart is Mine and ample provision, more than enough money, food and clothing are well within My will for you, so do not be afraid to ask for you have not only because you ask not. Just do not let the enemy steal your blessings by making you doubt Me or My word. That is the real danger because I only respond to the voice of faith. Doubt, fear and unbelief have no place in My kingdom or in My children.

Stop trying to reason everything out, for My ways are much higher than your ways, and My thoughts higher than your thoughts, but I will come through for you.

I fervently hoped I would not need the knowledge He was teaching me for long, I prayed I would begin to see the fulfillment of the promises He had given me for my life. Had it not been long enough? He knew I had never been a seeker of wealth or materialism. I had few desires past being able to pay my bills on time, driving a dependable vehicle I knew would not break down along the highway, and living in a decent house, other than wanting a small home of my own. Coming from a simple background, I had simple tastes.

YOU ARE NOT LIMITED BY ME, BUT I CAN BE LIMITED BY YOU

I was about to call my sister for a chat one night near the end of May when suddenly the Lord began to speak to me about the subject of provision, which was never far from my mind.

Indeed you are not believing Me for a place to sleep in a homeless shelter, so that will not be your reward. For many, that is all their small faith will allow, but you do indeed believe for much more, and this does indeed please Me for I truly want the best for all of My children who hearken to My voice and try to walk in My ways. My Son did not die that horrible death so you could all live miserable lives, but lives of healing and plenty. I have the power to grant you all that your faith can believe Me for, daughter. You are not limited by Me, but I can be limited by you. That is why I spoke to you that I wish for you to believe Me for more than you need at this time, that your testimony may be grand. Enough will spark faith, but abundance will spark great faith for far greater things in the lives of many of My people.

> *Use your voice and the weapon of praise to defeat fear, My child, for indeed the enemy cannot stand against you then, and I will be free to manifest all I desire to give you for My glory.*

I want you to go about your days proclaiming that all I have spoken to you is yours so that I may manifest it to you, that My name may be proclaimed throughout the land and My power known to those who do not know Me that I have called you to.

Use your voice and the weapon of praise to defeat fear, My child, for indeed the enemy cannot stand against you then, and I will be free to manifest all I desire to give you for My glory.

Far too few of My people understand truly the power of their words, and their lack of knowledge in this area will lead to their destruction if they do not learn. I have given man the power to make his living with words alone but they do not use it. The enemy uses every negative word you speak against you, My child, so guard your words carefully always. They are a snare to the unknowing ones. Do not let them become a snare to you also, and discredit My name. I want you to believe Me for you provision just as you believed your job for a paycheck. Remember how you told others they paid "on time, every time?" Do you think I will do less?

I kept pushing my faith higher, struggling to believe in the face of seeing nothing happening. Every day was like the one before it, and not one thing in my days showed any evidence anything was changing. None of God's promises were appearing. Had I left my family and friends in Oklahoma to come to Texas and sit alone in this small house?

One afternoon in late May, I was sitting on my air mattress, which was up on my bed frame, looking out my bedroom window and meditating on the Lord, when a loud POP jolted me back to reality, followed by the hiss of my air mattress deflating.

Okay, Lord, I know I've been praying a lot about my weight, and asking You to talk to me about it, but my air mattress popping with me sitting on it is not a very reassuring start to that conversation........

As the weeks passed and the days rolled into June, my life felt like a battle on every front, inside, outside, and everything in between. I constantly fought doubt and fear from reading the news reports of the terrible recession that had taken hold of the economy, and the flu that was spreading. I continued to press in during prayer by trying to pray longer and more fervently. Battling an onslaught of ants and tiny black beetles on the inside of the house I had rented, I barely walked outside for the swarms of wasps and hornets that awaited me there.

One day I was especially fearful. Job losses were soaring on every front, and suicides were frequently in the news, and I began to pray for help with the fear. As I began praying in the spirit, I noticed that whenever I was praying in tongues, the enemy did not seem to be able to put fearful thoughts into my mind, and I began to pray more in the spirit to shut out his attacks.

I knew praying out loud and thanking God for His help could be powerful in prayer, so I decided to add that to my prayer time as well. In 2001, I had begun praying scriptures out loud from a prayer list for the first time, and had come under immediate intense attack from the enemy. That was always a good sign that I had discovered a spiritual key he did not want me to know about. I decided to write out a prayer and begin praying it. As soon as I began praying it, I immediately came under attack, so I began praying it out loud daily. This was my prayer:

Lord God in Heaven, I know that in all of heaven and earth there is not another one like You. You alone are God. Show Yourself strong in my situation, Lord God! Nothing is too hard for You. You are the Most High, nothing is too hard for You. Show Your faithfulness. If there ever is lack in our lives, it is because we have not fully believed Your word for You love Your children more than all of creation. Show Your might and show Your power in My life and My finances that I may testify of You, and glorify Your Son Jesus.

A month earlier, reading back over the famine visions the Lord had shown me and the word He had spoken to warn His people, I began looking for ways to be obedient in telling others what He had shown me, and I posted the visions to some prophetic forums and shared His word there. As the weeks passed, I began receiving emails and requests for contact regarding the visions. Others wrote, telling me they had seen similar visions and believed the famine in America was not far off.

In my spare time, I began reading prophetic words on the internet, and watching videos of them on YouTube. I was hoping to find encouraging words to give me something to cling to in this terrible season of uncertainty. It had the opposite effect. Within three days, the spirits of fear and terror had attached to me to the point I was literally shaking with terror, and I had to cast them out again. Lesson learned. In prayer, the Lord spoke to me about it.

Keep your eyes on Me and learning of My ways, not on that which is coming to the world or America, for you cannot change My judgments and they are long past due, as you now know.

Know that I will guide and protect and keep you in those times until it is time for you to come home to Me. Do not sit and wring your hands and get into fear. Simply store up the knowledge you have been given for it is only that you, too, might not be deceived as others are that you have been shown these things. In reality, nothing has changed, you only know more about what already is.

I knew there were many who did not believe America had come under God's judgment, and He had spoken to me that it had. Though it is important to be aware of the prophetic voices the Lord uses to warn His people, there is a balance that must be maintained. If the words speak of sin in our lives and we feel conviction, then we need to address that sin, but we should never spend so much time chasing after the prophetic that we take our eyes off Jesus, and doing the work of the ministry that is before us today. We should at all times be concentrating on drawing closer to Him and walking the way He desires for us to walk, and keeping that our first priority, not whatever is coming in the future.

 Whatever I needed to know, I needed to trust the Lord to show me or speak to me. I was only torturing myself with fear. What good would it be to know what others had seen anyway? The prophecies might be true or they might be false, but I could do nothing about them either way, and I needed to keep my focus on my walk with the Lord, hearing from Him and doing whatever He had brought me to this place to do.

CHAPTER 9 – NEGATIVE WORDS

It was mid-June and I had begun assembling a collection of my newspaper columns to publish in a book, when my laptop suddenly began to malfunction because of the warmth and humidity in the room. I was trying not to run the air conditioner any more than was absolutely necessary to keep my utility bills down, because of not having a regular income.

Suddenly in my spirit, the Lord showed me that I was actually insulting Him by not believing Him for enough money to run the 110 air conditioners at least enough to be reasonably comfortable, as opposed to sitting in my house day after day sweating in the Texas heat while trying to conserve money. I immediately repented for not trusting Him more, and turned on the air conditioner in my office with great relief. Not once did He not provide the money for the electric bill, all of it, and on time. Just after that, He spoke to someone who knew me from my internet postings to send me a gift of money.

"Home is where you hang your heart," someone once said. As the days passed, it was clear to me I had left my heart hanging someplace else. I longed more and more to see my family in Oklahoma. I worried about the flu in the news, that one of them would fall ill with it. I worried about them surviving the recession we were in. I tried to tell myself living where God had sent me would all be worth it, that God would do something awesome in Princeton, and

"Home is where you hang your heart," someone once said. As the days passed, it was clear to me I had left my heart hanging someplace else.

that I would have a mighty testimony that would glorify Him, but inside I was still sad to be away from the family I loved. I clung to Psalm 22:5, that those who trust in the Lord would not be disappointed, but the tears wouldn't stop.

I especially missed my Mom and my grandson, and I longed to be near my sister as she cared for her husband in his illness. I missed my nieces and the way they always made me laugh. I simply wanted to be near my family. I didn't understand why He was not allowing me to, but I was trying to. I knew God did nothing without a purpose, and that sometimes His purposes could be difficult to see through the eyes of our pain, but my heart really grieved at times while walking through the wilderness so far from where I wanted to be.

Everything in me wanted to go back to Oklahoma where my people were. Waves of grief hit me all over again each time I thought of my grandson. My Mom had gone into a care home in 2006, less than a month after his father had died very suddenly, and now I was gone away as well. His life must surely have felt desolate at times. So many of the people he was closest to seemed to be taken away from him.

I know You will send people to take care of all of them, Lord. I just wish I could be the one to do it. I can't stand thinking they need me, and I might not be there for them. It hurts me that my calling costs other people so dearly. Please make it all turn out good, Lord, and please reward all of those who have suffered with me in this as well, I'm not the only one who is giving something up for this.

Would this heartache never end? Would life ever be anything but day after day of terrible struggle and heart wrenching emotions? My life had never even come close to ideal, but I knew many with much harder lives than mine, and the pain of the last ten years had been really trying. Maybe I felt the pain more because I was older and alone, but happy days seemed to be fewer and further between as the years went on and I sometimes wondered if everyone my age felt the same way.

I tried hard to refocus my mind on my goal, getting through the wilderness walk and doing what God had brought me here to do, whatever that entailed, learning more of His word, obeying. *Pray, trust and obey*, He had told me recently. Pray, trust and obey.

Okay, Lord, this is me praying, trusting and obeying. Please help me with this pain and grief, and please make all this somehow have a happy ending.

The next day, sadness and longing still filled my soul. I drove out by a lake and just sat on a log, looking out at the water for a long time, thinking about all that had transpired and praying. Something about the water calmed my soul. When I arrived back home, I spent the rest of the day cleaning house, grocery shopping and doing laundry, trying to not think about how much I missed my loved ones.

> *Did I really trust Him to come through for me? His timing always seemed so different than what I expected, what if I was wrong?*

I was down to taking one day at a time, and some days, even a day felt like a stretch to me.

My unemployment was set to run out the end of August. Did I really trust Him to come through for me? His timing always seemed so different than what I expected, what if I was wrong? What if He didn't come through? I would be in the streets with no income in less than a month. This was the biggest step of my life and no one I knew had the money to rescue me if I failed. Everyone I knew was going through a time of financial hardship themselves. This time I had no Plan B to fall back on.

Lord, if I really did hear from You, why is nothing happening?

Oh, but something is happening, My daughter, only you cannot see it yet. I have you in the palm of My mighty hand and you are safe there. You ask the hard questions tonight, but I think you already know My answers. Your times are in My hands, child. If you were to determine the timing of My promises being fulfilled, everything would go awry, for you know not the other pieces and people which must be put into place for My mighty plan to work out to perfection for you. Everything will happen as planned, but it is indeed My plan, and not yours.

I missed having a regular, predictable paycheck almost as much as I missed my family, but I also missed working. Work had given structure to my life, and I also began to see that I had gotten much of my identity and self worth from my vocation. Work had been my comfort and my husband for so long, I was somewhat lost without it. I had been a workaholic for years; it had been how I numbed my pain. Over the past several years, I had learned investing my energies in work paid a far better return than romance or partying ever had in my life.

Now, without the soothing balm of work until I was so tired I could do nothing but sleep, I was forced to face the pain of being away from my family and the terrible emptiness in my soul.

Two days later, as I caulked a huge crack I discovered where even more insects were coming into my house from outside, I was again being attacked by discouragement. I had walked with the Lord for thirteen years. *What if His promises another 13 years to manifest?*

I can't hold on that long, Lord. Please do something soon!

I did not understand God's timing and I don't know how to keep hoping . I wasn't sure how long I could keep holding the faith line if God didn't move on my behalf soon. It all looked so hopeless to me. I had no job, no husband, no savings, no career, no nothing, not even good health to cling to. All my proverbial eggs were in God's basket and right now He wasn't doing anything with any of them that I could see. Nothing appeared to be happening. At least my unemployment had been extended again, so I would have some income, even if it was not enough to pay everything. I had tried hard to hang onto every extra dollar I could to make the last of my tiny savings stretch. The last little bit I had would be gone in the next two weeks to pay bills.

I was so very tired, so worn out. I felt I had believed until my believer was worn down to a nub, and I did not know what else to do that I had not already done. I was in the Word for hours every day, in prayer for hours, and ministering to every soul the Lord place in my path in any environment, mostly people who emailed me, since I rarely left my house. Sometimes I felt as if I were carrying a thousand pounds on my back as I walked through each day. Life had become a burden, not a joy.

Is this all my life is ever going to be, Lord? Just more pain and struggle and loneliness? Surely You want better for Your children than this.

A few hours later as I was praying, I felt an angelic presence in my house. The Lord had apparently sent an angel to minister to me. What a beautiful feeling. The presence was so strong, I was surprised I could not see it.

That evening, my mentor Beverly called me with a word from the Lord that He had seen my weariness and my tears, that He had placed a very special creative gift in me, and that He was going to perform every single thing He had ever told me He was going to do. She also saw great abundance in my future, which rallied my hopes. She said that in the meantime, she saw my needs being met as I had them. A vision was opened to her as she prophesied over me, and she saw a huge golden chalice with red liquid flowing out of it on the right side like a fountain, and the number 7, but we were not sure what it meant.

After Beverly's call, I was greatly encouraged. I was so thankful to God for appointing her as my mentor. She was so powerful in the spirit, and walked in great love and wisdom, and though she corrected me when it was needed, she always did so with great compassion. I knew others who had mentors who were far less gentle and loving than she was.

The next day my hope was renewed, and my thoughts were back to normal. Apparently I had come under an attack of discouragement, something that seemed to be happen a lot when I was walking through the wilderness, but so far, God was showing Himself faithful.

Soon after the attack of discouragement, the Lord began speaking to me in my morning prayer time about my destiny.

The enemy desires you never see the culmination of your dreams, and he will attempt to dissuade you from following Me now. Do not listen to his slanderous lies that I will not provide for you in this time, My child, for truly that is much of the reason I brought you to this place – to prove My hand of provision in your life, that you might tell My other children of My greatness, My mercy and My generosity towards those who serve Me with their whole hearts. The biggest danger lies in listening to the lies of the evil one. Discouragement delays blessing, so entertain him not for I desire to greatly provide for you and bless you.

Concentrate on My promises to you, both written and spoken. Repeat them out loud until their truth permeates your heart and mind and you believe Me 100%, and you will indeed see the hand of your mighty God move, and your provision will manifest every time and on time. Were the ravens ever late to the Brook Cherith? Was I late in saving Joseph or David or Daniel at any time? Nay, and I shall not be in your case either. Believe only, and it shall be done for you also.

Only days after the Lord spoke this to me, the enemy brought an attack through a close friend, who cut off all communication with me. The loneliness I already felt was greatly increased, and I found myself once again consumed with despair. I begged the Lord to send my husband to me, or at the least to send me increased hope.

I continued studying God's word and reading books on subjects like authority in prayer and spiritual warfare. I kept putting one foot in front of the other and just taking the next step, spending hours each day in prayer and sitting in His presence. I fought my wrong thoughts, but as the days rolled slowly past and I still saw no change in my circumstances, it was difficult to continue believing what I could not see a single thing happening. Seeing the bills arrive in the mail each day only served as a constant reminder that I had no paycheck arriving with them to pay them with.

GIVING THE ENEMY ACCESS

> *He began showing me in my spirit that any area of my life I spoke negative words over, the enemy would be given access to.*

As the weeks passed, I continued to wonder why God was not doing more in my life. It was as if my life had just stopped suddenly. Lack of money kept me from doing any of the hobbies I normally enjoyed when I had time off. As I stared at the quiet nothingness my life had become, I felt despair in my soul. I would rise each morning, pray and read the Word, and look in the newspaper for coupons I could use to save money on food, or talk to my few friends on the phone where we would bemoan the state of the world or our financial situations together. Without a job or money for hobbies, I had no idea what else to do with my time.

One afternoon as I was lying on my bed for relief from the pain, the Lord brought to my remembrance what He had shown me several years before about someone else's negative words stopping the blessings from showing up. He began showing me in my spirit that any area of my life I spoke negative words over, the enemy would be given access to.

I sprung out of bed and drove to a local fast food place where I got two tacos for one dollar as a special treat to cheer myself up. When I got back home, I busied myself doing small tasks in the yard and washing my vehicle while dodging the wasps and hornets. Keeping busy kept my mind from dwelling as much on the negative, and gave me something to do besides call my friends and talk negative over the phone.

I spent little time outdoors, partly due to the wasp and hornet problem, and partly due to the constant noise of traffic zooming by on the busy road in front of my house, but later that evening I sat on my back steps watching the butterflies on the nearby tree and reading the Bible. The old tree by my back steps was slowly dying, but it was absolutely covered in butterflies. I had never seen anything like it, and I loved watching them softly gliding on the air, so delicate and beautiful. Sometimes they would even land on me, something that had never happened before.

I had begun watching teaching videos on YouTube to build up my knowledge of the Word. I didn't have television, and it helped take the place of the movies I could no longer afford to rent. I was especially interested in anything on destiny and despondency, because it seemed everyone I knew was suffering the same emotions I was while trying to stand on the promises God had given them for their lives. As I watched, I became even more convicted that my attitude had strayed a long ways from what it should be.

Watching the videos began to increase my faith and courage to face my situation. I determined to make progress every day in the future on walking with a positive attitude. I might not be able to change my circumstances, but I could change how I thought about them.

In the meantime, I had discovered books by Nancy Angove, a deliverance minister in Washington state. After reading a few of her books, I found them on Amazon and wrote review comments on them. I also wrote to her for more copies to share with others I knew needed what she was teaching. We soon became fast friends.

Several days later, still working on building my faith, and praying almost continually, the Lord again spoke to me.

You are entering a realm of My glory you have not walked in heretofore. Few of My children ever find it since it requires they lay down all for Me. You must sacrifice all of you to receive all I truly have for you and what each child receives is in direct proportion to what each is willing to give up or lay down for My name's sake, for each higher level will require more sacrifice from you – more of your flesh must be surrendered at each new realm I allow My children access to.

Those who cannot believe Me for even enough will never receive more. They become satisfied where they are and are unwilling to go higher, and so I am able to bless them very little. You asked for more and are willing to lay down all you own for more of Me, and indeed you shall have it. Do not faint on the way, My child. You know I often move at the last minute in order to more fully develop your faith. This stretching of your faith is necessary in order that you may fully receive all I have for you, and that you may walk in it.

Stand and keep on standing, Daughter. Honor Me by believing Me. Believe in My promises to you for My words do not return void unto Me, but shall fulfill the purposes for which I have spoken them.

During this time a kind couple in California who had seen the famine vision postings began sowing Christian books into my life. Being a book lover and having had no extra money to buy books, I was delighted, and I devoured the books one after another.

Some friends I had made on the internet began encouraging me around this time to share the end time visions the Lord had given me on YouTube to warn others of what was coming. I had no desire whatsoever to put my face out in cyberspace, but I did need to obey the command to "tell My people" the Lord had given me in every way possible so I made some slide show videos and posted them.

By the end of August, 2009, I needed hundreds of dollars to transfer and tag my vehicle in Texas and I had no idea where to get it. I had nothing to sell, I had donated 2/3rds of everything I owned just to move to Princeton, and with the Great Recession in full swing, I knew the chances were that no one would have money to buy anything I tried to sell anyhow. People everywhere were desperate for work, losing their homes, sleeping in tents, and going without necessities. To say we were living in a terrifying time was a gross understatement. No one in my generation had ever lived through anything like it and I desperately wished my Grandma was alive so I could ask her how she survived the Great Depression.

In the wee hours one morning after worrying over my lack of finances, I was praying and crying out to God and I angrily told Him I didn't want Him to tell me anymore how wonderful my future was, I needed Him to start bringing some of it into my present. I was about to be in big financial trouble if He didn't do something soon, and I just did not want to hear any more promises. As wonderful as they sounded, this time I needed action. I needed Him to move on my behalf, and I needed Him to do it soon. If He didn't, I would not be able to drive my truck without getting cited for expired tags, and my taxes would be beyond late.

Lord, I don't need more words, I need you to perform the ones You already gave me! Please! My faith is barely hanging by a thread and I'm about to go under! I need money to file last year's taxes – the extension is about to expire, and I have to hire a CPA to prepare them, plus I need money to transfer and tag my vehicle. Please hurry, Lord!

Later that day, I felt led to begin a fast of all solid food again, so I did. I didn't really ask the Lord what the fast was for, I just obeyed. The Lord seemed to lead me to fast when the enemy's attacks were getting to me the worst, or when I needed help with a particular sin. I never questioned the fasts. I had submitted my life to His plan, and if He wanted me to fast, then I would fast.

By the very end of August, I was battling overwhelming sadness and grief. I grieved the loss of my brother so many years ago, who had lived in the town the Lord had brought me to. My father also had lived here before his death, and my Grandma, who had passed away while I was working in South Texas. I missed them all terribly, and greatly wished I had more time with them now. For days I would sit looking out my window remembering them, thinking of happier times, with tears streaming down my face. Tears I had not had the time to shed before now because of working so much. Everything in the town reminded me of them. The grief sometimes took me so deep I wondered if it would ever come to an end. It seemed with all that time on my hands that all the unhealed pain was rising to the surface. I was in the place of my new beginnings, but I was seeing there was still much from the past that had never been dealt with.

During this time of contemplating deceased loved ones, I began losing my desire to read the Word. It did not seem to matter that I fasted since food had lost its appeal anyway. My life suddenly felt like nothing, and I wondered sometimes why God left me on the earth. If He was not going to take me into the bright future He had told me about, why couldn't He just let me go home? What could possibly be the use in this long torment? My faith was slipping, and it was slipping fast.

Although He had warned me the enemy would try to stop His plan for my life, He had also made me many promises about my life that would happen in this place of new beginnings. Since I did not see the promises coming to pass, I tended not to think much on the other words either.

Everyone I knew was feeling the same way. I had never witnessed another time when the faith of Christians was so completely tried as it was in 2009. My life felt so empty. I had almost no one to talk to, my days had no structure, and I was losing faith in all God had promised me because I was seeing none of it happen. I didn't want Him to tell me anything else about what was in my future, I wanted to see some of it. I had done my part, I had moved to this place on His word, and now I felt the ball was in His court. *It's Your move, Lord.*

My days felt like an endless succession of emptiness, and all my dreams had dried and turned to dust, blowing away in the Texas wind. I no longer cared if I ever fell in love again, if I ever worked again, or even if I did anything of note. I felt isolated, unlovable, and completely without purpose.

What had happened to my life? Who had turned out the light of hope that had once burned so brightly in my soul? It was as if a thief had come in the night and stolen away all my dreams. Or maybe I had only fooled myself into thinking I had ever had a life to begin with. All I had done for years was work and move and work and move.

Just when it seemed all my hope was gone forever, the Lord spoke to someone to give a small money gift to me. At almost the exact same time, someone wrote that the Lord had shown them my husband in a vision. The sun suddenly seemed to shine brighter, lighting up the Texas sky. Within a few days, my phone began ringing with family and friends checking on me and catching me up on all the latest, after weeks of it hardly ringing at all, and I felt encouraged again. If He could do this, then maybe I could believe for the hundreds of dollars I would need to tag and transfer my truck and have my taxes prepared. I rallied my faith to keep going a little longer.

On the fifth day of my fast, the Lord spoke to me during my prayer time.

Yes, My daughter, you know and see in your heart that I have not forsaken you, and truly I have not, and never will. You have desired I tell you of things to come that you may know, and yet you grow angry when they do not happen immediately in your time.

I'm sorry, Lord. I hung my head.

Indeed your life has been changing slowly into one you no longer recognize, and it is unfamiliar territory to you indeed, for you desire the security of your work and steady paychecks as so many of My other children do, and yet you have laid it all down to obey Me, even to the point of leaving your beloved Mother, on My word. Great and mighty shall be your reward for this, My child, for great is the reward of all who take up their crosses to truly follow me, the King of Kings.

Food also are you willing to lay down for My name's sake, and changes are being wrought in you even tonight which you know not of, for many of the changes I make cannot be seen with human eyes or felt with your heart. What I change, however, is still changed. Fear not.

I repented and asked forgiveness for telling the Lord I did not want to hear any more promises. I felt really bad for not believing more fully.

I have already forgiven you, My daughter. All that you have been through was to prepare you for your destiny just ahead. Go and tell the others, child. Tell them I am coming back soon! Get ready, My coming is sooner than My church thinks.

The first week of September, the Lord spoke to a distant friend to give a gift of money to me that covered my truck tag and vehicle transfer. I was thrilled, He had come through for me again! At the same time, He moved on the heart of a friend's husband who was a CPA to prepare my tax returns at no charge.

Soon after, I woke up with pain and swelling in one jaw. Apparently, I had an infected tooth, and as the early hours of morning passed, it was getting worse and worse. It had been many years since I had suffered anything like an abscessed tooth, and the enemy began to remind me of horror stories I had heard through the years of people who died from not getting treatment for them.

I tried not to think about the tooth, as I went through the rest of the day, and went on to bed that night. The next morning when I woke up, it was worse. In addition to making my entire body ill, I had now lost my appetite. Loss of appetite in any illness for me is truly the last straw because I really do like food.

I had no money for dental visits other than the small gift of money I had just received, and there were numerous other things I needed to use that money for. Suddenly I got really angry at the enemy, and began shouting at him that he was *not* going to get away with making me sick. I began to command the infection to die and come out of my body in the name of Jesus.

A few hours later it was still there and I began putting one finger on the gum where the pain was and commanding it with authority to be healed, for the infection to leave in the name of Jesus.

A little while later, I still had some doubts since the swelling did not appear to be lessening, so I decided to check the internet for dangers of an abscess just in case it didn't work, to make sure I wouldn't be dead by morning or anything. I suddenly realized the tooth that hurt was one I had had a root canal on. I should not be able to feel *any* pain in that tooth! Something was terribly wrong. What if my face ballooned out in the middle of the night and I couldn't get help? What if I died in my sleep because I didn't seek medical attention? I began to feel afraid.

Immediately I looked up the nearest dentist offices and found one that was open on Saturday not far away that was fairly inexpensive. I jumped into my vehicle and drove quickly, becoming one of the last patients they allowed in

> *I will make a way for you even if I have to part the Red Sea!*

that day. All the way there, I prayed against the pain and infection. About the time the doctor x-rayed my tooth, the swelling completely disappeared, along with all the symptoms of the infection including the pain. The dentist, of course, looked at the x-ray and saw nothing wrong. I paid for the visit and left feeling completely foolish.

I should have just had faith, Lord! That was a waste of time, energy and money!

If I had stood in my authority for one more hour, my healing would have manifested. I had listened to the enemy's fear-inducing lies, and I had acted hastily and spent money I needed for food and utilities for a dentist visit I no longer needed.

The key I missed was when I was commanding that healing with authority, was that I truly had faith for my healing. The faith and authority that rose up in me was the sign I should have kept standing against the infection. Sickness has no chance against the true faith of a child of God standing in authority!

After the dental incident, I returned to worrying over my daily expenses once again. My unemployment check being only half enough to pay my expenses, I constantly battled the fear over my provision showing up. As I was in the midst of struggling to believe, and worrying about upcoming rent and bills, I prayed constantly.

Lord, I believe you will make a way somehow, though I can't see how the things You told me about my future could possibly happen. I know You can do anything, and I'm standing on that.

I will make a way for you even if I have to part the Red Sea!

Suddenly I saw in my spirit that God saw me as no different than the precious children of Israel He had sent Moses to bring out of Egypt thousands of years ago. He cared just as much about me! I felt His love surround me when I saw that, and I hung on to His words with everything in me.

I DESIRE INTERCESSION

A few days later in my prayer time, I was praying in the spirit. I felt I was praying for America, then after awhile, it changed and I was weeping, I felt in my spirit it was for someone in my family who was lost, and then it continued, changing from time to time.

This is what I desire of you, My daughter, that you would spend your hours lying before Me in intercession. There I will reveal My glory to you. There I will reveal My truths to you. There I will tell you what to do as the days grow dark and this world approaches the end.

It is there I desire My people to be – ever seeking My face and to do My will, sharing My heart for the lost. For did I not send My only begotten Son for just that purpose? To save the lost? To bring them back to Me? It is here in My presence you will find peace. It is here that you will experience Me – here, crying out for those who do not know Me.

Lay aside the cares of this world, the thoughts about your needs. Did I not say in My word to seek first My kingdom and all the things you need would be added to you? Why then do you worry so for what you will wear or what you will eat? Am I not a wealthy father, well able to provide all you need and more? Am I not able to take care of you, My little flock? Stop wandering and wailing in the world and focus on __My__ purpose – to save the lost, and you will find your every need met in the earth and much, much more!

I am calling out to My intercessors – fall on your faces and cry out to Me! Wail for your lost loved ones, for your unsaved families and friends, for the lost you do not know! Call on My name – the only name that can save them from destructions to come!

Cry out! Weep for them, My children, while there is yet time for them to be saved. There is no better use of your time. Come – share My heart!

The message the Lord spoke to me was so powerful, and it was clear it was not just for me, but I was not sure what He wanted me to do with it. That night, as I told a close friend I had connected with through YouTube about the message He had spoken to me, another friend was in on our call. They both urged me to make a video and share it on YouTube.

"I am not putting my face out there in cyberspace! No way!" I replied.

They continued insisting, trying to persuade me. Finally, to get off the phone, I told them I would pray about it. When I hung up the phone, I did.

Okay, Lord, this is me praying about making the video.

I want you to make the video.

I had not expected Him to answer my prayer. *What? Lord!*

I want you to start making videos for YouTube. It will be your training ground.

Yes, Lord.

I was so shocked I didn't even think to ask the Lord exactly what it was I was training for, I just obeyed. Maybe it was my training ground to learn to preach. I knew I needed a lot of help in that area. I changed into a clean tee-shirt, combed my hair, and proceeded to make my first video.

That night I felt the angels back in my room again, protecting me. Over the following months, I continued to make many more videos to post to YouTube. I found I enjoyed sharing the revelations the Lord gave me, and I received many responses others were being helped in their own journeys by what I was sharing.

A few weeks later, as I pulled up in my back driveway after buying groceries one afternoon, I glanced up at the house as I put my vehicle into park. Though I had looked at it hundreds of times, I suddenly recognized something. Quickly I rushed into the house and dug through my journals, finally finding the one from January where I had scribbled the tiny sketch of the house I saw in a flash vision just before the Lord told me to begin packing to move.

I ran outside and took a picture of the back of my house and ran back inside. It was a dead-on match other than I had the dot for the doorknob on the opposite side! I had seen the house before the Lord had even brought me here, but I had never recognized it from the vision because I assumed what I saw was the front. What He had shown me was the back, where I always parked my vehicle. I seldom used the front driveway because the back was more convenient. It was one more confirmation I was in the right place in a time of great uncertainty.

My unemployment was set to run out November 8th, and I still didn't know yet how I was going to pay my rent on the 1st, but I turned my focus to holding on and enjoying Jesus for the time being. As I continued to spend time in prayer and worship, my tax return arrived in time to pay my rent, and my unemployment benefits were extended once more.

As the weather turned colder, I moved my air mattress into the living room to be near the heater, and began sleeping in sweats with a pile of blankets and quilts on me, trying to stay warm. Every night was a challenge, if I turned the heater on, I woke up red faced, ill, and with a migraine headache that lasted for days. If I left it off, I woke up cold over and over during the night. I began sleeping in snatches to solve the problem. When the cold awakened me, I would get up and turn on the heater for a while to take the chill off the room, then turn it off and go back to sleep until I was so cold I awoke again.

By the end of the first week of December, I was really feeling weary dealing with the cold house, being in pain, and constantly struggling to believe that God's promises for my life would somehow come to pass. The news was constantly filled with stories of people having to sleep in their cars or tents after losing their homes, and worse, those who had lost all hope and taken their own lives. One morning when I was in even more physical pain than usual, I wrote the prayer I prayed down in my journal, asking the Lord about healing.

Lord, my body hurts so bad these days, but I know in Your word says I have already been healed, so something in me must be holding up my relief. Please help me understand what I am doing or not doing that is keeping me from receiving my healing so I can get well once and for all. The pain is so bad today and this feels so hopeless that my eyes fill with tears even as I write this, and I am only an hour into my day. I know it is not Your will, because me hurting and eventually becoming disabled would not in any way glorify You or what Jesus did at the cross for me, for all of us. I must be doing something wrong because You are perfect in all Your ways. I'm sorry Lord for complaining so much, it's just that every time I move I hurt so bad. What am I missing, Lord? This pain has gone on far too long, and I don't want to feel like this every day for the rest of my life. I can stand the waiting, the rejection of this walk, the poverty, and the loneliness, but must I walk each step in so much physical pain as well?

Please have mercy, Lord. I have no one down here to help me and I need You to heal me. You are the great Healer. I have no money for doctors. Please help me. Everything You have told me for years says I am going up, but everything in my circumstances appears to be going down.

I waited before the Lord for a while but He was silent.

A sad and lonely Christmas came and went, and I wondered if 2010 held more of the same, or if things would ever get better.

Please, Lord, breathe life into this place for me. I feel like some kind of zombie, just going through the motions, and I don't understand why!

Where are all the things You told me were going to happen when I came here, Lord? I don't understand. I'm doing my best to walk in obedience, but nothing is happening. I know I heard from You to come here, there's no way I told myself to give away 2/3rds of what little I owned and move to a town where I don't even know anyone, hundreds of miles away from Mom and my family, not to mention going without solid food for 75 days. I did not tell myself to do any of those things. This has to be You, so what happened to all the promises? Please help me understand. Have You changed Your mind? Did I somehow blow the plan? Am I doing something wrong? Please tell me what to do, Lord. I don't understand this nothingness I'm walking in every day.

> *Tell Satan to release your financial harvest!*

I continued to search the internet every day for encouraging prophetic words and I clung to them like lifelines, trying to build up the tiny wisp of faith I was still clinging to. I continued to post videos to YouTube, often reading some of the more encouraging words hoping to encourage others. It seemed everyone was having a hard time, and making the videos was the only way I knew of to help others get through the dark valley we all seemed to be dwelling in at the moment.

I continued to minister to others who contacted me after viewing the videos I had posted on YouTube, writing long emails, and helping some by phone. Inside, I felt I was barely hanging on myself, but few knew the true extent of what I was walking through. I wondered if Moses and Aaron had felt so empty inside, trying to survive the desert themselves while ministering to those around them. Much later, the Lord revealed to me I had been in a season of sowing, for a harvest that would come in the future.

When you are in a season of sowing, you do the work to plant the seeds while continuing to stare out over the barren field longing to see some sign of your harvest. It is in seasons of sowing that we must encourage ourselves all the more not to grow weary.

GALATIANS 6:9

AND LET US NOT GROW WEARY OF DOING
GOOD, FOR IN DUE SEASON WE WILL REAP,
IF WE DO NOT GIVE UP.

One morning soon after the beginning of 2010, as I was just beginning to wake up, I heard one word in my spirit "Turnaround." I knew that was my word for 2010 – the Lord was about to turn my situation around!

I continued keeping my prayer times and spending time in the Word. Near the end of January, the Lord spoke to me during my prayer time.

Tell Satan to release your financial harvest!

He was telling me spiritual warfare would release my finances.

Lord, if that is really You, lead me to a confirming scripture.

I closed my eyes and flipped open my Bible. It opened to I Timothy 1:18.

1 TIMOTHY 1:18

THIS CHARGE I ENTRUST TO YOU,
TIMOTHY, MY CHILD, IN ACCORDANCE
WITH THE PROPHECIES PREVIOUSLY MADE
ABOUT YOU, THAT BY THEM YOU MAY
WAGE THE GOOD WARFARE,

That was all I needed. I began warring that night against the enemy, demanding he release whatever financial harvest I had coming that he was holding back, in the name of Jesus.

Three days later, a friend called to tell me the Lord had spoken to him to to sow his tithe to me for the next several paydays.

I began receiving more and more email from YouTube viewers asking for help or advice. Having friends across the miles to fellowship with even on the phone or the internet was a great comfort to me and my days became busier. Fatigued from long hours in front of my computer and on the phone, I began skipping my prayer times when I was too tired to pray.

One morning soon after, the Lord woke me up around daylight, even though I hadn't gone to bed until well after midnight. As I laid in bed wanting more than anything to go back to sleep, I knew He wanted me to get up and pray, and I guessed it was to make up for skipping my regular time with Him. I rolled over, burying my head in the soft pillow and protesting.

Lord, the birds aren't even up yet!

Just then birdsong erupted just outside my bedroom window from one little bird, but really loud.

Okay, Lord. I'm up.

It was the first week of February, and I was again two weeks away from the end of my unemployment benefits, but the Lord had recently told me He already had a plan for my provision when the checks stopped, and that reassured me. I had barely been able to squeeze out enough money to buy milk, eggs and potatoes. I was so tired of living in poverty. I spent over two hours that morning in prayer, praying for provision and increase.

February 9th rolled around and I was down to only a few dollars. When I logged into the website to file my weekly unemployment benefits claim, I discovered they had run out. I had thought I had another week at least, if not more, and it took every ounce of strength I had not to completely panic. How would I pay all the utility bills coming in? How would I buy food?

All afternoon, praying constantly and trying desperately to remember the faith that had brought me to this point, I reminded myself of what had happened to me years earlier when I got into fear.

I began to busy myself around the house. I walked out to the mailbox to check the mail. Hauling my stack of mail in, I sat down at my folded table desk to open it. Much to my relief, one of the envelopes contained my tax refund, which was enough to pay my utilities and eat. Just after opening my mail, I received a phone call from a close friend who had heard from the Lord to send me a small money gift as well. I breathed another sigh of relief. God had not left me destitute. Surely He would continue to provide.

Days later I got up thinking about the fact that I now no longer even had unemployment benefits coming in. They hadn't been enough to live on as it was, but at least they were steady, and every month the Lord had brought money from some other source to make up the difference. Not once in all those months had I received any response to the resumes and applications I had submitted for jobs, so I held little hope of finding work. Millions of people, most far more educated than me, were still unemployed and few job openings abounded anywhere, even those paying minimum wage.

Now would be a really good time for You to send me that husband, Lord. He could show up in a shiny white Dodge Ram truck and whisk me away to his farmhouse where we could live happily ever after...

> *I was a child of the victorious risen King, and I needed to get my words in line with that.*

Stop believing in man and believe in Me. This is not about your husband, it's about Me being your provider!

Oops.

Sorry, Lord.

Okay, so the husband showing up suddenly and making all the problems go away probably wouldn't be the ultimate way for this whole situation to glorify God, but it did sound good. To me at least.

Weeks later, in early March, I was fighting to keep a positive attitude and believe my provision was going to show up each time I needed it. The friend who had sown his tithe to me for several weeks had stopped, and I was becoming more afraid by the day, though I tried with everything in me not to fear. I longed for the security of a steady income. It took far more effort to constantly work at keeping my faith buoyed up than it would have to simply work a full time job, but so far the Lord had not sent me any job.

The spring air in Texas was heavy with pollens and I was ill with another upper respiratory infection, and still fighting the pain in my back. I bounced back and forth between fighting to stay positive and just wanting to give up. What if things never got any better? Was I going to be in this struggle forever? Why wouldn't He tell me what was going on?

I started looking up scriptures to confess over my situation. I had done that off and on ever since the walk began, but I thought maybe I could find new ones. A friend sent me a book by Dr. Daniel Rodes *Seven Keys to Victory*. I began reading it and applying the principles. One was praising. I realized I had not been doing that so I began right away. Immediately, I felt the spirit of heaviness lifting. I was a child of the victorious risen

King, and I needed to get my words in line with that. I tried to concentrate on praising and confessing to keep my mind off the overwhelming fear that threatened to take over my thoughts.

The following morning, illness seemed to take over my body. The illness made it especially difficult to fight the discouragement. I struggled to lift up praise to His name, to praise Him for more provision. I quoted the scriptures I had found, and I praised some more.

As I sat in my room praying and talking to the Lord about my situation, I was trying so hard to hang on, to keep moving forward and not give up, and I told the Lord that I wanted to tie a knot in the end of my faith rope and hang on, but I really felt there wasn't any more rope left to tie a knot in. I really just wanted to lie down and give up, but I couldn't do that either. There was no way I could keep going the way I was. I reminded myself that I had moved to Texas on His word, not on my own plan, so that meant He had guided me, which meant He would provide for me. *The Lord is my shepherd....*

I prayed for hours, studied my scriptures, confessed and prayed some more. Finally, I tried to busy myself with housework, still praying. On the way out to my mailbox to send a letter, I kept praying.

Lord, I know You are not going to let me down, I know You always provide where You have guided, and I do know You for sure guided me here. I am believing You will come through for me. You know I have no income now, no way to get money for myself to pay my bills and buy food. I am looking for work, but there aren't many jobs out there. I don't know if the oilfield has anything, but I have no travel money anyway, so it doesn't matter. Please show me I am still on the right path and I haven't taken a wrong turn somewhere. If I know I am doing the right things, I know I can rest assured You will provide. I may not know just how, but You've never failed before.

Back inside, I plopped the stack of mail down on my desk with a sigh. I sat down, making a mental note I needed to opt out of receiving so much junk mail, just as the pile toppled over sideways, sending mail and sale fliers scattering across my desk. I bent over to pick the mail up from the floor, and noticed one envelope addressed to me with no sender. I slit it open. Out fell a money order made out to me for a thousand dollars.

Did I just hallucinate? Did that say a thousand dollars?

I did a double take. *Was someone playing a joke on me?* It appeared to be real, and made out to me. I looked all over it but there was no name showing who it was from. It was postmarked Johnson City, Tennessee. I quickly researched the address on the money order. It was the address of a Post Office in Unicoi, Tennessee. I knew absolutely no one in Tennessee. Whoever had sent the money, they had wanted God to receive all the glory for their generosity. With tears in my eyes, I prayed over and over that the Lord reward them mightily.

God had done a financial miracle for me! Once again, He had confirmed that He was indeed in what I was doing, that I was in His will, and He was going to provide for me no matter how barren it might look in my life. I danced and praised with great joy over the great miracle and His mighty power to provide for His children. A thousand dollars when you have no income might as well be a million it looks so big to you. I immediately set about making a video about the new miraculous provision. I wanted to encourage others who were barely hanging on that God would come through for them as well.

It was almost one year to the day since I had moved into the house at Princeton. I was trying hard to be productive in the days while I waited to see what God would do about me having no income, because it felt wasteful to not do anything. I continued watching for Him to fulfill His promises, but still nothing was happening other than me alternating between trying to believe, and begging and pleading for His help.

Was I not ready? Did I not qualify somehow? I had wavered back and forth many times, maybe God had changed His mind. Could that be why the blessings were not showing up? I pleaded with Him to tell me what I was doing wrong. I had stopped talking to anyone else about the things He had spoken to me about my life, because I could not see any of it happening, and I knew by the way they went quiet on the phone that I wasn't the only one it wasn't making sense to.

On the one year anniversary of my move into the house at Princeton, I discovered a family of skunks freeloading under the house. I had grown up in rural areas, and that smell was really familiar to me. Judging by the loud squeals in the middle of the night, I figured one of them got stuck temporarily and sprayed under the house. It was days before my house smelled normal again. The second round of squeals at 3:00 a.m. that morning I saw as an opportunity to practice praising God for all things, so I did, but being awake most of the night against my will was not something I relished.

Two days before the end of March found me in terrible pain, being attacked in my body more ways than one, almost completely broke, with the rent due in two days. The thousand dollar miracle and small money gifts the Lord had spoken to friends to sow to me had carried me through much of the month and I had paid as many bills as possible with it, buying food sparingly.

I had also begun to pray fervently for a mattress and box springs. Whatever was wrong with my spine, the air mattress seemed to be making it worse. I walked around in so much pain that I was afraid of becoming one of those sour-faced people who never smiled. I continued to confess that the Lord is my shepherd and I believed He had guided me to Princeton, and that He would continue to provide for me there.

April 1st came and, I prayed fervently in my morning prayer time.

God must be planning a really awesome miracle for the money not to be here yet, I thought.

I tried to stay calm and focused on household tasks as I waited for the mail to run. I wasn't sure how He would bring the rent, but I knew He would bring it somehow.

When I saw the postman, I quickly walked out to the mailbox. I would need to drive the rent over to my landlord in a nearby town so it would not be late. When I opened the box, I found only junk mail.

Lord, what's going on? I am believing You for rent money. You have never let me down before. How am I going to pay the rent now? What am I going to tell the landlord? I've never paid him late before.

Silence.

Fear hit me full force, I was really scared now. I didn't even have enough money to buy a week's worth of groceries and now I could not pay my rent either. On top of that, my truck payment would be due in less than a week. For the thousandth time I wished I had not bought a new vehicle when I did. My car was breaking down and I needed one, but I thought I had enough time to pay it off before work cycled down again. I had been wrong. Then when work ran out, there was no way to even refinance it, because you have to have a job to refinance. I was stuck with the payment.

Lord, I know You led me here, and I have believed You to provide and all this time You have provided. What's going on? Are You moving me some place else? Because I can't stay in a house I can't pay for. Please tell me what to do!

Along with the fear, I was overcome by discouragement. I knew people who did not even attempt to walk in God's ways who were prospering as if there was not even a recession going on. I knew God rewarded His children, but it was hard not to notice the difference in their provision and mine.

I suddenly felt very lost, very stupid, and more afraid than I had ever been in my life. I had no idea what it would be like to be homeless and living in the streets, because I never had been, and no one in my family ever had been. Surely that was not His will for me.

What happened to all the things You told me we were going to do here in ministry, Lord? Please tell me what to do!

Silence.

Surely I had not believed in His strong hand of provision in vain. Surely.

I could just hear what all my friends would have to say about me falling on my face, how they had really thought me stepping out in faith was complete insanity, how secretly they had believed I was hearing things. Had it all been for nothing?

The past year had been one of the most difficult years of my entire life. The uncertainty of not having a steady paycheck was bad enough, but the chronic pain made it even worse. Pain wears you down, drains the life from you, and makes you feel like going to bed and just pulling the covers up over your head until it's gone. Only when it's chronic, it never leaves. It's there to greet you when you rise in the morning, and it's there with you when you go to bed at night. It's there when you awaken during the night. It's always there.

I was so weary of the constant fight to stay in faith and not give in to fear and the blow of the rent money not showing up was threatening to quickly destroying the small whisper of faith I had managed to hold on to through it all. I was so tired of living in poverty, not being able to buy even basic things that I needed. Doing without for a short time was never much of a hardship, but when poverty continued for months or years, it slowly drained your dreams and killed all the hope in your spirit.

Maybe someone's going to bring me rent this evening, or He's going to tell me something to do to make the rent.

I decided to just pray and try my best to remain calm.

Surely He had a plan, maybe He was just stretching my faith a little further.

Although I honestly felt like an overstretched rubber band about to pop under the strain, I determined I would wait, and pray, and just try to believe a little longer.

> *Doing without for a short time was never much of a hardship, but when poverty continued for months or years, it slowly drained your dreams and killed all the hope in your spirit.*

Maybe He was testing me to see if I would give up or hang on.

The next morning, I arose and prayed solidly, pleading with the Lord to supply my need for rent money. Maybe my provision wasn't missing, only late. Maybe someone hadn't obeyed when He spoke to them to give, and He had to speak to someone else. Surely it would come in the mail that day, or someone would call and say the Lord had spoken to them. So I prayed, and waited.

When the mail again brought no provision, my fearfulness went into overdrive, my spirit flew into turmoil and I fought everything in me to keep from going into a total meltdown. I had bet everything on God's plan and now it did not appear He was going to provide for me. Where would I go? I had no one to help me, and not even enough money to rent a storage stall for my belongings. I would lose all of what little I had left, all my keepsakes, everything.

What is going on, Lord? Please tell me why this is happening. You have always been faithful to provide when I believed. I wasn't in fear until the money did not show up, so why isn't it here? I don't understand. What did I do wrong? Did I not hear You that You were going to provide for me so I could minister to Your people and take Your words to them? I hope the provision is only late and I'm trying really hard not to panic, but I don't know what to do – You have always come through before!

Silence.

I began scouring the internet harder for job opportunities, as well as the classifieds in the local papers, searching in places I had not even looked before. If God wasn't going to help me, I had to find work, and I had to find it quick! I wanted to cry as I realized I had no clothes for a job, other than one suit I paid $2.99 for at the second hand store when I was invited to preach at a church in Dallas. Out of everything, though, the toughest part was that I had not seen the Lord's promises to me fulfilled. Had I missed it completely? Why then had His provision shown up all the months before? He had spoken to me in the same voice for years, and I had seen Him perform miracles when I obeyed it.

I called a friend on the phone and explained my situation to her and asked her to pray with me. She prayed, and then told me she felt I was angry at God. *Angry at God? Was I?*

After I hung up the phone, I sat back, thinking about what she said. *Am I angry at Him?*

I knew I was angry at my situation, but I didn't think I was angry at Him. As I examined my heart, I realized I was. I had never been truly angry at Him before, but I was now. I was angry that He had called me here and now He was going to let me fall flat on my face. But how could I be angry at the God I loved so much, that I had vowed to serve for all of my days? The same God whose mighty power I feared? I knew I was in a dangerous place, feeling anger towards the God who held all power.

As I thought about it, I remembered all the times I had surrendered all I had to Him for His use. I had asked Him to use my life for His glory and to serve His people. I had just assumed He would take care of me while I was doing those things. Did I have the right to be angry, knowing His ways were often different than I expected them to be?

Inside, I felt as if my trust had been violated. How could I ever trust Him again to provide for me when my rent had not come in? How could I possibly ever have the faith again to step out in another faith walk? I was afraid my heart would become hardened towards God because of the lack of provision.

Lord, please tell me why this is happening! Please tell me what to do!

Silence.

Had I laid everything down in vain? I didn't have much by anyone's standards, but it was all I had. I felt so discouraged, and so disappointed. Finally, I called my landlord with the bad news that I had no rent money yet. A kind man, he said he would apply my deposit to the rent I owed, which would cover me for the month, but stated clearly that if I did not have work in two weeks, I needed to make other arrangements.

I hung up the phone. *Lord, please do something quick. I don't even know how to be homeless. Please send me a job, or some money, or something!*

The next day as I began updating my resume and searching all over the internet for job openings, I struggled to figure out how much of what I had been believing was wrong. Something had gone terribly, terribly wrong and, while frantically seeking employment, I needed to figure out what it was so that I never, ever made the same mistake again.

I had moved from anger to bewilderment. God was God, and He could do whatever He pleased, but I was going to have to reassess what I believed. I had believed with my whole heart that He called me to Texas, and I had staked everything on it, had spent what little savings I had to move here and take care of myself. Now I was down to nothing. He had said He would provide for me, so where did I take a wrong turn?

I was no longer sure I could make videos and share on YouTube. If I could not live what I was teaching, I would not teach it, because I would not be hypocritical. I would not preach and spout scriptures and preach hope to hurting people if I could not believe in that same hope myself. He was still God, and I still believed He saved, but something was apparently very wrong with what I had believed about the provision part. If God came through for me, then I could still speak; if not, I would have to stop.

A close friend had been sharing my pain, and began to seek the Lord for a word for me. She flowed in the prophetic, and I knew if she got a word, it would truly be a word from Him. I also knew her heart, and that there would be no motive other than love if she got one. She did.

"He said, "*This is not the time to sit back, but to act, not to be afraid,*" she told me.

I felt it meant He was saying that it was His will that I went back to work.

I breathed a sigh of relief. Thank God! He was in this then. That meant everything was going to be okay. Maybe I had only misunderstood that I would never have to work again. I believed He had spoken to me the end of 2008 that my labors had ceased, but maybe I had somehow misunderstood what He meant. He would provide a job then, and the bills would get paid, and I would not end up homeless.

I stared at the pile of bills on my table. My phone bill was due that day and my water bill was due in less than a week, and I was trying hard not to panic. At least if God was in my situation, I could believe that He would somehow get me through everything. He would make a way somehow. Had He not told me He would part the Red Sea if He had to? My situation looked just as hopeless to me as the Red Sea must have looked to the

Israelites thousands of years before. It was a change of plans, that was all. I thought I would not work another secular job, and I was wrong.

I began searching through the house for even small things I might be able to sell online to make some quick cash. I owned nothing of any real value, but I listed books, DVD's, and other small items just in case I might get lucky. The recession was so bad I didn't think many people had money for buying extras, but one never knew. It was worth a try, especially since I had no other ideas whatsoever. At least it made me feel as if I was doing something to help my situation. I would need gas money for interviews, and food until I could find a job and get paid. My food supply was already starting to look slim but, having fasted so much, I wasn't afraid of missing a few meals here and there.

I spent the next two days applying for any job that looked even slightly promising that was within driving distance, praying constantly. I knew it would be tougher to get hired at my age, I was fifty years old now, not the young slim twenty-something I had been so many years before when I first worked as a secretary in the area, but I had maturity on my side now, and far more skills and experience.

The constant news of people seeking jobs and not finding any were not helping my confidence level, nor was the fact that I emailed and called company after company after company and got zero response, but I had peace about what I was doing, so I knew God had a plan.

A few afternoons into my frantic job search, I called a construction company running a job ad in nearby Plano, and the man who owned the company answered. His payroll girl had walked out on him, leaving him in real trouble for help. I had no experience with his software, but I had experience in a similar one. He had just placed the job ad and had one person to interview after lunch the next day. After a pleasant conversation, he told me he would call me back if she did not look promising. Desperate to earn money, I offered to temp for him and help keep his office running until he found someone if he did not hire the other lady.

I hung up the phone with more hope than I had felt in months. I had felt a real connection with him on the phone, and he sounded like someone I would really enjoy working for. I prayed the next day would bring good news.

The next day, I drove into Dallas and signed up with my old temp agency. They had never failed to put me to work in the past, and I was sure they would not this time either. As I waited my turn to be interviewed, I glanced at the faces of the other women waiting, and saw a frightening level of desperation in both the young and the old, but especially in the women near my age. I hoped that same desperation was not reflected in my own eyes. The news was a constant stream of bleak reports and stories of thousands losing their homes, sleeping in their cars, and the tent cities springing up in various places for those who no longer had any place to live.

> *Nothing I had done in the past to save myself was working this time.*

"Thanks, if we need you, we'll call you," the efficient young man said as he took my resume without so much as looking up. I walked out of the building thinking of the time and gas I had just wasted. I knew from his response and the full waiting room they would never call.

My friend John had invited me to lunch at one of our favorite restaurants, and I took great delight in ordering my favorite meal, something I had not enjoyed in at least three years. I was more than grateful to get to enjoy such delightful company and appetizing food. As I was driving away from the restaurant, I called the construction company, hoping they had not hired the other applicant, and that I could drive by and interview on my way home to save gas. A different man answered the phone and informed me the position had been filled earlier that day. My heart dropped. I had felt such a rapport with the manager there, and I was truly hoping that was my job.

I drove home fighting back tears over the one job opening I was actually interested in, and tired beyond belief. My mind was flowing with job history dates and job descriptions I had not needed to recall in many years. As I continued to drive, I began to pray.

My truck payment is due tomorrow, Lord, and I have no money to pay it. What do I tell the bank? I don't even have a job. How can I tell them when I will pay them when I don't even have work?

Silence.

To add to everything else, Mom was scheduled for minor surgery soon, and I had no money to be with her. Not only that, but with my rent not paid, I dared not try to borrow any to go, I had to find work and find it quick.

That night, as I sat writing in my journal, I felt so broken, and so alone. Problems I could do nothing about seemed to surround me on every side.

It seemed every way I turned, there was a wall. I was so weary of dealing with so much. I felt like giving up, but I didn't know how to do that either. I had never been through a more difficult time financially other than 1998 when the Lord had called me to Dallas the first time. Nothing in me wanted to keep fighting, to keep trying to find work, to keep believing, but it had been so long since I had lived any other way than believing and trusting God, that I could not remember how else to live. I desired nothing more than to crawl into bed and pull the covers over my head until things got better, but I couldn't afford to. There was no one else to fix my problems but me.

As the days passed, the thing that shocked me the most was the unrelenting fear that attacked me. I woke up numerous times every night, shaking with fear, terrified of becoming homeless. In the mornings, I would rise and apply my makeup, style my hair and dress for job hunting, and then fight fear all day, overwhelmed by the enormity of what I was facing. A giant loomed dark and menacing before me, and I did not understand how to defeat it. For years I had believed God to defeat my giants, and now He was not telling me what to do. Most of all, I was terrified because He was not giving me any direction.

I had always been able to find work, always able to find a way to pay my bills and take care of myself, always able to somehow make ends meet, and now it seemed as if every door was closed in my face, and I stood bewildered, staring at all the closed doors, wondering what else to try. Nothing I had done in the past to save myself was working this time.

Many mornings I sat frozen on the couch, terrified. I rebuked the spirits of fear and terror over and over, and tried to mobilize and do something – anything – to find some kind of work to bring in some income. I dropped off resumes everywhere, applied online for every job I was even remotely qualified for and some I wasn't, I called and tried to set interviews. No one seemed to have any jobs open. The few times I found openings, the waiting rooms were crammed with people interviewing for the same position. In all my fifty years, I had never seen such a recession. The mountain of joblessness loomed dark and unyielding before all of us, immovable, and silent.

Late one morning, I headed out my front door to go to the grocery store where some items I greatly needed were on sale. A friend had gifted me with a small amount of money, and I would be able to buy enough food for several days if I shopped wisely, and to put enough gas in my truck to go to a few interviews if I was lucky enough to schedule any.

I had been on the phone bemoaning my sad state of affairs to more than one friend in the past couple of days. I simply did not understand why God was not coming through for me and providing like He had before, and like He had told me He would. I was going through horrible suffering, and wailing about it to my closest friends made me feel at least temporarily better.

As I approached the truck, I noticed a folded flier had blown into my yard. *Great, everyone's trash is blowing into my yard, making more work for me.*

I tossed the flier into my front seat and drove off to the store. A little while later as I was putting away my purchases, I came across it again, and I glanced at it on the way to the trash can. The flier was from a church in Blodgett, Texas, 90 miles southeast of where I live. It was addressed to a man simply named "Scarecrow," who lived about 80 miles the other direction from me. The flier contained a story called "The Law of the Garbage Truck by syndicated columnist David J. Pollay about an experience he had twenty years or so before in New York City that changed his life. In the story, David J. Pollay talks about people who go around dumping their negativity on others like a garbage truck. He was so impressed by the revelation he got from his experience years ago that he had written a whole book on it simply called, *The Law of the Garbage Truck.*

I hung my head. I knew the Lord had caused that flier to fall into my hands, because I had been doing that very thing. I had always tried really hard not to be the kind of person who went around dumping all their frustration on others, I was just so miserable and felt so alone in my situation that I wasn't sure what to do with any of what I felt, but that did not make it right. I repented immediately and asked the Lord to help me stop spewing negativity everywhere. I did not want my friends and family to begin avoiding my calls because of my bad attitude, and I did not want to displease the Lord in any way.

That night, I broke down weeping before the Lord. I was way past the end of my rope, and terrified beyond words. I had no place to go if I did not find work, even the local homeless shelters were full. I could sleep in my truck, but not for long since I didn't even own that yet. I really wished I had bought a travel trailer when I was working and traveling. At least I could have lived in that without fear of being tossed into the streets to sleep under a bridge. Why had the Lord never allowed me to buy a home? I had prayed many times and asked, but He had never said yes and I knew if I bought one anyway that it would most likely end up being an albatross around my neck.

I had no more strength for the battle before me and I did not understand what He wanted me to do. I thought I had done all He had asked of me, and He had promised He would provide for me here, yet I did not have the provision I needed. I lay broken before Him, weeping, wanting nothing more than to just give up. At last, He spoke.

Just believe in Me a little while longer, My daughter, and I shall bring you out of this time of trying.

As the days drug slowly on, I scoured every possible job ad, though my hope was dwindling. It was truly frightening to see how few jobs there were, and how little they all paid. Hundreds of job applicants were showing up for jobs in some places.

I had tried so hard to be obedient, to lay everything down at His command, and now I felt almost as if I were being punished for it. My emotions vacillated between wanting to lay down and give up and wanting to scream "Why???" at the heavens, because I knew God had the power to fix my situation by as little as glancing in my direction. Why wasn't He helping me? I had too much fear of God to scream at the heavens and I was too close to sleeping under a bridge to give up, but that question was never far from my mind.

I was in one of the worst predicaments of my life, and He wasn't even telling me what I needed to do, that was part of what was so difficult. He had told me to hold on a little longer, but hold on to *what?* In a very short time, I wouldn't have anything left to hold on *to.*

Being rejected time after time after time for jobs made me feel like a complete failure in every way. It was obvious no one was interested in hiring an unattractive, overweight, middle-aged woman, no matter how good her typing skills might be. The days when I could easily find work had apparently passed years before without me noticing.

I could see where my situation might be further testing from God, but if I lost what little I still had, would I really care about that? I had worked since I was a teenager and I didn't own so much as a tiny broken down shack of a home to show for it. I was trying to do what was right, but none of the right things seemed to be happening to me. What happened to Him guiding and providing for me?

I had not had a panic attack since my early twenties when I was being abused, but I felt panic rising in me again and again as the days went by, and I fought not to have a full blown attack each time it did. I was afraid if

I had one, I would have to fight them constantly, and I was determined not to let the enemy win that battle.

The pain, the panic and the confusion, along with the constant mental agony were what made it so tedious when people who had jobs and savings accounts tried to quote a scripture and think they were solving my problem. They were sure it was just my lack of faith, or I was in sin. I was certain they felt very holy and self righteous quoting those scriptures to me in my time of pain, but they were not where I was. They were not facing an empty cupboard, an empty gas tank and, worse, no money for rent or to make my vehicle payment. I prayed that I would never minimize someone else's pain in their wilderness as others now did to me. It only made me feel more alone.

CHAPTER 10 – I SURRENDER ALL

LUKE 9:57-58

AS THEY WERE GOING ALONG THE ROAD,
SOMEONE SAID TO HIM, "I WILL FOLLOW
YOU WHEREVER YOU GO." 58 AND JESUS
SAID TO HIM, "FOXES HAVE HOLES, AND
BIRDS OF THE AIR HAVE NESTS, BUT THE
SON OF MAN HAS NOWHERE TO LAY HIS
HEAD."

All I wanted was out of the wilderness. I no longer cared about learning anything from it, I just wanted it to end, and the sooner, the better. During this time, I began to understand where so many older people I knew had gotten that look of terrible hardship in their eyes – that broken look like life had whipped them and left them laying in a heap on the ground. I was feeling that whip across my back as well.

So many times I had prayed, *"Lord, I will give You anything. You are my Lord, my God. All I have is yours."*

But was it? Was it really? Now I was terrified He was actually going to let me lose it all. Had I truly surrendered all? If I had truly surrendered all to Him, why was I so devastated at the thought of losing it?

I began to walk through my small house looking at the mementos on my wall. They weren't much, but they were all I had to show for my small life.

Mementos I had purchased while shopping with my sister, a plaque from a friend, figurines from my children. Such small things in the eyes of the world, but each one represented a time in my life I wanted to remember forever. As I stood before each thing, I asked myself, *Can I give Him this?*

Tears streamed down my face. Could I? Could I really give Him everything? What if it really was His will that I become homeless? What if He had some purpose in that, and that was what He was requiring of me? Would I turn back? Had all those times in prayer just been pretty words offered up to a holy God from the comfort of a secure life with a steady paycheck? Did I really mean them or didn't I? Would I really give up anything for Him?

Would I still call Him Lord if He indeed took it all after I had given it to Him so many times in prayer?

Everything in me broke at the thought of becoming homeless. There was nothing I wanted in life so much as my own home and I had tried so hard to hold on to my mementos for that glorious day when some tiny house came to me with my name on the deed and I could finally hang them up and never pack them away again. Just some humble little place where there was peace, some place I didn't have to leave. I was so very tired of moving. When I was a child, we moved every year and a half to follow my Dad's work. When I was married, we seldom stayed any place more than a couple of years. The last year I was married, we had moved four times. My work in the oilfield kept me constantly moving, every several months and sometimes after only a few weeks. I just wanted a place to call my own, and I had saved all of it hoping and praying that someday, that one dream would come true.

I didn't even own a tent. Where did homeless people sleep? Did you just find a bridge to sleep under and make your bed there? What did people do when they didn't have a bed to go to at night, or even a vehicle to make a bed in?

I knew we were living in the end of the end times, and at some point I truly believed Christianity would be outlawed in America, and that Bibles would become illegal. It sounded radical, but I had felt it in my spirit for over ten years, I knew it was coming and many other believers also felt it. If I couldn't lay something like this down for Him, what would happen in that time? What would happen if at some point my soul depended on whether I could lay down my life for the glory of His name?

Tears flowed freely down my face as I stood in front of one of my favorite pictures. I realized I had no right to withhold anything from Him. I knew I had to lay it all at the feet of my King. Wave after wave of such intense pain hit me, I thought I would surely stop breathing as I whispered, *Yes, Lord. The answer is yes.*

If it is Your will, You can take it all, I won't fight You on it. I have nothing You did not give me anyway. Do Your will in my life. I will still call You Lord.

Silence.

I wept. I was beyond broken. I felt so alone. I had no place to go, and no way to support myself, and I had no idea what to do about it but continue on the path He had led me on, and hope I had not been wrong. In that moment, everything left inside me was crushed. Every dream, every hope, and every condition I had placed on my belief in Him, as I offered up the last dream I had held dear.

As my heart shattered into a million pieces, I realized He had shown me what was in my heart.

DEUTERONOMY 8:2

AND YOU SHALL REMEMBER THE WHOLE
WAY THAT THE LORD YOUR GOD HAS LED
YOU THESE FORTY YEARS IN THE
WILDERNESS, THAT HE MIGHT HUMBLE
YOU, TESTING YOU TO KNOW WHAT WAS
IN YOUR HEART, WHETHER YOU WOULD
KEEP HIS COMMANDMENTS OR NOT.

That day, I realized my faith in Him had been conditional all along. I expected Him to keep me in a house, in at least a decent amount of comfort, if He was going to be my Lord. Before that evening, I would never have guessed my faith in Him had conditions on it. Suddenly, I realized I needed to tell the others. They needed to check their hearts, so they would not have to journey through this terrible wilderness like I did to find out. My friends needed to know what I had been shown.

I pulled myself together enough to make a video and share with my internet friends and viewers what I had learned. I also wanted to tell them that since I might become homeless in the next two weeks, I would likely not have internet access, so they would understand if I suddenly disappeared.

This wilderness walk had broken me above all the others. I had never felt the level of brokenness I felt this night. I felt like I had been crushed by giant boulders, but somehow continued to breathe and speak.

As I recorded the video, I broke all over again. Soon, I might not be able even to do this, to make videos from this small house to share with my friends. About an hour after I posted the video, comments were already coming in. Many offered encouragement and prayers, and many told of similar experiences.

Other messages also arrived, emails from Christians accusing me of not having enough faith, or of being in sin. If I was in sin, it was the sin of being afraid of being homeless, and I did not know how not to be afraid of that. One man called me a 'religious diva.' I wasn't sure what that was, but it didn't sound positive. I wondered if divas could be my age. It was hard sometimes to understand how people arrived at their perceptions. Wasn't a diva someone who was young and beautiful?

I knew it was just like the enemy to kick you when you were down, so I tried to ignore the added pain those judgmental messages inflicted. I prayed the Lord would help them to become more compassionate towards those who were being broken. A few friends who lived in the far northeast even offered me a place to stay. My eyes filled with tears as I read messages from my brothers and sisters in Christ who, though they had never met me, were willing to open their homes to me. I had never experienced anything like that before. Through their love, I felt the oneness of the Body of Christ. The warm and caring comments were like a gentle embrace that made me feel I could keep going just a little longer, a little further.

As I sat on my sofa a little while later thinking of the big question mark I had found in my own heart where there should have been a period, I suddenly felt the gift in my hands. At the end of every wilderness journey, He always places a gift in your hands. I knew my gift was the revelation that my faith needed purifying, refining into gold. It had been conditional and I had not seen it. Secretly in my heart I had believed He would never take away the basic creature comforts from me if I always tried to do what was right. He had shown me He was God, and that I thought I had given Him everything while secretly holding back part of it. He had shown me that the things I owned, however small they might be, were not my life, but that in my mind they represented it. He showed me I had to lay those things down as well, and let Him decide whether He would let me keep them or not, according to His will. I was bought with a price, and everything in my life was His, not just some of it.

I felt illumination hit my spirit, and I knew then I was on my way out of those dark mountains, out of the wilderness. I probably wasn't going into the Promised Land just yet, but at least I would be given a reprieve from the fiery desert.

That night my air mattress popped and I slept on my couch cushions on the floor. I had no money to replace the air mattress, but that was the least of my concerns. At least the Lord had shown me I would be getting out of the wilderness soon. That was really all I cared about anymore. It had been one of the longest battles I had ever tried to stand through and I was worn down and very weary.

Within three days of making that video, it was clear the Lord was speaking to people from all over to give. I began getting emails and messages asking for my address. Some found my PayPal address on my channel where my book was listed and just sent money anonymously. I was beyond surprised when money arrived even from other countries. My God was a God of miracles, I should not have been surprised at all. Some of the money gifts came with notes that the Lord had spoken to them before to give but they had put it aside or forgotten. I took eight dollars and bought another air mattress so I wouldn't be sleeping on the cushions on the floor that night, and rejoiced at the mighty hand of my God to provide for me.

Though I delighted over the gifts that came to me, I still was unable to pay my rent, and I still needed a job. The fear had not left, but seeing the provision coming in so unexpectedly had buoyed my faith higher to keep going. I knew the Lord had shown me in my spirit that I was on my way out of the wilderness. Now, I just had to hang on as He brought me out. I was sure I would receive a job offer in the next several weeks.

As the excitement over the sudden provision receded, I again began waking up during the night sometimes eight or ten times, terrified out of my mind and shaking violently knowing I was approaching the time when I had to be able to tell my landlord I had a job or I would be forced to move out of my house. My nerves tied in knots, I would fight to go back to sleep so I could wake up early and search for a job again.

I had been going on every possible interview for any and everything that looked like a paying job. I would have worked at McDonald's if I had thought they would hire me. Every morning I got up, dressed, fixed my hair, and looked for some place to interview or take a resume, and then sometimes I would find myself paralyzed with fear. I had money to buy food temporarily and keep the utilities on, but nothing I did or said was getting me a job, and that had never happened before. I was terrified. I tried to keep going, to keep moving forward. The Lord had said hold on just a little while longer, I just wasn't sure whether I would still have a roof over my head at the end of that little while. Still, the word I had received through a friend indicated I needed to take action, and action to me meant get up and go to work, so I would just hold on until God opened a door for me into a job somewhere.

Please, Lord, open a door soon. I don't know how much longer I can keep going like this. I feel like I'm falling apart. Please help me!

Silence.

The other terrifying aspect of where I found myself was not being able to hear His voice. As long as I could hear Him and He kept guiding me, I could keep going, but when He stopped, I panicked. The fight in me had come back briefly the day after I made the video, and then left again as I went on the few interviews I could schedule, or sat frozen on my sofa, paralyzed with dread.

My desperation increased as several more days passed and I still did not have so much as a good lead on a job. In complete desperation, I began posting my resume even on oil and gas job sites. The big problem was, I had no travel money and I had no credit cards either, since I did not like using credit. I wished I had had the foresight to get at least one major credit card because it now appeared from those sites that there was work. Maybe I could find some close enough to drive to, and I could commute back and forth to my house until I began getting paid. In the oilfield, it is common to wait six weeks to receive your first paycheck, but if I had work, I felt sure my landlord would work with me. I had never once been late on the rent before. I would take anything, and I would work without food for however long I needed to if there was some place I could go and make money.

I considered whether I should try to come up with enough money to buy a tent. It was looking very possible I would need one to live in soon, but I didn't know how to put one up, or where to go to camp out. I had camped out one night in my entire life, and it was during the first year of my marriage. I was fairly certain living in a tent would terrify me, but I doubted it would be any more terrifying than sleeping under a bridge with a bunch of strangers.

I reached out to my family asking for prayer and to seek any advice they might have, but most of them were battling serious problems and illnesses of their own. It seemed half the people I knew were in the wilderness.

FIGHTING BACK AGAINST FEAR

The next day, after spending another long night battling fear and terror, I had decided that Satan was going to lose the battle to make me afraid. However my situation turned out, I didn't have to put up with being afraid as well. I had already given it over to God, and He could take all I had if He chose to, but that did not mean I had to be Satan's doormat while it happened. I began fighting him with a vengeance. Every time he came at me with fear, I began quoting II Timothy 1:7 out loud to him, over and over, until the fear left.

II TIMOTHY 1:7

FOR GOD HAS NOT GIVEN US A SPIRIT OF FEAR, BUT OF POWER AND OF LOVE AND OF A SOUND MIND. (NKJV™)

I also began fasting. I desperately needed God to intervene in my situation, and I knew fasting was a powerful weapon both for the purposes of God and against the enemy.

The next day after I began the fast and began standing up to the enemy, I received a phone call. An oilfield services company near Ft. Worth was looking for people with oilfield experience. They had seen my resume and were interested in hiring me. I resisted the urge to scream with glee while doing the happy dance on my desk as I calmly scheduled an interview for the next morning. The man on the phone warned me their interviewing process was multi-level, and difficult to pass. I didn't care. At least I had a chance. I began to pray harder while searching through my clothes for something suitable to wear. All I could find was the suit I had paid $2.99 for at the thrift store. I would have preferred it be one size larger for comfort, but it was all I had that was appropriate for an interview.

That night was a constant battle with fear and terror attacking me over and over again. The physical pain and apprehension of interviewing were bad enough, but the fear would not let me rest. I lost count after the tenth time I awoke, as I slept in short snatches between attacks.

I rose early and worked hard on my hair and makeup. I applied coat after coat of concealer trying to hide the black circles under my eyes from lack of sleep. There wasn't much I could do with my hair since I could not afford a professional cut or color, so I simply curled it and pulled the top back and prayed it looked good enough. I carefully applied the rest of my makeup, trying to use a light hand so I would not look overdone. My hands shook the entire time. There was so much riding on this interview, and I had to get this job.

THE INTERVIEW

I left the house two hours before time for the interview to be sure I could find the place in time. The trip was 55 miles one way, through heavy traffic, and over a toll-way. I prayed all the way there.

Please, Lord. I really need this job. No one wants to hire someone my age around here, please, please give me favor in this interview. Please let me go back to work, I can't go any further on this faith walk right now. Please, Lord. Only You are mighty enough to bring a good paying job in the midst of a horrible recession to someone like me with no college degree, no beauty, no nice clothes to wear, but You are well able. Your arm is not too short to save me out of this wilderness. Please, I don't have enough faith to go any further. Please let me work again.

Silence.

I had to believe He was in this. I had to believe because there were almost no jobs anywhere, and here He had brought me an interview for one that was actually in my preferred field – energy services. I had to believe this was it, and I was coming out. I was so weary of this wilderness experience, of being in constant pain, of sleeping on the floor, of being afraid. I just wanted out. I didn't care anymore about learning, I just wanted relief from the hellish fire I had been walking through for far too long.

I prayed that the long drive, and the fact that my pantyhose were cutting me in two would not cause my thrift store suit to wrinkle and make me look unkempt. I prayed my hair and makeup looked okay. I prayed I would pass whatever tests they gave me. I had not checked courthouse records in two years, what if I didn't know the answers to whatever they asked me? But surely I could, the Lord was in this, surely He would help me.

When I got to the street, I was nearly half an hour too early so I drove to a fast food place and freshened up. The ride was long and my suit was trying to wrinkle. The food smelled so inviting, but I was fasting, and I had no money for fast food anyway. I got back into my truck and kept praying, watching the clock. Finally, it was time to go to the interview.

My apprehension grew as I walked around the first floor of the building and could not find the door with the address number on it. I would be late! I tried not to panic but adrenaline was flowing through my veins. I *had* to get this job, or I was going to be homeless. There were no other options. I had to walk out of this building with a job!

Please, Lord, show me where the door is! There is no door with that number on it! Please help me!

Tears were starting to fill my eyes as I continued walking in high heels that made my back scream, but there was no door with the number given. I tried calling the phone number and got a recording. My panic was rising.

Please, Lord! Help!

Just then the unmarked door beside me opened and a kind faced young man asked me if I was waiting to interview. I felt all the breath go out of me as I smiled and tried to hide my previous panic. He ushered me into an office full of long tables lined with people sitting in front of laptops, all working quietly.

The first level of the interview was with an attorney who questioned me on various terms. He looked surprised as I answered each question with an almost textbook definition, and I only had trouble remembering one of the answers. I explained that I had been a Petroleum Land Person and trainer at my previous broker. He messaged the big boss to see if she was ready to see me. He warned me she was tough.

"I've heard," I said, praying silently in my heart.

Lisa was a beautiful blonde woman with a warm, inviting smile. I immediately felt comfortable with her. Was this the tough sell they had warned me about? She was a doll!

As she read over my resume, I looked at the carpet and began picking out the place where I planned to kneel to beg for the job if it looked like she was going to send me away. I had absolutely no problem begging and the minute I heard anything that sounded like no come out of her mouth, I would be in that floor in two seconds. I had never done that before, but desperate times called for desperate measures. I would gladly beg. I had to have this job.

"You have nine years experience in the oilfield?" she asked.

"Yes," I answered, and went on to explain my various jobs further.

She got quiet again.

Please, Lord. I have to have this job. I'll beg. I don't care anymore, I have to have this job. It will make my knees hurt really bad to get down on that floor but I'll do it if she says no, please give me favor. And please help me get back up off the floor in these high heels without toppling over if I have to do that!

> *Please, Lord. I have to have this job. I'll beg. I don't care anymore.*

"We start new people on Mondays and Wednesdays. When would you like to start?"

Did I just hallucinate?

I looked at her. She was looking at me and smiling, obviously waiting on me to answer, so she must have said that. My mouth dropped open. I pulled it closed again, trying to hide my shock.

"Monday. Can I start on Monday?" Monday wasn't far away.

She smiled. "Yes, I'll need you to bring your paperwork over tomorrow and review the contract. Now let's get you over to see your new manager."

It seemed as if sunshine had invaded the entire office then. I had a job! I was working again! I wasn't going to have to be homeless! And it was an energy services job! Not only was I going back to work, but I would be working in energy services! God hadn't just come through, He was showing off!

Thank You, Lord! Thank You! Thank You! Thank You!

When I got back out to my truck, all I could do was thank Him over and over again.

Okay, Lord, I have no gas money or money to eat for the next six weeks until I get paid. I have no idea how I will keep my utilities on either, but if You are mighty enough to bring me a job in the midst of this recession, and even the field I preferred without travel money, then money for gas and utilities and food to eat won't be anything at all. You probably won't even have to get up off the throne to do that. I'll just believe You to bring it to me!

All the way home, I praised Him, my eyes filling with tears again and again. I was so relieved to have work, so grateful that I was not going to become homeless.

That weekend, I thought back to the torturous ordeal I had just come through. I had failed so many parts of the faith test. I thought I was so much stronger than that, but as it turned out in some things I behaved like a lukewarm, weak Christian would have. There was certainly no Sister Super Christian living in *my* house!

Again and again, God had showed me His mighty hand of provision and again and again, I fell back into fear, doubt and speaking negatively over my circumstances. Would I never learn to trust Him? And now, in spite of all my failings, He had yet again shown Himself faithful on my behalf. Not only had He brought me a job, He had brought me one in my chosen industry.

I dredged through my closet and all my old clothes trying to find enough things that fit to make work outfits from. In my previous job, I had worn jeans every day. I didn't think jeans would work for an office environment, and they no longer fit me anyway. I found a few odds and ends, but nothing very promising.

During my time off, I had gained weight and none of my old clothes fit. The pain in my back had made exercising nearly impossible for fear of making it even worse, and eating the least expensive food was not helping my waistline either.

I managed to scrounge together a couple of outfits for my training days, but they looked like the thrift store throwbacks they were. There was nothing I could do about it though, they were all I had. I would just have to make the best of it for now. When I got caught up on my bills, I would buy a few things some place really inexpensive. In the meantime, I would have to wear the ill-fitting pieces I had and just make the best of it.

THE BOOK

Right before I was hired for the job, a young man I knew from YouTube emailed me and felt the Lord told him to tell me I was supposed to be writing a book. I thought about it, and began praying. I knew the Lord had told me I would write many books, but I honestly could not imagine what I could possibly know enough of to write a book about, other than maybe the wilderness experience. About a month before, I had seen a flash vision of a book that I knew in the spirit I had written, and I could see that the book was helping people, but I was not shown anything else in the vision. In my spare time, I began going through old journals and making notes on my wilderness experiences, just in case that was the book's subject matter.

EXTREME COMMUTING

Over the next several days, my body felt the true impact of my extreme fifty-five mile commute. It left me so exhausted, that it was all I could do to answer a few emails, eat a few bites of food, and fall into bed when I arrived home each evening.

I planned to move closer to my job, but after two weeks, I began looking at how long it might take me to save up enough travel money to return to title work in Oklahoma, and just praying I could survive it that long. The office environment was not a good one, and people were being let go left and right. I held no hopes of surviving there for long, and continually prayed I would not make anyone angry enough to fire me before I had even gotten started.

For a good week straight after accepting the job, I received numerous emails and phone calls from my resume posting, all of which I turned down. All of them were traveling record checking jobs and I had no money for travel, but it gave me hope that there was at least work again in my chosen field. All I needed was some savings.

Those first two weeks of commuting nearly killed me. By the time I drug through the door at home on those nights, I barely knew my name. Many evenings I was so exhausted my mind would just blank out, as if there were an electrical short in it. The pain in my back was excruciating, and I carried over-the-counter painkillers with me to take during the day to make it bearable. As the weeks passed, I noticed I did not seem to be very proficient at my job. My coworkers also did not seem very friendly towards me, other than a couple of them. I thought it might be my shabby clothes or the some other aspect of my appearance. I thought it might be the fact that I was a Christian. Whatever it was, I had spent the majority of my life not fitting in, so it was nothing new. I spent most of my work time in silence, head down, and working, but there was definitely no joy in my new job other than the paycheck it provided. Morale was low, and workers were constantly being berated for not completing this or that form correctly, etc.

When Mother's Day weekend rolled around, I had no money to buy a gift for Mom. It broke my heart not to give, although I knew there was probably nothing she needed all that badly or even wanted, but I wanted to be able to give her something nice. She was an excellent mother, and worthy of honoring and celebrating, and I wanted to her to know how much I loved her and honored her at every possible opportunity.

As I sat that Mother's Day thinking over all I had just come through, I realized that all I thought about now was surviving, nothing else seemed to matter anymore. Just don't let anything happen to the job. Go to work, pay the bills, keep putting one foot in front of the other and taking that next step. But there was no joy in any of it.

Before my latest wilderness experience, I had always encouraged others in their faith. Now, whenever I heard others talk about starting faith walks, I wanted to scream at them not to do it; I wanted to plead with them to cling to their normal little routines and their boring jobs for dear life, and not to give up what they had, but I couldn't. I couldn't, because no matter how hard it was, I knew God was in it, and that He had brought me out with a gift in my hands.

I came out of this wilderness walk more changed than after before it. I no longer believed anyone would rescue me if I fell on my face other than God Himself. I no longer had conditions on my faith in Him. If He chose to take everything I had, it was already His anyway, and He could take it. I had determined I would still call Him Lord, and I would still praise Him if He chose to do that. Before, I had thought being homeless could never happen to me because I was a hard worker, now I knew beyond any shadow of a doubt that it could. It could and it almost had. It had happened to many people all across America and other nations in this terrible recession we were in. There were no guarantees any more. The illusions I had walked into the wilderness with could not withstand the heat of the fire I had walked through. I knew I would never be the same.

I finally understood why people who had survived the Great Depression held on to every scrap of anything they owned. The fear did that to you when you walked through that dark place. It had done it to me as well, and for months after, I could not throw anything away. Finally, I prayed for the Lord to help me with it, because I did not want to become a pack rat. I was determined to remove the imprint of lack the enemy was trying to stamp my mind with.

Though I was exhausted beyond reason from my commute, having received a second prophetic word through someone who barely knew me that the Lord wanted me to write a book, in the evenings I sat before my laptop and began making notes on my wilderness experiences.

In late June, I finally had enough money to pick up a used mattress and box springs at a local flea market. I was overjoyed at finally being able to retire my air mattress.

By July, my accumulated fatigue was worse than bad. I was falling ill again, and I had almost been involved in vehicle crashes numerous times. I decided to fast for a breakthrough. I did not have the travel money I needed to go back out on the road, but I hoped the Lord could grant me a job that paid in less than six weeks or somehow make me have enough money to change jobs anyway. I knew if I continued the fifty-five mile commute much longer, it was likely I would end up not coming home at all one night.

As the days passed, two more people were let go at work and the atmosphere became even more tense than usual. Everyone was afraid of losing their job that the fear in the air had become palpable. As I sat in my office going over paperwork, I prayed constantly. Suicides were on the rise in the news again. So many people out of work. My heart broke each time I heard of one. People had been out of work for so long that many were just giving up. Knowing the job market, and seeing so many people being let go at the office, I was constantly afraid I would also become unemployed again. In addition, I began sensing in my spirit that my job was not secure, although no one had ever said so, and I began praying about it.

Lord, something about this job doesn't feel secure, and it's not just that others are being let go. Something doesn't feel right. Please get me out of this place. Please send me another job.

I began scouring the internet for record checking jobs. When the weekend arrived, I began calling friends I knew in the business and emailing resumes again. The energy field was getting busier than it had been in awhile, surely someone somewhere needed a record checker.

Finally, one morning at work, I got an offer from a company in Oklahoma. I walked outside to take the call. They needed someone to check records at courthouses in Central Oklahoma. I walked back into the office, and sat down calmly in my chair, thinking of how to let them know I was leaving. I doubted seriously anyone would care, I had not been there that long, and plenty of others could do my job. When I gave notice, my supervisor showed little reaction.

On Sunday, while packing to go back on the road the following week, I was already in a lot of pain with my back. The past week, something had happened with my hip and I had spent two days walking with a twisted limp, but there was no money for doctors or chiropractors, so I had tried to hide my limp at the office, and had begun sleeping on the floor in my house, hoping whatever was wrong would right itself.

TO ABASE AND ABOUND

As I walked past the pallet I had been sleeping on, I asked the Lord about being so far out of my comfort zone, because I had been way out of it for over a year and a half, and I knew where I was could not possibly be His best for me, so there must be a reason. It wasn't that I expected to be comfortable all the time, I just wanted to understand His purposes so I could work with Him and not against Him in them. As I was praying, He answered.

So you can learn to abase and abound, that I may use you freely without complaint. In my spirit I saw the word 'adaptable.'

Okay, Lord. Thank You for telling me.

At the end of July, my ex-husband fell ill and was life-flighted to Oklahoma City. We had not spoken over the last few years. I wanted to rush there to be by his side, but I knew if he could hear me, he would be upset by my presence, and I was torn over what to do. I knew he still loved me, and that he hated being vulnerable. He would not want me to see him like that. But he was comatose and I desperately wanted to be there for him if he was dying. Regardless of how bad our marriage had been, our love had been real, and it had been deep. I expressed to my daughter that I wanted to come, but I was afraid my presence would kill him.

"Mom, they said he's dying. At this point I don't think it will make much difference."

"Okay. I'm already packed. I'm leaving right now!"

All the way there I pushed the speed limits and prayed. It was three and a half hours from where I lived in Princeton to Oklahoma City but it could vary if there was road construction or heavy traffic. I tried never to speed, but this was an emergency. Today I prayed for light traffic. I knew he didn't have long and I knew he would probably not even know I was there, but I would know. I wanted so much to be there for him when he crossed over to the other side, even if all I could do was stand there and hold his hand while he left this life.

> *Pain wracked my soul as I looked down into the face of the man I once believed I could never live without.*

I kept watching my Garmin for how much longer on the way to Oklahoma City. When I was twenty minutes from arriving, my phone went off. It was a text from Chrissie.

Better hurry was all it said.

Please, Lord, help me get there before he leaves the earth. I can never do anything else for him, but I want to be by his side when he leaves this life. Please help me get there in time!

Tears filled my eyes and threatened to spill over but I refused to break down that close to the hospital. There would be plenty of time for that later. Right now, I needed to be there for him, and for Chrissie and my grandson.

Finally, I arrived. I practically ran out of the parking garage into the hospital to ICU. Chrissie had a friend waiting in the hall to take me straight to his room to save time.

I had to put on a gown and glove up before entering the room. When I walked in, he looked so small in the bed and there were tubes everywhere. His face was frozen into a pain-filled mask with his head turned to one side, and a huge tube was running out of his mouth.

I felt my knees go weak and grabbed for a nearby wall.

Please, Lord, don't let me faint. They don't need another patient, and I need to be conscious for this! Please help me!

Tears filled my eyes as I walked to the empty side of his bed and reached down to brush the hair back from his face. Pain wracked my soul as I looked down into the face of the man I once believed I could never live without.

I took his hand in one hand, and stood caressing his hair and his face with the other. At least I could hold his hand as he made his journey to the other side, hoping it would comfort him if he could feel my presence somehow, because we never forget a loved one's touch. My grandson arrived soon after and stood beside me, his heart breaking with grief. Hours later, we were still standing by his side when his heart began to slow and his blood pressure dropped. I knew he would soon be gone forever.

Tears rolled down my cheeks as I realized how many hopes and dreams I still had for him. I had hoped for years we could at least share a friendship. Disabled by some mystery disease that made his feet and legs numb, he had lived in poverty in a lonely rent controlled apartment for the last several years. He had trouble staying warm and I had planned to make him an afghan the next Christmas as a surprise. The final blow had come when he fell in his front yard and broke his hip. As I stood there trying to comfort my grandson and reliving so many painful memories of better times, his heart shut down for the last time, and the monitor flat-lined.

I knew he was gone forever. I would never get to make him that afghan now, never get to hear his laughter again, never share another cup of coffee or news of the kids. His life was over, and the end had been even sadder than I knew, and I grieved that even more than I grieved his passing. He was only fifty-five. He had been one of the most handsome men I had ever seen in my life, and the most tormented.

I stayed in the city in a motel room that night to go to the funeral home the following day. The funeral home required a family member to ID the body again before cremation, which was his desire. He hadn't wanted the fanfare of a funeral, or even a grave. After answering questions for the death certificate, the funeral home director led us through to a separate building and into the room where he was.

We walked in and he was lying there on a gurney, looking like he was asleep. This time there were no tubes, and the pained expression was gone from his face. He looked like my Rick. A tsunami of grief hit my gut and my knees tried to buckle as I grabbed for a nearby wall to hold myself up.

As tears streamed down my face, I couldn't decide which was harder, the pain I was in, or the pain I felt watching my daughter say goodbye to her father.

That evening I drove north to my job location. I was already a day late and working with a new broker. I didn't know what else to do but go on to work. That evening, alone in my motel room, I wept for hours. All I wanted was to go somewhere where I could grieve, and not be at work, but I couldn't afford to stop and grieve, and I knew what I was feeling wouldn't end in the usually allotted three days anyway, so I kept going.

That week I worked in Enid, Oklahoma, and stayed at a bed and breakfast. I would work at the courthouse during the day, making trips to the restroom in the basement about once an hour when I could no longer hold back the tears. In the evenings, I returned to my room, wrote in my journal, prayed and cried myself to sleep. The grief was overwhelming. More than the loss of him, I grieved the sad, lonely life he had led the last several years. I knew him well enough to know he had to have been terribly lonely, and his disability must have terrified him. The final blow came when he had fallen in his front yard trying to get to his car to go get food. Unable to get up, he had laid there until a friend saw him and helped him up. For ten days, he tried to take care of himself not knowing he had broken his hip. When he finally sought help, they operated right away. Six days later he went into septic shock and they hadn't seen the symptoms in time to save him. He coded that night in ICU, never regaining consciousness. It would be weeks before the grief became even manageable, but I never missed another day of work after that Monday.

Three weeks later, as I was driving to Oklahoma to begin another work week, my niece called to say my sister had been rushed to the hospital. I made a turn and headed for Duncan soon after, calling my broker on the way. I arrived at the hospital and was heartbroken to see my beautiful sister looking so helpless. Her faith was so strong, she wasn't even fearful. The doctors said she needed to be life-flighted to Oklahoma City. I offered to stay with her so other family members could go on ahead and she would not be alone when she arrived in the city. She was calm and I appeared to be, but inside I was devastated. I was terrified things would never be the same for her again. Everything was changing and it was changing too fast for me to keep up.

I felt so helpless standing there on the ground watching the life flight take off with someone I loved so much inside.

Please, Lord, take care of her. She is so precious to me, to all of us!

I headed for the city to meet the others, calling on the way that she had taken off and would be arriving there within minutes. My mind was having a hard time handling so much so soon after Rick's death. All I knew to do was pray and pray hard, so I prayed all the way to the city.

All day and into that evening at the hospital, family and friends kept arriving until the waiting room could not contain them all. In between worrying about my sister and greeting family members I hadn't seen in ages, I was worried about paying for my motel room in Enid. If I didn't work, my room would not be reimbursed. My room was guaranteed, so I had to pay for it, but I wouldn't be able to charge it to the job. I was barely scraping by waiting to get paid as it was, I did not need any additional expenses.

I woke up early the next morning in Enid in terrible pain. The left side of my face was swelled up like someone had hit me and I had pain in my ear that extended up onto my scalp. In addition, I had big knots on my neck and behind my ear. I called the nearest walk-in clinic and made an appointment. The doctor prescribed me antibiotics and I went on to work at the courthouse.

That evening after work, I drove back to the city to see my sister, although inside I felt so sick I just wanted to go to bed. Everything hurt. I was taking the antibiotics, but I was still miserable. That evening, her doctor came into the room with the results of the tests. As it turned out, there would be no surgery and she would be going home soon.

Before my sister was rushed to the hospital, we had all planned to surprise Mom with a birthday celebration in Western Oklahoma.

Having already told my grandson I was coming, at the end of that week, I drove there, though I still felt awful physically. My grandson was grieving over the loss of his grandpa, and he wanted to drive over to the apartment where he had lived. When we pulled up to the apartment and got out of the truck, I immediately sensed a terrible heaviness present, and the Lord spoke to me.

Anoint this apartment and command the evil spirits to depart so they do not torment the next resident to move in.

Yes, Father.

I got my anointing oil out and told my grandson what we were going to do. As young as he was, he already knew how it was done. We went window to window and door to door anointing the apartment and commanding all the spirits to leave. I felt the atmosphere lighten considerably.

In the front, a gentle breeze rustled the leaves of a big tree. I wondered how many times Rick had sat alone in that apartment listening to the lonely sound of that tree. My heart grieved for how alone he had been the last several years. I wished so much I had been able to take care of him.

The pain I saw in my grandson's eyes was almost too much to bear. He had seen far too much loss in his young life, being only nine years old when the father he adored had passed away suddenly in 2006, and now this. I remembered visiting his father's grave and finding letters addressed to heaven from him. I wanted so much to protect him from the pain, but there was nothing I could do.

"Nana, will you take me to see my dad tomorrow?"

"Sure, honey."

> *I began to wonder if the suffering would ever end.*

When I was visiting, he often wanted to visit his father's grave 30 miles away.

I was feeling worse the following day physically, but I generally only get to Western Oklahoma once a year, and I didn't want to ruin the time my grandson had so looked forward to, so we headed out to his dad's grave.

When we got there, he walked over to the grave, and I hung back for awhile to give him some time alone. His father had been a loving and friendly man with many friends. He had been a musician on the side, and my grandson had inherited his talent. As I watched quietly, he took his French horn out of its case and played a sad song over the grave. My heart broke every time I saw how much he missed him, and I prayed his father could hear in heaven the beautiful song he was playing for him on earth.

Driving back, the pain I was in increased until I could bear it no longer and I pulled into the emergency room as soon as I could get there. After a short wait, the doctor took me off the antibiotics I had been taking and gave me two very strong ones to replace them, and sent me home. An allergic reaction sent me back to the emergency room the following day. I began to wonder if the suffering would ever end.

I loaded my truck early the next morning for my 4:45 a.m. departure, only to find my battery had gone dead. It had been five weeks since I had been paid, and the dead battery was the last straw. Everything in me wanted to give up, but I had no idea how to quit. Having already called in the day before, and after missing a day when Rick died, and another one when my sister was rushed to the hospital, I truly feared losing my job. I was ill in my body, grieving my ex-husband's death, worried about my sister, and now this. I wasn't sure how much more of my life's drama my boss would be willing to deal with. I knew I could get roadside assistance more quickly later, so I went back into the room and slept awhile. Several hours later, they jumped my truck off, and Iwas finally on my way.

I worked that afternoon, then went to the motel and unloaded. The next morning the battery was dead again. I'd had it tested the day before and it had tested good, but it was dead. I had no idea where to get the money to have it replaced, but I believed God could get it there. The estimate was over $200. I dropped off the truck, got a ride to work, and sat praying like crazy for provision to pay for it to come in.

Please, Lord. I need money to pay for the new battery. It will be ready in a couple of hours. Please help me!

Fifteen minutes before my truck was ready, the Lord spoke to someone to send me a money gift via PayPal. It covered the whole cost of the repair. He had answered! When I picked up the truck, the mechanic told me he had no idea how I had driven it in even after jumping it off because from what they found in the battery's condition, that wasn't even possible. I smiled, took my keys from him and told him I knew exactly how I had driven it in there, by the power of the mighty God I served.

CHAPTER 11 – NEW LEVELS

The grief I was suffering made me feel as if my wilderness journey had been extended, or that I had entered a wilderness of emotional pain instead of my former financial wilderness. Days after the death of my ex-husband, I received an email from my friend Ardith, who I knew through YouTube. Ardith is very prophetic and everything she had ever received for me was extremely accurate, and always confirmed something the Lord had spoken to me or that I had been praying about. She knew what had been going on with me, and she shared a vision she had been given a couple of years earlier that my experiences reminded her of. I share it here with her permission because we both believe anyone walking through the wilderness will be encouraged as they read it. Here is what she wrote:

In the vision I saw levels. At the first level there was a giant and the first battles with him were difficult, but with each battle the Christian grew in strength and in size. When at last he overcame the giant, he advanced to the next level. There the giant was bigger and stronger and more fierce than the last was. He easily defeated the Christian.

Each time the Christian came back, even after defeats, he was stronger, wiser, and larger in comparison to the giant. At the last battle he was the same size as the giant and easily defeated him.

The Christian went to the next level and there again was a new giant to overcome – crafty, larger, more deceitful, and stronger than the last. Again, the Christian battled and battled until he was able to easily defeat the giant.

The people of the Lord following Moses were sent into the Promised Land. When the scouts returned with their reports, they came speaking of a land full of giants. Their attitudes had defeated them as soon as they saw the giants. Even though the Lord had led them, fed them, kept them well, they still were more influenced by what they saw than by what they knew of the goodness and mercy of the Lord. Two were not discouraged and wanted to go on into the Promised Land. It is not unlike our walk with the Lord.

The Lord knows we are fighting battles that are too hard for us. He goes with us and as we grow stronger, sometimes it feels like He has pulled away and we are fighting for our very lives. We wonder, Lord, where did You go? Why are You not helping this time the way You did last time?

It is because of the struggle we grow stronger and learn. We grow closer to becoming the people God made us to be. He is there watching over us, helping us, sometimes in ways we cannot comprehend until after we've won the battle. He is always faithful and true. As we progress, we realize that the Lord was with us every step of the way, catching us if we fell, loving us, leading us.

Through all of this, either our love for Him grows stronger, or we grow bitter and have to redo some lessons.

I believe the speed of the difficulties you have been experiencing has to do with the level you have stepped in to. At first the battles were not so hard, not so fast. Now the only way to stretch you and keep you growing into the place God has for you is that the battles become more difficult. Faster makes it harder to stay positive and to win. This is the understanding I believe the Lord gave me about this level and other levels.

BLOG TALK RADIO

About a week later, I received an email another fellow YouTuber who got one word for me – *BlogTalk.* He felt it meant I was supposed to start a Blog Talk Radio show. I had never done radio before, and had no idea how to do anything related to audio, but I began praying about it. I felt in my spirit it was a word from the Lord, and that He did indeed want me to begin a radio show.

One of my friends, Vonda Brewer, a dream interpreter, was having a prophetess guest on her Blog Talk Radio show, *In Your Dreams,* the next day and taking callers who had questions. I had told her I would be calling because I had a situation in my life that I really needed to hear from God on, and I had not gotten an answer I was sure of yet.

All evening I prayed that I would hear from the Lord. I had prayed and asked Him about my situation myself, but He had not answered me.

Lord, I am really exhausted from all this traveling, and from being so ill. If it is truly Your will for me to begin a Blog Talk Radio show, I'll be glad to do it, but I don't know how I can do that and be out here on the road. At home I barely have time to straighten the house, do my laundry, go through my mail, and repack for the next week before I leave again early Monday. I need You to give me a job I can do from home, Lord, and I need a word from You when I call in to that show tomorrow.

When I arrived home the next evening and checked my mail, I found the check I had written to the clinic in Enid had bounced. I had thought I had enough money to cover it, but all those weeks of paying for motel rooms, gas, copies and food, plus trying to keep up the bills at home had emptied my checking account and I was still waiting to get my first check from my new broker. Among other things, I would not be able to return to the job the next week with no money.

I was beside myself over the returned check. I had always been extremely careful about such things. The last time I could remember having a returned check was in 1998 when I had made a mathematical error in my checkbook. I must have forgotten to write something down. How was I going to pay for that check when I hadn't been paid in over a month?

I can't go on like this, Lord. Something's got to change. The travel is exhausting, not to mention the money problems that come with it. If You truly are telling me to start a Blog Talk Radio program, I need You to give me a job I can do from here. I know it sounds unlikely, since the only broker that truly knows my work doesn't have anything, but You're God, You are the mighty Jehovah that parted the Red Sea for the Israelites! There is nothing You can't do!

I had just finished unloading when it was time to call in to Vonda's show. I had been praying all day that I would hear from the Lord. I got through on the show and Vonda announced the Lord had shown her a vision when she had prayed for me. She went on to describe a vision of washing hands at a kitchen sink and said that the message was, whatever job I was on, I was finished with it. I nearly broke out into the happy dance right there when I heard that. I had not told her anything about my situation, so I knew it was a true word from God.

The next day, Vonda called with another word the Lord had given her for me during her prayer time. The word was that I had to lay the job I had on the altar if I wanted to receive the job He had for me.

After almost becoming homeless in April, and with so many thousands of people still out of work, it was frightening to think of just quitting a job, but I felt in my spirit the word was from the Lord, so I sat down at my desk and composed an email to my broker telling them I would not be returning on Monday. I was out of travel money anyway, and I had just completed my current assignment, so the timing was good.

Lord, before You bring me the job, can I please have a couple of days off? I really need to organize my house, and I'm so tired right now!

That weekend, I decided to believe for nothing less than a job working from home. As a step of faith, I spent all of Saturday evening setting up a work area in my living room, the only room I could find enough space in to set up two folding tables.

Okay, Lord. I have the work area ready for my new job working from home. I don't know how You're going to pull this one off, no one knows me well enough to let me work from home except my old broker from years ago, and they don't have any work for me, but You're God, and I believe You can do anything!

> *Release your tithe and I will send you your job.*

On Monday, I began sending out emails and calling friends, telling them I was looking for work I could do from home. In between calls, I prayed. When I got done calling everyone I knew, the Lord spoke to me.

Release your tithe and I will send you your job.

My paycheck finally arrived. When the Lord spoke that, He showed me which ministry to give to and I immediately wrote the check and mailed it. I found out shortly after that the small ministry I sent my tithe to was in dire need, and my tithe made a big difference that month for them.

Later that day, I got a call back from a friend who knew of a possible job with a broker in Oklahoma City, but the job required travel. Still, I did not want to close any doors until I knew for sure.

The following day, the broker called, and I set a time in Oklahoma City for the next day to interview. I hung up the phone and began praying.

Okay, Lord. We both know I don't have money to be running back and forth right now, so I am believing You to bring me a job where I will be allowed to work from home, whether it's this one or another one.

At the interview the next day, I stepped out in faith, telling the owner of the company I was looking for a job that would allow me to work from images at home. Because of my length of experience and because I had been recommended by a highly trusted professional in the field, he was willing to take a chance on me. I was hired that day, completed a short training program and drove back to Dallas. I had dreamed of working from home for years. God had answered again!

Where God guides, He will always provide, and any time He assigns you something to do, He will also make you able to do it.

WORKING FROM HOME

Over the next several weeks as I began my new job, it turned into an unbelievable challenge. What normally was easy to me, grew into a greater challenge than anything I had done in years in the way of work. At the same time, I developed sciatica in my back, and between doctor visits costing hundreds of dollars every couple of weeks, I wore a back brace as tight as I could get it for over a month, day and night, loosening it only about a half hour each day. The pain was absolutely unbearable otherwise. In the meantime, a new family of critters moved in under my house and fleas took over the entire neighborhood, creeping into my house and biting my legs every morning. I thanked God I had no carpet, they would have been so much worse then. I sprayed so much bug spray I nearly made myself ill, but no matter what insecticide I used, they seemed impossible to eradicate.

Lord, what is going on? Just when I thought things were about to get easier, more challenges show up!

I have you in a season of growth, healing and change. You asked Me for change, and you shall have it.

Late in October, I really began to press in for more understanding about all the critter problems at the house. I had lived in many older houses growing up and when I was married and I had never, ever experienced anything like I was experiencing at the house in Princeton. I worked hard to keep my floors mopped, the dishes washed and the house clean. Why did I still have an insect problem? And why were none of the usual remedies working? Suddenly as I prayed, the Lord showed me in my spirit. I saw that the critters and the insects had not been sent by Him, but by the enemy. The enemy knew I was in Princeton on an assignment that involved revival, and he did not want me there. He was trying to run me out of town before I could complete what the Lord had sent me to do.

Immediately, I stood up and canceled the attacks sent against me in that place. If I had correctly interpreted what I had seen, the critters and insects would begin to leave.

Over the following months, I struggled not only with my new job but to learn how to produce audio for my new Blog Talk Radio program, Straight Talk. Week after week, I would almost cry sitting at my table trying to splice the audio clips together, not understanding one whit of what I was doing. At times I would hit a wrong key and lose an entire show, forcing me to start over. I did not understand at all why God wanted me on the radio. I wasn't even sure what to talk about on the shows, but I continued to trust Him. If my friend Vonda had not eventually taken pity on me and walked me through editing audio over the phone, I think I would have just given up. By early December, the sciatica had finally ended, the fleas had left and the critters disappeared. In addition, I began understanding enough about basic audio editing to at least produce something that resembled a radio show.

WINGS OF PROPHECY

During the last two weeks of the 2011 the Lord began giving me prophetic releases for the Blog Talk show. I had just recorded one and within two days, He gave me a second part to it. The next night on December 30th, before I had part 2 recorded, He gave me a third.

Lord, what's going on? I don't even have Part 2 of that last word recorded yet.

Start a blog and post the prophetic words I give you there. Link it to the show. Make it subscribable. I will use you in this way.

Yes, Lord.

Over the next two days, I created the Wings of Prophecy site.

On New Year's Day, the Lord sent me a word that He was going to take me out of my job. Immediately, I felt panic rising up.

Please, Lord, not so soon after almost becoming homeless! Please! I don't think I can go through that again!

During my morning prayer time a few days later, the Lord began speaking to me.

If you will truly do My will and not your own, all those things I have shown you shall surely come to pass. Do not fear, My daughter, for did I not say to you that to fear dishonors My name?

Did I not fully provide for you in the past as I walked with you through your last fiery trial?

What you did not know was, had you not feared, the trial would have been shortened. Walk in faith, My child. Know that I love you, and I will not let you down in any way! Know that I shall not only provide for you, but I shall also give you seed for sowing besides, because I love you and I desire for you to live in fullness and abundance.

I have called you to ministry, not the oilfield. The oilfield was only a vehicle I used while you were in it. I desire so much more for you than this. I know you do not despise the day of small beginnings, but it is not My desire that you stay in this place or in slavery to a job you hate.

> *What you did not know was, had you not feared, the trial would have been shortened.*

I desire you to spend more time in prayer and fastings, and crying out for the lost souls of America, so that I may save them before it is too late. I desire all My people to intercede, if only for five minutes per day, but few of My people are willing to spend their precious time in this way. They desire to be chasing the things of the world. But great is the reward for intercessors, for I hold them in high esteem, for they truly have My heart for the lost.

This change is coming soon, but everything will be provided for you. When you need money, money will be here. It is truly easy for Me to cause money to appear for you, so it should be easy for you to believe Me for it, for is anything too hard for Me?

Begin to purify yourself more for Me, daughter. The purer you are, the more of My power I shall pour out on you. This is why so many claim My promises and see no power in their lives. Their hearts are not pure before Me, and their hands are not clean.

Over the next year, the Wings site grew to over 50,000 hits per month and the Blog Talk Radio program, becoming more prophetic-oriented, often ranked in the top ten in the religious category site-wide. I continued to work, but the Lord spoke to me and told me it was never His intention for me to return to work in 2010. My job never got any easier, and at times it even became more difficult. When He confirmed it was never His intention that I return to work, I knew why all of my jobs since returning to work in 2010 had been so difficult, I had been out of His will for my life. He had allowed me to work, possibly because my faith ran out, but it was not His will. I had moved from faith into fear, not seeing the provision when I thought it would appear. I had not enjoyed my work as I had in the years before because He had taken His anointing off me to be in those jobs. He had also not truly given me favor at work. I could have the job, but there would be no favor, and no joy in any of it. Being out of His will was miserable business.

> *The purer you are, the more of My power I shall pour out on you. This is why so many claim My promises and see no power in their lives. Their hearts are not pure before Me, and their hands are not clean.*

Like the Israelites so long ago, I had gotten into fear when the Lord did not show up when I thought He should, and I had quickly put everything I had into building a golden calf to lead me out of the desert. My golden calf had been my work, my ability to earn my own living. He spoke to me near the end of February and told me simply that the book I was writing must be finished "by the end of this year," or He would give it to someone else to write. Trying to juggle working, writing my newspaper column, producing the weekly Blog Talk show, and writing the book, plus keeping up with the volume of emails generated by the YouTube videos and the Wings site was an enormous task which left almost no down time at all. I often had to take long breaks from writing the column, and hold off on making new videos to get everything else done. Before the year was up, I was no longer able to keep up with both working and writing while doing all the rest, and the book took precedence.

I did finally come out of not only the financial wilderness, but the emotional one that followed, while writing this book. As I have written, I have lifted thousands of prayers to the Lord that what is contained herein will help you survive your own wilderness walks, because the wilderness teaches you things you can learn no other way, though they are far from being enjoyable experiences.

I pray also that your journeys will be shortened by what you learn here as you partner with God to achieve His purposes in your own journeys. What follows are the lessons I learned in my own trips through the desert.

May the Lord clearly lead and guide you through your own desert experiences, and may you pass all your tests with flying colors. Though the wilderness seasons often feel as though they will never end, we have His promise that they will.

PSALM 34:19

MANY ARE THE AFFLICTIONS OF
THE RIGHTEOUS, BUT THE LORD DELIVERS
HIM OUT OF THEM ALL.

May your wilderness take your faith to levels you never dreamt of, and may it result in praise and glory and honor to our Lord and King, Jesus Christ.

I PETER 1:6-7

IN THIS YOU REJOICE, THOUGH NOW FOR A
LITTLE WHILE, IF NECESSARY, YOU HAVE
BEEN GRIEVED BY VARIOUS TRIALS, SO
THAT THE TESTED GENUINENESS OF YOUR
FAITH—MORE PRECIOUS THAN GOLD
THAT PERISHES THOUGH IT IS TESTED
BY FIRE—MAY BE FOUND TO RESULT
IN PRAISE AND GLORY AND HONOR AT THE
REVELATION OF JESUS CHRIST.

CHAPTER 12 - THE SEVEN TEMPTATIONS OF THE WILDERNESS

In the summer of 2002 as I was writing an article for my newsletter, the Lord gave me a message entitled *The Seven Temptations of the Wilderness.* This section of The Wilderness Companion is designed to help you identify the various temptations of the wilderness, and give you suggestions to increase the likelihood of passing your own tests.

TEMPTATION #1 – TO WORRY AND BE FEARFUL

NUMBERS 13:32-33

SO THEY BROUGHT TO THE PEOPLE OF ISRAEL A BAD REPORT OF THE LAND THAT THEY HAD SPIED OUT, SAYING, "THE LAND, THROUGH WHICH WE HAVE GONE TO SPY IT OUT, IS A LAND THAT DEVOURS ITS INHABITANTS, AND ALL THE PEOPLE THAT WE SAW IN IT ARE OF GREAT HEIGHT. 33 AND THERE WE SAW THE NEPHILIM (THE SONS OF ANAK, WHO COME FROM THE NEPHILIM), AND WE SEEMED TO OURSELVES LIKE GRASSHOPPERS, AND SO WE SEEMED TO THEM."

NUMBERS 14:1

THEN ALL THE CONGREGATION RAISED A
LOUD CRY, AND THE PEOPLE WEPT THAT
NIGHT.

In all my walks through the wilderness, my biggest temptations were to worry and be fearful. I was especially fearful about provision, as I moved to new cities, worked low paying jobs, or walked through wilderness times with no income at all.

At one point in my walk when I was under a particularly heavy load and really bound up in fear and worry, the Lord spoke this to me:

Daughter, when your burdens are too heavy to bear, bring them to Me, for I desire you would live a life free from fear, worry and anxiety.

My friend Conrad, who recently entered a faith walk himself, wrote this in an email to me, which describes so well what stepping out in faith really feels like:

"You know that moment people talk about when you are a kid ready to jump into Dad's arms in the swimming pool? Walking by faith is like that, isn't it? We know Dad will catch us, and He won't let us down, to even think such a thing is ridiculous. But we are still scared. Scared to leap off of the ground that supports us, into the wind where only birds are meant to fly." - Conrad (*www.bethefew.com*).

Most of the Christians I have discussed the wilderness experience with stated fear was their biggest battle. What a marvelous thing to learn to trust the Lord for all our provision, but what a terrifying walk trying to learn to do so!

Let's face it, we live in a paycheck system. We work, get paid, and pay our bills. We grow up learning about the system, and we go to school so we can join it. Coming out of something that ingrained is not an easy or painless process. We step out into the faith walk after hearing God say "I'm going to provide all you need," feeling like Brother or Sister Super Faith, and before we know it, we're just begging Him to let us go back to work some place. Any place. Just let me out of this wilderness, Lord! I begged hard for a job when that happened to me, and I'm not ashamed to admit it. I was terrified! That paycheck was my golden calf, and sometimes I had whole herds of shiny golden calves, before God started thinning out the herd.

Fear is faith running the wrong way down the road. It's believing more in a bad outcome of our situation than in a good outcome. It's faith in what the enemy is whispering in our ears, the disasters he tells us are going to happen to us.

As someone once said, fear is **F**alse **E**vidence **A**ppearing **R**eal. Satan will try to make that false evidence appear real to you, too. He will tell you all the reasons why the bad outcome is going to happen, to try to get you to believe in it because he knows if he can get you to believe in his outcome instead of God's promises, the door will be open for him to bring them to pass.

> *Everything that has worked for us before suddenly becomes ineffective. It becomes ineffective because He wants us to be where we are.*

Have you ever noticed that the longer you stare at a problem, the bigger it seems to be? There is a great temptation when we are in the desert places to stare at our circumstances, trying to figure out what to do next. When we find ourselves in the desert, whether we walked there voluntarily by His command, or we just woke up there one day, when the heat starts turning up and the pressure is building, all any of us really want is out. As humans, we are problem solvers. We have the power of reasoning, and the natural response to discomfort is to reason or solve our way out of it. Most of us find in the wilderness that the solutions we normally have success with no longer work. Everything that has worked for us before suddenly becomes ineffective. It becomes ineffective because He wants us to be where we are.

There is more for us to see, and where we are is the only place we will be forced to learn what He wants to teach us about Himself. There are some things you just can't learn out of a book. Bicycle riding is an example of one such thing. You can read all about how to balance as you turn the pedals and propel yourself forward. You can review it in your mind over and over, and think you understand the dynamics of how a bicycle works, and that you know how to ride. But do you? No. Real understanding comes in applying what you have read. It is the same with the Word of God. We think we know it. We think we know how to apply what we know, but we don't really know unless we can apply it with success. Faith without works is dead. If your faith isn't working, it's dead faith, and He wants you to fix it so it will work. If you don't know it's broken, you'll never get around to fixing it, will you?

> *Terrorism started with Satan. He loves to terrify God's children.*

Fear drains your strength and steals your joy. It makes you too weak to fight the enemy. That's why fear is the enemy's #1 weapon, and that's one of the reasons we need to stand up and refuse to fear.

Any time we become fearful, it is a sign we have been staring at our circumstances, not at our mighty God. Fear is a big red flag that we have believed some lie the enemy told us. Otherwise we would still believe God's promises, wouldn't we? There is nothing to fear when we believe God, and not the enemy. Fear means you believe more in the enemy's power to make you fail than in God's power to help you succeed. Our fear dishonors our mighty God.

God wants us to look to Him for whatever we need, whether it is financial provision, healing, help with unruly children, or whatever else we are facing in our desert seasons. He has the solution to every problem. Whatever you need, He has it. It's kind of like one-stop shopping. Go to God, get it all.

Recently, the Lord spoke to me and said, "In quietness and trust is your strength." Later, I found something similar stated in Isaiah 30:15.

ISAIAH 30:15

FOR THUS SAID THE LORD GOD, THE HOLY ONE OF ISRAEL, "IN RETURNING AND REST YOU SHALL BE SAVED; IN QUIETNESS AND IN TRUST SHALL BE YOUR STRENGTH." BUT YOU WERE UNWILLING,

Many times, He has told me, "Only believe." It is up to us to "only believe," and stop allowing the enemy to speak doom and gloom into our thoughts, causing us to doubt. It is up to us to stop his scenarios of ruin from running through our minds. We must realize that we cannot add one cubit to our stature through worrying, and know that it is Satan's goal to destroy our strength to stand through his fear inducing tactics. Terrorism started with Satan. He loves to terrify God's children.

> *You cannot hear the voice of faith while listening to the voice of fear.*

If God brought you to where you are, He is well able to bring your through where you are. And if you brought yourself, He is still your loving father, and He will not leave you without help. He is a very present help in time of trouble. If you get off track, He is well able to reroute you. Though we must strive to remove sin from our lives, He isn't going to leave us to starve if we commit a sin while walking through these difficult places. When the Israelites sinned in the desert, the Lord God Jehovah still fed them, and although they suffered for their sins, He continued to lead them, and He will you and I, too.

You cannot hear the voice of faith while listening to the voice of fear. The last thing we want to do in the wilderness is cut ourselves off from the ability to hear the Lord when He speaks or leads us. It is difficult enough to hear when we are traveling through the desert places because of the screaming of our flesh and our emotions. When we get bound up in fear, we also run the risk of binding up the blessings that may be on the way to us. We must turn away from the enemy's voice and refuse to hear it, if we want to hear from heaven.

Our eyes must be fastened on the Lord as well. This is how we keep our peace in the wilderness places.

ISAIAH 26:3

YOU WILL KEEP HIM IN PERFECT PEACE,

WHOSE MIND IS STAYED ON YOU,

BECAUSE HE TRUSTS IN YOU. (NKJV™)

It is human nature to feel afraid when we can't see our provision, and can't figure out how we are going to pay rent or make the mortgage payment. Usually by the time this comes up, we have come to the end of our own provision, and we do not know any way to provide for ourselves. We have never lived this way before, and it is natural to fear the unknown. It is important to remember that if you get into fear, you're no longer walking, you're standing still. You're no longer receiving, because your faith in God's power has been replaced with faith in the enemy's power. Eventually you won't even be standing still, you'll be moving backwards. It is human nature to be afraid in these situations, but God wants to replace our fearful human nature with His faith-filled nature.

God wants us to be more interested in Him than in His plan for how He is going to get us out of the wilderness we're in. When we are out in the wilderness, all we really want to know is how we are going to get out of our mess. We want things to calm down and go back to being predictable and comfortable. We want our garlic and leeks and onions back. (Numbers 11:5) Our old way may not have been the best, but at least we knew what to expect. Now here we are out in the desert and nothing is predictable any more, nothing is comfortable, nothing seems solid. We want to know when and how He is going to rescue us!

What God wants from us is not that we would be looking at how He's going to save us, but at Who it is that's going to save us. If we realize that He is right by our side in the situation, that He is our healer, our provider, our banner, our strong tower.... If we *really* realized He is all these things, would we still fear? Would there be any need to worry or be anxious? No. That is where He is trying to get us - out of the land of Where's My Promise to the land of I Know Who Holds My Promise.

> *Your faith may feel at times like the proverbial mustard seed, but after God leads you through the wilderness, it will be a mustard seed the size of Goliath that can easily stare down any mountain in your path.*

In a wilderness walk where you are relying on the Lord for all your provision, fear will try to take over all your thoughts, both waking and sleeping. You must exercise your faith constantly, building your faith daily by reading scripture, praying and declaring back to God those things He has promised you. Like a weight lifter building muscle, what you don't constantly use, you'll lose, and your faith is the muscle God is trying to build up in the desert. It's a constant cycle of pushing and pulling your emotions until He gets you built up to the next level of strength.

The wilderness is designed to turn the little faith you have now into giant-killing faith. Your faith may feel at times like the proverbial mustard seed, but after God leads you through the wilderness, it will be a mustard seed the size of Goliath that can easily stare down any mountain in your path.

> *The desert seasons are tests to see if you really believe God is faithful, or if you just think you believe He is faithful.*

The desert seasons are tests to see if you really believe God is faithful, or if you just think you believe He is faithful. Each day of your walk, you will choose faith or you will choose fear. Which one you choose helps determine how long you stay in the wilderness. When fear knocks at your door, your faith needs to get up and answer it.

Since fear and doubt are likely to be your biggest challenges in the wilderness, it pays to have a battle plan. Here are some of the methods I used to fight them.

- Declare God's promises back to Him. This is something the Lord told me to do, and I kept forgetting. These can be personal promises to you, as well as the promises found in scripture. A promise book is also useful for this. Whenever I did remember and declare the promises back to God, it turned out to be a knock-out punch to the fear that plagued me.

- Pray for others in need, and get others praying for you – commit to pray for each other. Buddy up! Pray the prayer of agreement over each other's needs. There is strength in numbers.

- Find someone you can help. If you are busy helping someone else, you have less time to be in fear and doubt over your own situation. Do something for someone else and get your mind off of yourself. Sow it as seed to the kingdom, and the kingdom will rain a harvest back down into your own life.

- Fast – and you can fast other things besides just food. There were numerous times when the Lord had me fast television or other activities. It's still a sacrifice for your flesh and He will reward you for it. God always honors fasting.

- Get into His word – God often speaks to us through His word.

- Worship. Worship wins the battle when the enemy is too big for you to defeat alone. If all you see are armies of problems marching towards you, fall on your face and worship! No matter where we are, He is still God, and He still deserves our worship.

- Praising God for everything you can think of that He has done in your life, and for what He is doing even now for you behind the scenes that you don't even know about (Phil. 4:6).

GET YOUR PRAISE ON

Praise is especially powerful against the spirit of fear. The most difficult time to keep praising the Lord is when you feel there is not a word of praise anywhere in you - when you just lost your job, received the foreclosure notice, when your child just called you from the police station, when the doctor just delivered the worst report of your life. You may feel like there is no possible way you can praise God in that dark moment, but in the darkest valley is where your praise becomes the most anointed, and the most powerful. In darkness is where praise shines the brightest. When the enemy taunts you in those moments of loss, of terror when you cannot see how anything could possibly ever work out, when it seems all hope is gone, that is when God is most likely to show up in your situation. He is never far away from His children when they are hurting.

In October 2011, the Lord spoke this to me during prayer one night:

If only My children understood the value of just praising Me! If only they would look to Me instead of the world for their needs!

Ruth Ward Heflin, in her book, *The Glory, Experiencing the Atmosphere of Heaven,* told the story of how her mother, whenever there was a great need, would tell all her children to answer the door and phone that day, that she was going to praise the Lord. She would then proceed to walk back and forth throughout the house the entire day praising God. Ruth Ward Heflin said the only times her mother did that were when there was a serious need, and there was not a single time that God did not answer her mother's praise day prayers.

The Lord spoke this to me about praising when I have a need:

When I tell you to praise Me, keep praising until the answer comes!

The key to praising Him is don't just offer one or two praises, praise Him until the answer comes!

When Jesus hung on the cross, it looked to all the world as if the enemy had won. When He cried out "*It is finished!*" and commended his spirit to our Father in heaven, it seemed He had done all the good on earth he would ever do. His ministry was over, and the Pharisees breathed a sigh of relief. In the natural, it appeared to be game over, but in the spiritual, it was anything but.

THE SHOUT OF A KING

There is a beautiful verse of scripture in the Old Testament that is perfect for pulling out in the dark moments in life. This verse comes from the story about Balak, the son of Zippor, trying to convince Balaam to curse the Children of Israel. Balaam explained to him that God was with them, in the form of the shout of a king.

> NUMBERS 23:21
>
> HE HAS NOT BEHELD MISFORTUNE IN JACOB, NOR HAS HE SEEN TROUBLE IN ISRAEL. THE LORD THEIR GOD IS WITH THEM, AND THE SHOUT OF A KING IS AMONG THEM.

The shout of a king is what brought down the walls at Jericho when the Israelites marched around them. The shout of a king is what was in David's heart as he slung the rock that killed Goliath. The shout of a king is what Jehoshaphat and his praise band had that caused God to answer their prayer, and caused the armies coming against them to turn, and slaughter each other.

> *The shout of a king is the victory shout that says "God's got this!" "We win!"*

The shout of a king is the victory shout that says "God's got this!" "We win!" "Nothing is too hard for our mighty God!" No matter what, as long as we have Jesus, we do win, and we do have something to shout about. The enemy can't curse you when you have the shout of a King in you!

The enemy hates praise and worship. He hates it because he desires to take God's praise and worship for Himself. The Lord told me once that He really rejoices whenever one of His children ignores the taunts of the enemy by praising Him, and laughing instead of listening to the enemy's fear tactics. Your praise shouts in the dark moments of life confuse the enemy, just when he thinks he has you. Shout!

Carry the shout of a king in your heart. Use it often. Use it in the dark times, and watch the walls of fear come tumbling down. Fear is an illusion Satan sells us to steal our faith. But God says He is with you to deliver you.

TEMPTATION #2 – TO GOSSIP OR BACKBITE

NUMBERS 12:2

AND THEY SAID, "HAS THE LORD INDEED SPOKEN ONLY THROUGH MOSES? HAS HE NOT SPOKEN THROUGH US ALSO?" AND THE LORD HEARD IT.

NUMBERS 14:2

AND ALL THE PEOPLE OF ISRAEL GRUMBLED AGAINST MOSES AND AARON. THE WHOLE CONGREGATION SAID TO THEM, "WOULD THAT WE HAD DIED IN THE LAND OF EGYPT! OR WOULD THAT WE HAD DIED IN THIS WILDERNESS!

One of Satan's favorite tactics to get your attention off God, and off of any sin in your own life, is to get you looking at someone else's sin, and judging them. He also hopes you will gossip about them to others and encourage them to jump on the judgment bandwagon with you. "Can you believe she said that?!" "Well, I'm going to call her and say this...! We'll see what she has to say for herself then!" "I heard just the other day that he was...." "Can you believe he posted that on Facebook?!" and on and on and on. It's a never ending trail of deadly seeds that will spring up in your own life as others talking bad about you in return.

When the enemy has you staring at the sins of others, you aren't looking for any in your own life. Gossip is tale bearing and the Lord hates it. Scripture has much to say about tale bearing or gossiping. To be a tale bearer means to be a *scandal monger.*

When we gossip, we are passing judgment on another and the word says whatever measure we use to judge others we will also be judged by. Judging others comes out of the spirit of pride, and pride will keep you in the wilderness, or buy you a return trip back there like it did me.

ROMANS 2:1

THEREFORE YOU HAVE NO EXCUSE, O MAN, EVERY ONE OF YOU WHO JUDGES. FOR IN PASSING JUDGMENT ON ANOTHER YOU CONDEMN YOURSELF, BECAUSE YOU, THE JUDGE, PRACTICE THE VERY SAME THINGS.

When the adulterous woman was brought before Jesus, His statement was that he who was without sin should cast the first stone. If we are not without sin then, we should not be casting any stones.

JOHN 8:7

AND AS THEY CONTINUED TO ASK HIM, HE STOOD UP AND SAID TO THEM, "LET HIM WHO IS WITHOUT SIN AMONG YOU BE THE FIRST TO THROW A STONE AT HER."

One evening some time back I was praying for someone I knew who seemed to constantly talk negatively about others. As I was praying, the Lord spoke to me.

He who casts stones will find himself on a rocky path.

He proceeded to show me a vision of this person. Each time they spoke against another person, a large black seed pod would drop out of the air and fall on the ground near them. As the vision continued, many seed pods covered the ground. Suddenly without warning, all the seed pods sprouted and grew up very quickly into large black stalks. They surrounded the person and began covering them. The person began to cry, but the harvest had already begun and the seed pods kept sprouting.

PROVERBS 6:12-15

A WORTHLESS PERSON, A WICKED MAN,
GOES ABOUT WITH CROOKED SPEECH,
WINKS WITH HIS EYES, SIGNALS WITH HIS
FEET, POINTS WITH HIS FINGER, WITH
PERVERTED HEART DEVISES EVIL,
CONTINUALLY SOWING DISCORD;
THEREFORE CALAMITY WILL COME UPON
HIM SUDDENLY; IN A MOMENT HE WILL BE
BROKEN BEYOND HEALING.

We need to remember any time we gossip or slander that we are planting a seed of the same type that will sprout into a harvest in our own lives. No good result ever comes from talking bad about someone else. It does not matter if it is true information or not, if the person you are speaking of can be recognized by what you say, it is gossip. Ephesians 4:29-32 is very clear about speaking only that which edifies another. Gossip and tale bearing never edified anyone and they do not minister grace to the hearer.

It is common for Christians to repeat scandalous information about someone under the disguise of asking for prayer, when the real intent is to gossip and bear tales while appearing not to sin. The Lord sees the motives of our hearts and our motives make us guilty whether we do it under the guise of asking for prayer and trying to hide it, or not.

Gossip divides people and destroys reputations. To slander someone is to assassinate their character, to murder their reputation. It is an act of hate, not love. Wrong use of our tongue can also render us useless in kingdom work.

JAMES 1:26

IF ANYONE THINKS HE IS RELIGIOUS AND
DOES NOT BRIDLE HIS TONGUE BUT
DECEIVES HIS HEART, THIS PERSON'S
RELIGION IS WORTHLESS.

Gossip also shows we are prideful. Any time we gossip about someone else, we are implying that we, the wonderful Christians we are, would never, ever do what they did. Don't be so sure, because the Lord has a way of setting up circumstances to show you what is in your heart and whether you will keep His commandments or not (Deut. 8:2). Gossiping and tale bearing may not be listed in the Ten Commandments, but they are very serious in the eyes of the Lord. Satan is the accuser of the brethren. Any time we accuse, even lightly in gossip, we are doing the devil's work instead of the Lord's.

> *Any time we gossip about someone else, we are implying that we, the wonderful Christians we are, would never, ever do what they did. Don't be so sure, because the Lord has a way of setting up circumstances to show you what is in your heart...*

One of the most difficult aspects of gossip is when you are trying to stop gossiping, and others gossip to you. Scripture says that where there is a lack of wood, the fire will go out (Prov. 26:20). As Christians, we should refrain from participating in gossip altogether. I have found it helpful to say something good about the person being slandered, and also to let the other person know gently that the Lord is not pleased with gossip and I must refrain from speaking or listening to it. Then smile and excuse yourself.

As I was writing this book, the Lord spoke to me many times about what He wanted it to convey. One of the things He spoke to me was this: *"I want them to understand there are no perfect Christians except My Son who ever walked the earth. There are only believers who think they're perfect."*

Sometimes gossip has become a habit in our lives and we need to break it. When that happens, it is helpful to confess the scriptures daily that help us with matters of the tongue and also to remember how displeasing it is to the Lord. Gossip sows discord among the brethren. Sowing discord is one of the seven abominations listed in Proverbs 6:16-19.

PROVERBS 6:16-19

THERE ARE SIX THINGS THAT THE LORD HATES, SEVEN THAT ARE AN ABOMINATION TO HIM: HAUGHTY EYES, A LYING TONGUE, AND HANDS THAT SHED INNOCENT BLOOD, A HEART THAT DEVISES WICKED PLANS, FEET THAT MAKE HASTE TO RUN TO EVIL, A FALSE WITNESS WHO BREATHES OUT LIES, AND ONE WHO SOWS DISCORD AMONG BROTHERS.

WHEN OTHERS GOSSIP ABOUT YOU

Another experience many believers encounter as they walk through the wilderness is becoming the subject of gossip and backbiting themselves. Sometimes they are friends or others who turn on you suddenly, and sometimes they are family members who are concerned about your situation.

Many will gossip about you when you step out in faith, or when you are suddenly plagued with calamity in your life, not understanding the Lord is at work in a special way. The enemy often brings attacks of slander against you as well, to further weaken you, and his favorite method is to attack through those closest to you, because it wounds you more deeply. Either way, gossip and slander hurt and add to the pain you are already walking in. It is easy during these times to let our emotions get the best of us, and to strike out at those who hurt us. It is helpful to be aware ahead of time that these attacks are likely, and consider how you will respond. Forewarned is forearmed.

In the wilderness, our emotions are often all over the place with the uncertainty of how things already are, without slanderous attacks being launched at us to add to our pain, but these attacks are commonplace in the desert seasons. They will generally be untruths spoken about you in a vicious manner and circulated in the worst possible place - either at your workplace, at church, your favorite social media site, or in some other public forum. It is Satan who accuses the brethren and it is helpful if you find yourself reeling from one of these attacks to remember it is actually him attacking you through other people. He looks for the weakest links around you and then goes to work trying to cut you down.

Jesus, when falsely accused, answered not His accusers. Pride will make you want to answer back, and answer fiercely, but this is not the way the Lord wants us to react in these situations. Attacks of slander are hard to take, but we as believers have someone to fight our battles for us. The Lord spoke this to me on this subject:

> *He who casts stones will find himself on a rocky path.*

The less you answer your accusers, the more I will take up for you. Answer them not, and I will take up your cause and defend you completely, for is My name not Jehovah-Nissi?

Jehovah-Nissi means The Lord Is My Banner (Ex. 17:15), and the Lord is our banner, and our defender at all times. His banner over us shows that we are His. If we truly trust Him, we will let Him vindicate us when slanderous attacks come. If you find you are defending yourself, you may not be fully trusting Him to answer the attacks for you. The enemy of your soul desires to draw you into strife through false accusations, and you would do well not to answer his lies. Strife is difficult to stop once it has started (Prov. 17:14). God is well able to show the accusations to be false, and He will repay those who make them against you. You must remember this, if you launch an attack against your accusers to defend yourself, then you cannot expect God to also defend you.

BEING RIDICULED FOR YOUR FAITH

Wilderness Walkers learn to endure the ridicule of those who say the Lord no longer speaks to His people, because Jesus clearly stated in John 10:27, "My sheep hear my voice, and I know them, and they follow me." His sheep do hear His voice and sense His leading, and if they are truly His, they will follow wherever He leads.

There are many who will mock and say if you hear a voice, it is not His and you need to have your head examined, but I say the miracles that follow obeying that voice speak for themselves. I have nothing to prove to anyone and no longer feel any need to defend my actions or words, I am a witness to the power of the mighty God I serve, and that is all. None of this is about me, it's about Him. It's about Jesus and what He died to give us all. I am only the messenger, Jesus is the message. For those of you receiving similar criticism, be encouraged, there will always be Pharisees out there. It is up to us to remain humble and just keep doing whatever the Lord leads us to do. Others will think and say what they will, but the mission remains the same. Rejoice in persecution, because every time you are persecuted or mocked, it increases your reward in heaven. Many mock simply because they do not understand.

There will always be mockers, there will always be those who don't believe and those who do not wish to see the truth. There will always be the Pharisees who believe they do everything right and no one else can enter in. There will always be those who fear what they have not experienced, and therefore do not understand. After all, if you hear His voice and they do not, and some of them have been years longer in their walk with Him, how must that make them feel? You must remember as you enter the wilderness place following His voice that if Jesus was not able to convince the Pharisees, then you and I certainly will not be able to either.

The Lord spoke to me as I began writing this book and said there are no perfect Christians; that only Jesus was perfect; He said there are only believers who think they are perfect. When you step out in faith in ways others fear to do, you will encounter many believers who think that you are just crazy, and that you are making bad decisions. People understand pursuing wealth and prestige, they do not understand pursuing spiritual growth at the cost of it because what you are attaining is not tangible or measurable in their eyes. Be encouraged, because as you walk higher and higher with Him in the wilderness, their voices will become fainter. Their opinions will cease to matter, as His becomes stronger and stronger in your spirit.

TEMPTATION #3 – TO MURMUR OR COMPLAIN

EXODUS 16:2-3

AND THE WHOLE CONGREGATION OF THE PEOPLE OF ISRAEL GRUMBLED AGAINST MOSES AND AARON IN THE WILDERNESS, 3 AND THE PEOPLE OF ISRAEL SAID TO THEM, "WOULD THAT WE HAD DIED BY THE HAND OF THE LORD IN THE LAND OF EGYPT, WHEN WE SAT BY THE MEAT POTS AND ATE BREAD TO THE FULL, FOR YOU HAVE BROUGHT US OUT INTO THIS WILDERNESS TO KILL THIS WHOLE ASSEMBLY WITH HUNGER."

It is human nature when we are suffering to want to talk about it, to complain to others who care about us, and to be comforted by their sympathy, but the Lord views our complaining quite differently.

When we are walking through a difficult place, it is especially important to keep a guard over the door of our lips. Complaining about our situation and our hardships is the equivalent of telling God He is not doing a good enough job taking care of us.

EXODUS 16:8

AND MOSES SAID, "WHEN THE LORD GIVES
YOU IN THE EVENING MEAT TO EAT AND IN
THE MORNING BREAD TO THE FULL,
BECAUSE THE LORD HAS HEARD YOUR
GRUMBLING THAT YOU GRUMBLE AGAINST
HIM— WHAT ARE WE? YOUR GRUMBLING
IS NOT AGAINST US BUT AGAINST THE
LORD."

Maybe right now you are forced to live some place where you would
rather not reside. Or maybe your job is not a good fit, but it was the only
one you could secure at the time. Possibly your standard of living has
dropped considerably from where it was before, your spouse has left you
or you are battling a terrible disease. Choosing not to murmur and
complain does not mean denying the fact of what is happening, only
denying those facts a voice to help them gain power in your life. Anything
we speak, we establish.

The Lord taught me this
lesson through a friend
years ago who seemed to
have nothing positive to say
about anything or anyone in
her life. One night I was
praying for her in my prayer
time.

> *Our negative words can send our
> blessings back to heaven before
> they arrive in our lives. We cannot
> be double-minded, confessing
> victory one moment and defeat
> the next.*

*Lord, please help her to stop
complaining so much. I don't know how to help her when she constantly
confesses the enemy's victory over her circumstances.*

And the Lord replied: *Every time she speaks out her misery, she establishes
it in her life.*

The last thing any of us want to do when we are in that miserable desert
place is to establish the misery we are trying to get out of. Our words

hold great power to either establish or tear down what is making us unhappy. We would be wise to keep that in mind and speak accordingly.

Our negative words can send our blessings back to heaven before they arrive in our lives. We cannot be double-minded, confessing victory one moment and defeat the next (James 1:6-8).

We must choose a side. We can wallow in our misery and help establish it with our words, or we can confess that God's power will rule in our situation regardless of what we see with our eyes, and establish that. I fought this temptation again and again and most likely could have come out of the wilderness long before I did. Don't let your words be stout against the Lord, keeping Him from blessing you (Mal. 3:13).

Few areas of our Christian walk look so innocent and yet carry so much power as our words. With each word we speak, we are establishing either the good or the bad, there is no in between. Our words are either bringing life or they are bringing death to our situation (Prov. 18:21).

We should also strive to keep in mind that those we complain or murmur to are not at all edified by our complaining and misery, but burdened by it. When I would visit with my always complaining friend, I often left feeling as if someone had put a two-hundred pound weight on my back. She felt better and lighter, but I felt as if the whole world had been added to my burdens.

We should always put forth every effort not go around like the proverbial garbage truck, dumping all our miseries on those closest to us, burdening them with our pain and woes. Those who complain and murmur constantly will eventually find their friends and even family will begin avoiding them out of self defense. It is enough that our complaints are perceived by God as being against Him, we do not want to also make others turn away from us.

TEMPTATION #4 – TO TRUST IN AN IDOL

EXODUS 32:1

WHEN THE PEOPLE SAW THAT MOSES
DELAYED TO COME DOWN FROM THE
MOUNTAIN, THE PEOPLE GATHERED
THEMSELVES TOGETHER TO AARON AND
SAID TO HIM, "UP, MAKE US GODS WHO
SHALL GO BEFORE US. AS FOR THIS MOSES,
THE MAN WHO BROUGHT US UP OUT OF
THE LAND OF EGYPT, WE DO NOT KNOW
WHAT HAS BECOME OF HIM."

When we are scared and hurting, or when everything in our life feels like it is sitting on shaky ground, it is human nature to grasp for any kind of comfort we can find. That is the natural reaction of our flesh, and that is the problem with comfort seeking. It is our flesh, not our spirit, that seeks it. This was my other biggest temptation, and other wilderness walkers have expressed they found this one very difficult as well.

The Israelites got tired of waiting on Moses to come down from the mountain when he was busy getting the Ten Commandments so they approached Aaron, the next in command, and said "make us gods." Aaron, also apparently was unsure of whether Moses was coming back or not, wanted to placate the masses who looked to him to guide them in Moses' absence. He had them bring their gold jewelry to him, and he fashioned for them an idol they could worship, since it seemed the great God Jehovah had left on vacation, possibly taking His friend Moses with Him. They then began to worship the golden calf, giving it the glory for bringing them out of slavery in Egypt instead of God, who actually had. In fact, God had also given them the jewelry they used to make the calf, when He spoke to them to borrow it from their neighbors before leaving Egypt.

We must be careful about demanding God make an appearance at a certain time, for His ways are much higher than our ways. Faith is being certain of what we cannot know in the natural, that God is with us and for us, whether He is answering our prayers in the way we hoped or not. It is the uncertainty when He does not answer like we expect Him to that makes us afraid. That uncertainty can make us want to run for the nearest security blanket, whether that security blanket is a prospective mate, a job He doesn't want us in, or a habit or addiction that comforts us

> *For awhile, our security blankets make us feel warm and cared for. We feel almost at peace – until we lift the edge of our blanket and see the shiny golden calf lurking beneath it.*

momentarily. For awhile, our security blankets make us feel warm and cared for. We feel almost at peace – until we lift the edge of our blanket and see the shiny golden calf lurking beneath it.

One of the many uses of the wilderness experience is to reveal to us the idols in our hearts. The world is filled with so many things that demand our time and attention, that beg to be our idols, from jobs and careers, the perfect family, the perfect mate, the perfect ministry, sports teams, even children and grandchildren.

Anything that gets more of our heart than God does, or that tempts us enough to compromise what we know is right, is an idol. Anything we love so much we are willing to give too much of our time and attention and finances to, when we know some of that time, attention and money should go to the work of the Kingdom of God, is an idol. When we are alone out there in the desert, He can get our attention long enough to point out our idols to us so we can offer them up to Him. There may be idols hidden amongst our stuff the Lord wants us to see that we would otherwise never examine.

GENESIS 31:34

NOW RACHEL HAD TAKEN THE
HOUSEHOLD GODS AND PUT THEM IN THE
CAMEL'S SADDLE AND SAT ON THEM.
LABAN FELT ALL ABOUT THE TENT, BUT
DID NOT FIND THEM.

Perhaps I have idolized the steady income I get from my work, and never realized I have made my paycheck the god of my provision instead of Jehovah-Jireh, my provider. Maybe I have idolized having the perfect family and been so busy tending to their needs and wants that I have ignored the family of God, the one He has called me to serve in and to love. Is it possible my constant work has hidden from me the idol of wealth and the security a fat bank account can bring me? Has my ministry become more important to me than the One whose name I minister in? It is important to search your heart for anything you may have more affection for, or dependence on, than God.

Our God is a jealous God, and He will have no rivals for His place in our hearts.

> *The intense pressure we are under can make cows look like saviors, and gold look like God. In our anguish and uncertainty, Satan can make wrong people look like right ones.*

RUNNING TO WRONG RELATIONSHIPS FOR COMFORT

Watchman Nee once said, "*Emotions Are the Believers Biggest Enemy.*" Romantic relationships or companionship are often idols in the lives of single people. One mistake I have seen over and over again, and which I also fell into, was running to a wrong relationship or marriage in the midst of all the uncertainty in my life. Our burdens seem lighter with someone else sharing the load, and no one knows that better than those of us who walk alone.

If you are believing for a godly mate, Satan knows it, and he is going to send as many counterfeits your way as possible to try to get you to marry the wrong person. He knows the Lord has someone who is a perfect fit for you, and that there is strength in the unity you will share with that person. Suddenly, someone who looks just like what you want appears in your life. They talk about God, they are also looking for a mate, and ... what a coincidence! A lot of the qualities you are praying for in a mate even appear to be in that person! What great timing! Just when you needed rescuing, right? Better look again.

The heat of the desert makes mirages appear, and things and people suddenly look like something they're not. The intense pressure we are under can make cows look like saviors, and gold look like God. In our anguish and uncertainty, Satan can make wrong people look like right ones. Marriage is serious, and wrong mates are miserable business. Another sharing the burden lightens the load, but not if it's the wrong one sharing it, and if that person is wrong for you, then you are also wrong for them, so both sides lose. It is better to be alone than to end up wishing you were.

One of the earmarks of this type of relationship is the confusion it brings. Idolatry always opens the door to confusion in our lives.

ISAIAH 41:29

INDEED THEY ARE ALL WORTHLESS;

THEIR WORKS ARE NOTHING;

THEIR MOLDED IMAGES ARE WIND AND
CONFUSION. (NKJV™)

Wrong relationships in our desert seasons will always have elements of confusion in them. That's what makes us confused about them....we feel not *quite* sure. When we worship the Idol of Companionship, our spirits become confused, because we were created to worship only the living God. Scripture tells us that God is not the author of confusion (I Cor. 14:33).

Satan delights in sending counterfeits into our lives, and getting us into confusion. I call them decoys, because they are used for the same purpose. A decoy is something fake that looks like the real thing, like the wooden decoy ducks used by hunters to lure real ducks to their death. They look like ducks, and they float like ducks, but they aren't real ducks, there isn't any life in them. And just like the counterfeits the enemy sends to you, you won't know until you get really close to them, that what you thought was real is just a cheap, lifeless imitation. Sometimes by then it's too late.

Another enemy tactic I have seen used over and over, is to convince you the other person needs your spiritual help, or to convince you that God has a plan of ministry for the two of you to do together. I have seen these same lies used repeatedly in decoy situations to entrap God's people, and the enemy has also used them on me. Don't fall for his lies and snares. He is setting you up to be tempted.

Wrong relationships will not only delay your destiny, they can have terrible consequences. Never rush into a serious relationship when you are in a wilderness season. We aren't in our right minds when we are going through so much anguish and uncertainty, and questions as important as 'Should I marry this person?' have no business being decided while we are walking through a painful desert season. If the person was truly sent by God, there will be no confusion, and they will wait.

When confusion enters into the situation, it can also cause the other person to think they have heard from the Lord that the relationship is a divine appointment. We should never take the word of anyone else for our answer to whether we should marry someone. The enemy can and does use this tactic with success. God is well able to tell us anything that important regarding our lives. The enemy will also try to convince you of "signs" that prove the decoy was sent by God and is a divine appointment. Do not let mere coincidences convince you to enter into anything as serious as a marriage covenant. Counterfeits sent into your life by the enemy during wilderness seasons are seldom what they appear to be, and may have even been sent to bring destruction into your life or ministry. If you are not walking closely with the Lord, or are not yet mature in your faith, it will be easy for the enemy to ensnare you in this way.

Beware too, if you suddenly feel called to move to a city where someone you have romantic feelings for lives. God will always position you for success and Satan will always try to lure you into moving where you are not supposed to be. Your divine appointments and provision are both tied to your location. When Elijah was sent to the Brook Cherith, God had already commanded his provision to be there at that brook. Not just any brook. The Lord specifically sent Elijah to the Brook Cherith.

I KINGS 17:4

YOU SHALL DRINK FROM THE BROOK, AND
I HAVE COMMANDED THE RAVENS TO
FEED YOU THERE.

God ordained Elijah's provision ahead of his trip. The ravens have been commanded to feed you where you are supposed to be as well. Your calling and your provision are both linked to your geographic location. Don't move until God moves you.

THE ENEMY WILL EXPLOIT YOUR EMOTIONS

In a wilderness walk, you will likely go through the whole gamut of emotions. Many days when I was in the intense heat and pressure of the wilderness, my emotions felt like a runaway horse. One minute I felt totally confident and full of faith that God was going to come through for me and the next minute I was filled with fear, and certain I was headed for ruin.

GENESIS 12:8

FROM THERE HE MOVED TO THE HILL COUNTRY ON THE EAST OF BETHEL AND PITCHED HIS TENT, WITH BETHEL ON THE WEST AND AI ON THE EAST. AND THERE HE BUILT AN ALTAR TO THE LORD AND CALLED UPON THE NAME OF THE LORD.

When Abraham was out in the wilderness, in Gen. 12:8, he camped between Bethel, which means House of God, and Ai, which comes from a word that means ruin. In the wilderness, we often feel as if we are somewhere between where the Lord wants us, in His house, and total ruin.

My toughest battles were against fear and worry. I needed to learn how to stop staring into my unknown future and just do what was before me each day, each hour if necessary. God will, after all, be just as present in all our tomorrows as He is in today, and as He was in our yesterdays.

Sometimes our wilderness experiences are filled with change after change after change. Change stirs up all kinds of emotions in us. Sometimes changes cause us to remember things we would rather forget, thus forcing us to face issues from the past and deal with them at a time that is not at all convenient for us. Some people simply do not enjoy changes at all, and they try to avoid it at all cost. If you are a stranger to change, the wilderness experience will lead you into new emotional frontiers in your life, casting you adrift on raging waves of change you can do nothing about.

As the stormy waves of change rage through our lives, it seems all we have known and felt secure in for so long is tossed up in the air on the waves and then comes crashing down, and we are left to pick up the pieces and try to put our lives back together again. The most effective way I found to deal with constant change was constant praise, constant prayer and constantly keeping my eyes on Jesus. If you look at the waves crashing around you, you will likely faint in your mind, but if you look at the One who has the power to calm the waves, you will stay strong. This is easier said than done, but it can be done with enough practice. The key is to capture any fearful thought as soon as it presents itself to your imagination, and cast it away from you. Replace it with the promises of God by deliberately thinking a powerful scripture in its place. Do this every single time and soon you will laugh in the face of change!

WHEN TEMPTATION COMES

Jesus was led into the wilderness to be tempted. We are tempted in the wilderness, too, so it is important we become wise to the ways the enemy tempts and ensnares us, and that we learn to be vigilant at all times.

When the heat is turned up, and the pressure is on us in the wilderness, it is tempting to run back to the sins and wrong relationships of our past for comfort or relief. Whatever your weakness is, the wilderness will expose it, and try it. Any sin you refuse to give up is an idol. It is an idol because you are choosing the sin over God, therefore it is more important to you than God is, and that makes it an idol. Since we know we will be tempted in the wilderness, let's talk about temptation, and about sin.

DEALING WITH SIN

The Lord often gives us revelation when we least expect it. Many years ago when I was still struggling to be free of old strongholds, I was praying for a friend who was heavily addicted to drugs.

Why won't he let You deliver him from his problem, Lord?

The Lord answered and said:

The same reason you won't let Me deliver you!

Ouch. Sometimes the truth really hurts, and the truth is this: sometimes we cling to a sin because we like it, and we don't want to give it up. I did not want to give up smoking cigarettes when the Lord first spoke to me.

Two weeks later, I was still arguing with Him about it, trying to cling to my sin. I did not realize He would also take the desire to do that sin from me.

Like the Israelites, we find comfort in sins that please our flesh whether it is drinking, smoking, drugs, sexual sin, overeating, or whatever, but the Holy Spirit desires to be our source of comfort. He knows every time we sin, we open ourselves up to further attacks from the enemy, and we put distance between ourselves and His holy presence as well. It is the renewing of our minds through reading God's word that transforms us.

ROMANS 12:2

DO NOT BE CONFORMED TO THIS WORLD,
BUT BE TRANSFORMED BY THE RENEWAL
OF YOUR MIND, THAT BY TESTING YOU
MAY DISCERN WHAT IS THE WILL OF GOD,
WHAT IS GOOD AND ACCEPTABLE AND
PERFECT.

It helps to remember that any time there is a sin problem, it is an indication that some area of our mind has not been renewed, and some part of our life has not been surrendered.

HOW SATAN TEMPTS US

The enemy works far in advance to set up just the right circumstances to get you to sin. One of the things he often does when he is setting a Christian up to fall is to begin drawing them away from the word of God and away from worship. Those are the two things that strengthen us most against temptation. When he succeeds at drawing us away from God, we are already weakened spiritually when the attack comes. Another popular tactic of the enemy is to plan his attacks for when you are worn down, weary, exhausted and distracted by other things going on in your life.

He will begin to speak softly to you, luring, enticing, persuading, flattering you.

JAMES 1:14

BUT EACH PERSON IS TEMPTED WHEN HE IS LURED AND ENTICED BY HIS OWN DESIRE.

We are dawn away by our own appetites and desires. The word entice in this passage comes from the Greek word *deleazo* meaning to delude or entrap, and comes from the root word *dolos*, meaning trick, decoy or deceit. Satan uses circumstances to weaken our resistance, and then he moves in with thoughts of temptation to trick us or deceive us into believing the sin he is dangling before us will make us happy and fulfilled. He puts up a decoy, something fake that looks like the real thing such as fake comfort, fake peace, or fake joy.

> *The war against sin is not fought in your body, but on the battlefield of your mind, where all sin is conceived. Your behavior is born out of your thoughts. If you don't let your thoughts get into sin, your behavior won't either.*

Satan will always try to minimize sin's effect while he's selling it to you. Around 2002, the Lord gave me a vision of Satan where he was dressed like a street peddler. He held up brightly lit beribboned packages that were so shiny and looked so beautiful, and the Lord showed me that when you opened them, they were empty and ugly inside.

When Satan is recounting all the wonderful pleasures committing the sin will bring, he fails to mention that he himself, the accuser of the brethren, is going to be in your face condemning you the moment you have done it. He fails to mention that he is going to make you feel shame and regret

and condemnation for doing the very thing he tempted you to do. He fails to mention that, after the brief pleasure of sinning, you will be tormented for weeks or months or years by the guilt and consequences of what you have just done. He also won't tell you that some sins carry consequences that last a lifetime, and that every time you compromise, it costs you something. He wants you to look only at the momentary pleasure of the sin he is tempting you with - the bright shiny lie he is trying to sell you.

He says things like "Go ahead, no one will ever know." "It's only a little sin," "Just this once won't hurt," "You're strong, you won't let it go too far." One of his favorites is "You won't ever be able to live without *that*." And then there are some of the old standards: "You can't help that, it runs in your family," "Look at all the good things you've done lately, this one little sin won't count against you," and the two that have served him well for so long: "There's plenty of time, you can always repent," and "A loving God would never send people to hell!"

The enticement comes when Satan moves in with the bombardment of tempting thoughts to your mind. The war against sin is not fought in your body, but on the battlefield of your mind, where all sin is conceived. Your behavior is born out of your thoughts. If you don't let your thoughts get into sin, your behavior won't either. This is why we must take every thought captive and bring it into obedience to Christ. (II Cor. 9:5)

> *God is far more concerned about your character than He is your calling, and He will stand patiently by and wait for you to clean up your act before promoting you, no matter how long it takes. You cannot have it both ways. If you desire to pick up your mantle, lay down your sin.*

The enemy hates you and if God would allow him to, he would kill you this very instant and you would never finish reading this page. Since God is not allowing him to do that, he tries to get you to destroy yourself, or destroy the credibility of your witness, through sin.

ARE YOU CALLED TO LEADERSHIP?

Satan works especially hard to tempt those who are called to leadership in the Body of Christ. The reason is because you can't live a sinful life and lead others, and the enemy knows it. Many who are called to positions of leadership are still refusing to lay down their sins. Do not deceive yourself into thinking God will promote you when you are going around acting like the devil. God is far more concerned about your character than He is your calling, and He will stand patiently by and wait for you to clean up your act before promoting you, no matter how long it takes. You cannot have it both ways. If you desire to pick up your mantle, lay down your sin.

If you are called to a healing ministry, or you have asked God for a healing anointing, you should also be aware that healing is connected with holiness. In many instances, Jesus healed a person by casting out demons. Obviously, demons are connected to sin. Whatever area the enemy consistently attacks in your life is exactly what God desires to use in you.

Leadership is about doing things correctly, and leaders must lead by example. Leaders will always be attacked in areas of purity – honesty, integrity and sexuality will be especially hard hit during times of temptation if you are called to lead.

Refusing to give up sin will only keep you in the wilderness longer, or cause you to have to go back. Years ago, I was praying for a friend I had seen in the spirit was being set up to sin. The person could not see what was happening, and continued to pursue a particular friendship in spite of my cautioning them. I was frustrated at not being able to stop the train wreck I saw heading for my friend's life. As I prayed about it, the Lord said this to me:

When a child refuses instruction to come away from the fire, only the fire can teach it what it needs to learn.

The fire is what we feel in the wilderness. Shortly after that, the person I prayed for did fall into sin, and then entered an extremely difficult wilderness season. Sin promises you everything, but it delivers only death and destruction.

HOW TO STOP LOVING YOUR SIN

It is by falling in love with Jesus that we fall out of love with the world and the pleasures of sin. Jesus said if we love Him, we will keep His commandments (John 14:15). Being in love with our beautiful savior is exactly what draws us away from the pleasures sin has to offer. As our love for Him deepens, we can no longer bear the wall that erects itself between us and our beloved when we get into sin. We cannot bear the silencing of His voice when we go out after other gods. We cannot bear for Him to take His holy presence from our lives, because He is essential to our happiness. As we spend more time in His word, in praise, and in worship, we fall more and more in love with Him, and out of love with whatever the world is tempting us with.

ONLY BELIEVE – HOW UNBELIEF AFFECTS SIN

> *Unbelief that we can stop sinning stops us from stopping the sin in our lives.*

Sometimes we fight giving up a sin because we honestly do not think we can stop sinning in that area. If you have smoked cigarettes, committed fornication, indulged in pornography, or taken drugs whenever you felt like it for twenty years, that sin has most likely become a stronghold in your life, and it will be difficult for you to imagine or believe that you can truly live your life without it. The Bible talks about strongholds in II Corinthians 10:4-5.

Addictions are born out of a need to feel better. We adopt behaviors that take us out of the present, or alter our moods, because we are not enjoying where we are. Addictive behaviors are a way of comforting ourselves, of feeling better. If we find some activity or substance that brings us temporary comfort or happiness, it is human nature to want to return again and again to that activity or substance so we can experience the comfort again, and that tendency is especially strong in the heat of the desert seasons.

The Lord told me once that the lie the Spirit of Addiction sells its victims is that they cannot live without the thing or behavior they are addicted to. As we commit the same sin over and over, the enemy moves in to set up a stronghold of lies in that area. He begins to tell us that there is no way we can ever stop doing the sin; we can never give up the drugs, the smoking, the sexual immorality, the alcohol, the pornography, or whatever our weakness is. As we return to the sin over and over again, he whispers, *"See, you can never live without this!"* If you believe his lies, the stronghold is erected. You begin believing that sin will always be a part of your life, and that you are too weak to stop. You are not weak, the enemy has just talked you into not fighting.

If you apply truth of God's word to that lie, you can tear down the stronghold and the addiction cannot remain in place. We are no longer required to be slaves to sin because the blood of Jesus has set us free. If you are struggling with a sin, find scriptures about your freedom and confess them over and over. When the truth gets deep into your spirit, you will be set free.

ROMANS 6:17-18

BUT THANKS BE TO GOD, THAT YOU WHO
WERE ONCE SLAVES OF SIN HAVE BECOME
OBEDIENT FROM THE HEART TO THE
STANDARD OF TEACHING TO WHICH YOU
WERE COMMITTED, AND, HAVING BEEN
SET FREE FROM SIN, HAVE BECOME
SLAVES OF RIGHTEOUSNESS.

JOHN 8:34-36

JESUS ANSWERED THEM, "TRULY, TRULY, I
SAY TO YOU, EVERYONE WHO PRACTICES
SIN IS A SLAVE[A] TO SIN. THE SLAVE DOES
NOT REMAIN IN THE HOUSE FOREVER; THE
SON REMAINS FOREVER. SO IF THE SON
SETS YOU FREE, YOU WILL BE FREE
INDEED.

Cast those unbelieving thoughts down and stand on the truth that if Jesus says you can be free, then you can be free indeed. He wants you to be free of sinful thoughts and behavior, free to serve Him with your whole heart and your whole mind.

The key here is this – we must only believe, and not also doubt in the back of our minds. Only believe. Belief that is pure, no matter how small that amount of belief may be, is more powerful than a lot of faith mixed with a lot of doubt. Most of us believe a little and doubt a lot, while thinking we believe, and then wonder why nothing we are believing for happens.

Unbelief that we can stop sinning stops us from stopping the sin in our lives. God's word tells us we can do all things through Christ (Phil. 4:13). If we say we cannot stop, we are lying against the truth of the word of God.

The Son of God has set us free from sin forever. We do not ever have to give in to it if we are willing to stand against it and claim our freedom.

TEMPTATION #5 – TO BLAME OTHERS FOR OUR SITUATION OR PROBLEMS

EXODUS 32:24

SO I SAID TO THEM, 'LET ANY WHO HAVE GOLD TAKE IT OFF.' SO THEY GAVE IT TO ME, AND I THREW IT INTO THE FIRE, AND OUT CAME THIS CALF."

When Moses came down off the mountain with the Ten Commandments, and confronted Aaron about the golden calf, the first thing Aaron did was blame it on the gold and the fire (Ex. 32:21-25)

We will get out of the wilderness far more quickly if we will take responsibility for our sins and not try to blame them on others. God cannot help us do better if we will not admit what we have done.

It is difficult to understand too, when we find ourselves in the middle of the barren desert why those we have helped do not run to our rescue. Do they not remember? Have they so quickly forgotten the times we were there for them? We always thought they would be there, that if the chips were ever truly down, they would be the ones to have our backs, right? What about our church? Shouldn't they be doing more in our times of need? What about the company we have served faithfully for twenty plus years? The list of those we can blame goes on and on.

When the enemy begins tempting you to blame, he is setting you up to become offended, bitter and unforgiving. His intent is to suggest someone else is to blame for where you are. If we say someone else is to blame for our situation or misery, then we are also saying only they can fix it, and we are making them like God by attributing power to them.

> *The Lord may not be allowing anyone else to rescue you, and He may have even hardened their hearts to keep you where you are so you will truly learn to rely on Him for help.*

You are in the wilderness to be tempted, humbled, and proven because God wants to establish your testimony and use you in a greater way than ever before. He won't be able to use you if you begin pointing fingers, casting blame on all those who have not rescued you from your misery.

The Lord may not be allowing anyone else to rescue you, and He may even have hardened their hearts to keep you where you are so you will truly learn to rely on Him for help. Many times I have prayed about helping someone I knew was in a fiery trial, and the Lord told me not to do anything, that He was refining them. In some cases, He added that if I helped them or gave to them, I would only prolong their time in the wilderness.

You won't be promotable if you become bitter, blaming others for what you are going through. Don't let the enemy get you into blame, bitterness and offense. It will eventually lead to unforgiveness.

TEMPTATION #6 – TO TRUST MORE IN OURSELVES THAN IN GOD

EXODUS 16:20

BUT THEY DID NOT LISTEN TO MOSES. SOME LEFT PART OF IT TILL THE MORNING, AND IT BRED WORMS AND STANK. AND MOSES WAS ANGRY WITH THEM.

How is it that we can trust so much more in our own frail ability to provide for ourselves than in the ability of our magnificent God who created the entire world in only six days? Why is it so hard for us to believe that God will provide for our needs? Even after He showed us He was willing to rain down manna for the Israelites for decades? We panic if we are $500 short on our bill money, as if moving an entire sea and holding it out of the way wasn't as hard as sending us $500 to cover our bills.

PSALM 23:1

THE LORD IS MY SHEPHERD, I SHALL NOT WANT.

That word *want* also means lack. If the Lord is your shepherd, then He is guiding you. A shepherd guides his sheep to where there is provision, that is his job. So wherever He guides you, He will also provide. If at first you don't see His provision, look around you. It's there some place.

Our own foolish pride and our unbelief can cause us to believe more in our own ability to provide than in God's. Our lack of trust causes us not to want to depend on anyone else, and in truth many people cannot be trusted, but the Lord God can be. He is faithful to His children.

My friend Conrad recently wrote in a blog that the more he worked, the deeper in debt he got, but the more he sought God, the more God provided for his needs.

MATTHEW 6:33

BUT SEEK FIRST THE KINGDOM OF GOD AND HIS RIGHTEOUSNESS, AND ALL THESE THINGS WILL BE ADDED TO YOU.

LACK OF PROVISION – SOME OF THE WAYS WE COPE

As I thought about the Children of Israel, I realized that manna didn't come for them until they had passed through the Red Sea, and they could no longer turn and run back to Egypt. Not until they had passed the point of no return, and they were on the other side of an un-crossable ocean from their old way of life, when they could no longer run back to what was familiar. God doesn't send us manna until we are truly in the desert, out of provision, and unable to provide for ourselves.

Once you have truly crossed over into the wilderness and you are beyond being able to rescue yourself, you will only have what He feeds you from heaven. The wilderness becomes a place barren of anything you can make your own way from. For most of us, this is the only way He can teach us just how faithful He is to provide.

The most terrifying aspect of the desert experience for me was my fear of a lack of provision, and other wilderness walkers have expressed the same sentiment. Our human response when our income stops and our savings dry up are often one of the following:

a. We sell our belongings. Obviously there is nothing wrong with selling belongings if we have excess items, but if we are selling things we really need to provide for ourselves, we are not truly trusting God to bring us provision. This is the old trap of trusting more in ourselves than in Him.

b. We overextend ourselves on credit and go into debt. Not only is overextending on credit making your own provision, but it is making the wrong kind of provision. Scripture says the borrower is a slave to the lender (Prov. 22:7). God is trying to bring us *out* of bondage, not take us in deeper.

FINANCING YOUR TRIP THROUGH THE DESERT

I made the mistake of financing my first trip through the desert on credit because I simply did not see any other way to pay my expenses. I had not yet developed real Bible faith for provision.

Living on credit is not the same as trusting God for your provision. Trusting God is believing Him to bring the provision, not borrowing to bring it to yourself. When Abraham returned from Egypt after God sent him on that faith walk, he did not come out in debt. He came out wealthy. That doesn't mean we will all be financially wealthy, but I don't think God means for us to come out deep in debt from trying to provide for ourselves when He is trying to build our faith in Him. Living on credit gives you faith in plastic, not faith in God.

If we are living on credit or credit cards, we are still finding our own way instead of surrendering to His. As long as we're providing for ourselves, even if it's by over-extending our credit, we're still walking our own path and trying to take care of ourselves. Though we believe we are surrendering, we aren't. No surrender, no manna. God will wait patiently by and let you continue to take care of yourself until you finally run out of ways, and realize He is your provider.

God doesn't want us to find our own way, but to seek His way for us. He wants to be our provider, our Jehovah Jireh. He wants to provide for our

He is trying to build our faith in Him. Living on credit gives you faith in plastic, not faith in God.

every need, and all He requires is our faith and our trust in Him to do it. The longer you keep making your own way, the longer you extend yourself on credit, the longer you prolong the wilderness experience because as long as you are finding your own way, you are still relying on you, not on God, and you haven't passed the test.

Looking back on the times I prayed for provision, I can see patterns. The times when I simply believed and did not fear, the Lord answered my prayers. The times when I had an extreme need, and I planted a seed into good ground and believed without fear, the Lord answered my prayers. The times I got into fear, it seemed like my provision was held back. During times when all I thought about or sought after was the Lord, it seemed my provision was constantly increasing. I was seeking first His kingdom, and He was adding all the things I needed, including some I only wanted. (Matt. 6:33)

Examine your heart and be honest with yourself. Where is your faith – really? When you think of the bills coming due, what is the screen of your mind showing you?

As I was writing this book, the Lord spoke this to me: *"Tell them I desire they would trust Me more to provide for them. Who do they think I am? Am I, or am I not, the great God Jehovah? Why then do you all doubt Me so?"*

TEMPTATION #7 – TO FAINT AND WANT TO GO BACK TO EGYPT

NUMBERS 11:5

WE REMEMBER THE FISH WE ATE IN
EGYPT THAT COST NOTHING, THE
CUCUMBERS, THE MELONS, THE LEEKS,
THE ONIONS, AND THE GARLIC.

NUMBERS 14:4

AND THEY SAID TO ONE ANOTHER, "LET US
CHOOSE A LEADER AND GO BACK TO
EGYPT."

When we find ourselves in the dry blazing heat of a barren desert, we look back on our days in Egypt through rose colored glasses. Suddenly we remember the delicious garlic and leeks and onions and forget the many lashings we suffered from the harsh taskmasters there. We remember the security of sleeping in our own beds and forget that our time was not our own because we were slaves. We remember that we never had to worry for our food or shelter and forget it was because Pharaoh owned us. We forget the despair of our former lives, while longing to go back to our comfort zones. We forget all about the fear, the lack of peace, the sleepless nights, the emptiness we knew there. We forget how we pleaded with God to take us higher and refine us, to walk us into our destiny in Him. We forget having told Him all we had was His and how we covenanted with Him to do His good pleasure and promised to follow His leading.

But then we thought He would lead us some place comfortable and warm where we would be prospered and honored, didn't we? Not this poverty stricken place of rejection and scorn we find ourselves in now. Not this hot dry desert where we can no longer find the comfort of His voice! We thought He was taking us some place fun and like spoiled children, as soon as the heat is on, we want to run from the discomfort. We assumed His idea of taking us up higher was the same as ours, forgetting He told us in His word that His ways and thoughts are higher than ours.

> *We assumed His idea of taking us up higher was the same as ours, forgetting He told us in His word that His ways and thoughts are higher than ours.*

And that's human nature. He doesn't fault us for that, but He knows that's coming so He waits to turn the heat up very high until there is a wall of ocean behind us where we can no longer run back home. If He didn't, we would probably all bail out of the race and run straight back to Egypt.

Never before have I heard from so many people who are truly at the end of their rope. Many saints have been in their current battles a very long time and everyone is battle weary. No one could blame anyone else for feeling like there is little use in pushing on when everything around them only seems to keep getting worse.

WEARINESS WHEN THE JOURNEY GROWS TOO LONG

The Bible talks about how in the last days Satan will wear out the Saints. I believe he has been doing this for some time, but it appears to be increasing. Discouragement and weariness have become rampant.

The enemy loves to set us up for weariness and then tempt us with sin when we are weary or afraid. We are far more vulnerable when we are tired or when we are out of our comfort zones and facing great uncertainty about our lives, because our human tendency is to try to find something to hold on to. The Lord wants us to cling to Him in these times. He wants to show us He is all we need. He wants to be the one we turn to to calm our fears and comfort our souls.

We cannot see in the desert where He is taking us, or why He is allowing so much pain and affliction in our lives, and we are afraid. If He loves us so much, why are we being afflicted? Are we being chastised? Is He going to bring us out of this terrible mess? All these thoughts run through our minds, leaving us fearful and seeking some form of earthly comfort to get us through.

> *If anyone is to blame for our being stuck in the wilderness so long, it is us.*

The bottom line here is that God does not work in our ways, or in our time frame, but in His. If you are in the desert, there is a reason. There is a work the Lord wants to accomplish in you while you are there to help you go up higher with Him. You may be begging Him to put you in ministry and fulfill all the promises He has given you, but before we can be given authority, we must learn to submit to it. You may be praying for a godly marriage, but you are not yet godly marriage material. Perhaps He has promised to promote you and exalt you, but you are refusing to lay down all of your sin so He can. Perhaps He has placed a gift of leadership in you, but you have refused to become the godly example He wants others to follow. There is always a reason.

Whenever the Lord gives us promises, it seems as if they will surely come to pass the very next week. I know mine certainly sounded that way, and I truly believed I was ready for them to. In the dark nights of my wilderness walks, the Lord revealed to me just how ready I wasn't. As the wilderness drug on and on, I often grew weary waiting and hoping for the fulfillment of those promises, but in all honesty, those promises were what kept me trying to submit to the pain of the refining process. Whenever I would feel like fainting, the promises would appear before me, like a shiny golden carrot. Jesus, too, kept going for the joy that was set before Him.

HEBREWS 12:2

LOOKING TO JESUS, THE FOUNDER AND PERFECTER OF OUR FAITH, WHO FOR THE JOY THAT WAS SET BEFORE HIM ENDURED THE CROSS, DESPISING THE SHAME, AND IS SEATED AT THE RIGHT HAND OF THE THRONE OF GOD.

As humans, we always think we are ready for greatness before we are, but He can see we are nowhere near ready. We can easily spot the flaws in others walks, but we can rarely see them in our own. We feel the gift He has placed in us rise up and think we are ready to go preach to an auditorium of 10,000 people. It is tempting at these times to run out ahead of God and try to make the vision come to pass ourselves, but that is the equivalent of the house built on shifting sands.

In truth, we cannot see the wickedness that still resides in the dark corners of our hearts. We cannot see that we will not keep His commandments though we promise Him we will. We cannot see that we will deny Him as Peter did when the going gets too rough, that we will whine and want to run back to Egypt when we run out of garlic, and leeks and onions. We cannot see our own weakness because the enemy has deceived us into thinking more highly of ourselves than we should.

God in His infinite wisdom knows if He were to answer our prayers and exalt us before we are actually ready that we would become easy targets for the enemy to gleefully destroy. He would need only to exploit one of our weaknesses to not only bring us down from our lofty perches and high opinions of ourselves, but to destroy any ministry the Lord had raised up through us in one fell swoop.

God would rather our character be strong and right even if we never do a single work for Him, than that we attempt great works with weak character. We don't need to be stepping up onto a platform in front of thousands when we cannot even lead in our own households by example. If anyone is to blame for our being stuck in the wilderness so long, it is us.

> *We cannot see our own weakness because the enemy has deceived us into thinking more highly of ourselves than we should.*

And so we hope for the prize set before us as we submit to the refiner's desert fire. And we wait. We wait. And wait. And wait.

We wait and we keep trying to submit because the promise of the vision He has given us is so much greater than anything we can ever hope to achieve on our own, and because we know we can never do it by ourselves. We wait because we are in love with a savior so magnificent, so majestic, so loving, so gentle and so merciful, that there is no place else to go. We wait, because our waiting is nothing compared to what He has done for us, and because we desire to please Him.

We wait, because, no matter how difficult our circumstances, He truly has the words of life and there is no other life for us to return to.

And because He who promised is faithful, and we know He will show Himself faithful in our situation as well.

WEEPING IN THE WILDERNESS

PSALM 84:5-6

BLESSED ARE THOSE WHOSE STRENGTH IS
IN YOU,

IN WHOSE HEART ARE THE HIGHWAYS
TO ZION.

AS THEY GO THROUGH THE VALLEY OF
BACA

THEY MAKE IT A PLACE OF SPRINGS;

THE EARLY RAIN ALSO COVERS IT WITH
POOLS.

Baca means weeping. It means to bewail, or mourn. This Psalm is about those who walk through the valley of tears, and those who have walked in the wilderness know that place well.

I have yet to encounter a single Christian who walked through a long, painful wilderness season who did not weep through at least some of it. I wept through all of mine. The Israelites wept during theirs as well. If you are weeping in your desert season, you are not alone.

The wilderness is often a place of broken dreams. It is a place where changes are taking place, and parts of our lives are being left behind including homes, friends, jobs, relationships, and places we would sometimes rather not let go of just yet. It is a place of loss, and loss brings grief. The desert is a place of suffering in our flesh, and often it is also a place of mourning.

MATTHEW 5:4

BLESSED ARE THOSE WHO MOURN, FOR
THEY SHALL BE COMFORTED.

The only good news about mourning in the desert is that we have His promise of comfort when we mourn. There is very little that truly comforts us when we are suffering full blown grief. When we face a loss so great that our world feels completely shattered, and we truly doubt the sun will ever shine in our days again. God beseeches us to run to Him because He is the comforter of our souls. He sends others to encourage us during these times, to love us and comfort us, to lift us up in prayer. He is the God of patience and consolation.

Romans 15:5 calls Him the "God of patience and consolation." To console means to make "less sad or disappointed." II Thes. 2:16 calls His consolation everlasting. He has given us consolation without end.

The wilderness is often a place of broken dreams.

Consolation comes from the Greek word that means solace and comfort, which comes from another word that means "to call forth, to order or command." God calls forth consolation for us when we are in mourning, when we are disappointed, and when we weep in the night seasons.

In 2003, my family prayed that my sister would be healed, and we knew she had a prophetic word from God through a stranger who did not know the nature of her illness that He was willing to heal her. We wanted so much for her to receive her healing and stay here with us, but we also knew that she was ready to go home. She had battled heart disease most of her life, and her life had not been an easy one. We knew that if she prayed to go home instead of praying to receive healing, her prayers would take precedence over ours because the illness was in *her* body.

When she left us to go to her heavenly home, we were left to walk through the valley of the shadow of death. The valley of tears.

PSALMS 23:4

EVEN THOUGH I WALK THROUGH THE
VALLEY OF THE SHADOW OF DEATH, I
WILL FEAR NO EVIL, FOR YOU ARE WITH
ME; YOUR ROD AND YOUR STAFF, THEY
COMFORT ME.

Often during the times of deepest mourning in my Christian walk, the Lord has answered some prayer dear to my heart that I had prayed years before. It is almost as if He saved some of the desires of my heart to grant me when I was at my lowest, to help me when I had to walk through the valley of the shadow of death. Answers to prayers so big they had the power to distract me at least temporarily from even my deepest grief.

When my younger brother, the sibling I was closest to, committed suicide in 1987, I felt as if half of my soul went with him. I have never felt such all encompassing pain and grief, and it felt as if it would never end. Two months later, the Lord opened the door to set me free from the abusive marriage. The one thing my brother wanted most for me, and that I wanted most for myself and my children, was to be free from the abuse, and God answered.

Whenever God answers a really big prayer like that that you have prayed for years, it's as if a little glimmer of light shines down into the valley of shadows and brings you comfort as you walk along the path of mourning.

The enemy is hoping you will turn away from God in anger, blaming Him for your situation, that you will stop believing in His love for you, or His goodness, or that what you are experiencing is for your benefit. The enemy is hoping in your pain and misery that you will stop doing whatever you are called to do, that you will stop witnessing about God's power and grace in your life, that you will stop your own destiny, and forfeit your blessings. If he can't stop you, he's hoping he can delay you, to keep you from witnessing to anyone *today*. Tomorrow he will try again, and the next day he will try again. He hopes to steal not only the joy today could bring for you, but tomorrow's rewards as well. He can't ever have any of the rewards that await us, and he doesn't' want us to have them either.

DROWNING IN SORROW

I PETER 5:6-8

HUMBLE YOURSELVES, THEREFORE,
UNDER THE MIGHTY HAND OF GOD SO
THAT AT THE PROPER TIME HE MAY
EXALT YOU, CASTING ALL YOUR ANXIETIES
ON HIM, BECAUSE HE CARES FOR YOU. BE
SOBER-MINDED; BE WATCHFUL. YOUR
ADVERSARY THE DEVIL PROWLS AROUND
LIKE A ROARING LION, SEEKING SOMEONE
TO DEVOUR.

The word translated *devour* in that scripture means to *completely drown.* That is exactly what the enemy wants to do to you in your pain, he wants to drown you in it. He wants to constantly remind you of it so it never leaves your mind. He wants to incapacitate you with it so that you will not witness about God's love or His mighty power, so that you will not stand strong in your faith, and so you will be no threat to *him*

Resist what the enemy is trying to do to you. Resist giving in to temptation when he is trying to weigh you down so heavy in your grief and sorrow that you feel walking with God is no longer worth the effort. Resist him because he tries that trick on every Christian. Every one of us must walk through the valley of shadows as our faith is being refined, if we want to go up higher and reach new levels in our walk with God.

> *It is in our minds that we are in danger of fainting. If we can win the battle in our minds, we will not faint.*

It is in our minds that we are in danger of fainting. If we can win the battle in our minds, we will not faint. It is in your mind that the enemy is going to attack you and try to bring you down and make you want to give up. So your mind is what you must strive to keep strong.

Luke 18:1 talks about praying and not fainting. So we need to pray and draw strength from God. It is in our weakness that His strength is made perfect. We connect with Him by prayer, and draw our strength from Him when ours is running low.

When we are being wearied and are walking through those fainting times, we are definitely suffering. God wants to hear from us when we are hurting. It's okay to tell Him about your pain.

Many Christians feel they should be strong and stoic no matter what is happening, but God sees our hearts, we can hide nothing we are feeling from Him. It is okay to weep before Him when you are mourning, even if it is due to the refining fire in the desert. He is not upset with us for hurting, only glad when we bring our pain to Him.

He is truly the God of all comfort. He will wrap you in the warm embrace of His presence as you weep, and He will sustain you there in that dark place. He knew we would walk through the valley of sorrows and that our pain would sometimes make us feel like giving up.

The Lord knew we would have seasons of weeping. He even included a promise to us in His word for those very times. It is one I hold close to my heart, whether I am in the wilderness or on my way to the Promised Land.

PSALM 126:5

THOSE WHO SOW IN TEARS SHALL REAP
WITH SHOUTS OF JOY!

EPILOGUE

Writing The Wilderness Companion was a journey of remembrance for me, at many times a very painful one. There were a number of times when reading back over the pain of the past caused me to stop and just weep. Late one night after writing through a particularly painful part, I prayed:

Lord, going back through my journals is so painful. Is it really necessary to do this to write The Wilderness Companion?

Yes. I can heal many through the pain of one. Are you willing?

Yes, Lord.

I did not ask again after that night. It is my prayer this book will change the way you look at and travel through your own wilderness experiences forever. I pray your journeys will be easier because of the knowledge contained here. It is my prayer that you can learn from my mistakes, and not be in the desert as long as I sometimes was, or make as many return trips.

As of the time of publication, I am still in the little house at Princeton. I have learned to keep my eyes on the King of Kings, and to spend more time in prayer, worship, and praising Him than ever before, no matter what is going on in my life. Sometimes I still dream of having my own home, but it is no longer an idol in my heart, because I know there is one in heaven with my name on it. It is enough that I have Jesus. He is all that really matters in the end.

May God richly bless you and yours, and keep you through all that is to come. May you keep your eyes on Him, and may your life be totally surrendered at His feet.

May all God's best be yours,

Glynda Lomax

P.O. Box 127
Princeton, TX 75407
wingsofprophecy@gmail.com

Websites

Straight Talk With Glynda Lomax on Blog Talk Radio:
http://www.blogtalkradio.com/glyndalomax

The Wilderness Companion Blog:
http://www.thewildernesscompanion.com

Wings of Prophecy Site: http://www.wingsofprophecy.com

My YouTube Channel: http://www.youtube.com/user/texasauthor1

Made in the USA
Columbia, SC
13 September 2023

22846052R00139